PRAYER WARRIOR BOOTCAMP

A Reflective Study of

The Necessity of Prayer by E.M. Bounds

&

With Christ in the School of Prayer by Andrew Murray

Reflection Questions and Leaders' Guide written by Rodney Jetton

Also by Rodney Jetton

7 Pitfalls of Power

Success Can Kill You - One man's story of success, failure and forgiveness

Son of a Preacher Man - Growing up in the Seventies and Eighties

Cussing Christians: We Love Jesus (but we cuss a little) – A short discussion on the language we use outside of church

Why Receive the Holy Spirit and How to Receive Him by J.E. Stiles (adapted by Rodney Jetton)

The Recovering Politician's Twelve Step Program to Survive Crisis (edited by Jonathan Miller)

Targeted Communications
18140 Twelve Oaks
Dexter, MO 63841
www.rodjetton.com

Ordering Information:

Special discounts are available on quantity purchases by churches, associations or individuals. For details, contact - rodjetton@gmail.com

ISBN 978-0991312634

Cover design by fiverr.com/Lisaarts

Printed in the United States of America
First Printing July 2016
Second Printing February 2017

Unless otherwise indicated, all scripture references are from the King James Version of the Bible.

Targeted
Communications
Content that Connects

DEDICATION

To Ed Kleiman of Pray Bold ministries, (www.praybold.org) who the Lord sent to help me get back on the narrow way after I allowed my pride to take me down the broad way that leads to destruction. Since 2010 Ed has encouraged me to stay close to the Lord by reading my Bible and praying. His teaching, encouragement, and prayer conferences have been a huge help in my spiritual walk, and I am so very grateful to God for bringing him and his ministry into my life.

CONTENTS

Theme – Prayer is Faith in God

Verse- Therefore I say unto you, what things soever ye desire, when ye pray, believe that ye receive them, and ye shall have them. -Mark 11:24

Class 6- **Word**- Fruit

Theme- Faith and obedience lead to fruit bearing.

Verse- Ye have not chosen me, but I have chosen you, and ordained you, that ye should go and bring forth fruit, and that your fruit should remain: that whatsoever ye shall ask of the Father in my name, he may give it you. - John 15:16

Class 7- **Word**- Intercession

Theme- Believing and persistent prayer for His kingdom.

Verse- And this is the confidence that we have in him, that, if we ask any thing according to his will, he heareth us: And if we know that he hears us, whatsoever we ask, we know that we have the petitions that we desired of him. - 1 John 5:14-15

Class 8 – **Testimony Time**

OVERVIEW OF COURSE

This course has been designed to explore the promises in God's Word regarding prayer by reading as authors E.M. Bounds and Andrew Murray reveal what Jesus said about prayer in the Bible. Too many Christians in today's churches spend little time in prayer, resulting in few obtaining the joy and power of answered prayer. Many live in a sea of doubt about their faith and wonder if God really answers prayer.

Our Savior not only spent much of His ministry in prayer, but also left detailed instructions on how we were to pray. Prayer was of primary importance when the Lord was teaching the disciples how to live the Christian life. This nine week course will help you better explore the teachings of our Lord in this most vital area of our Christian walk and most importantly, it will require you to spend time praying!

We will start with examining *The Necessity of Prayer* by E.M. Bounds. These 14 chapters will help us understand why prayer is so important in the believer's life. Each day we will read a single chapter and answer the reflection questions. These 14 days should increase our faith that God hears and answers the prayers of His obedient servants, while adding a newfound desire and fervency to our petitions.

After 14 days, we will begin looking at Andrew Murray's 31 lessons in, *With Christ In the School of Prayer.* Our faith in God's promises to answer our prayers will grow as we finish each of these lessons. As we focus on what the Master taught about fasting, forgiveness, perseverance and boldness in our prayers, our desire to spend more time with the Lord will increase. We will finish with the command to become intercessors responsible for bringing the kingdom of God and His blessings to our fellow man here on earth.

Each week we will meditate on our Lord's words by memorizing a scripture verse dealing with His instructions or promises concerning prayer. Hiding Jesus's words in our heart will assist in strengthening our faith in the promise of answered prayer. It has been said that any habit can be formed after 21 days. It is our hope that the reading and prayer required in this course over the next 49 days will help us all form a habit of daily meditating on God's word as we take our petitions to the Lord.

All of us need to earnestly seek the Lord during these nine weeks by reading God's word and spending time with Him in prayer. We must ask the Master to send His Holy Spirit to lead us during these lessons on communicating with our Lord.

HOW TO USE THIS WORKBOOK

We have included all the necessary reading (entire books) from E. M. Bounds and Andrew Murray's books in this workbook. Each day has a new chapter followed by the reflection questions and answers. It is designed for recruits to read the chapter, answer the questions, study the weekly memory verse and spend time in prayer asking God to implant His words in our hearts. The workbook is divided into one orientation class followed by eight separate classes on key lessons about prayer (total of 9 classes). After each seven-day period there will be a class section. The final class will be a testimony time where new prayer warriors can share their answered prayers and the key lessons they learned in the class.

We encourage recruits to highlight, underline or make notes in this workbook as God reveals His insights on prayer in our lives. Each day's reflection questions will leave space for writing our impressions on how to implement what we learned about Christ's teachings on prayer.

This class is designed for no more than eight participants and is most effective with three to six participants. It takes time to effectively share testimonies, learn the memory verse and pray for each other's needs, and any group larger than eight will make that difficult. We also recommend that recruits pick an accountability partner from the group so they can go over the daily reflection questions and keep each other on track with their reading and daily prayer time.

Five Parts in Every Class

Each class is designed to take approximately one hour and we recommend breaking it into five separate segments. (This is only a guide, as you should allow the Holy Spirit to lead each class.) We will discuss the key points from the week's readings and share what we learned (15 min.) before giving testimonies of our answered prayers (15 min.). Next, we will spend a few minutes memorizing the weekly scripture verse (10 min.) before previewing next week's class (5 min.). We will finish by praying for all the recruits in the class (15 min.).

1. Opening Prayer
2. Lessons Learned
3. Testimonies
4. Scripture Memory
5. Next Class Preview
6. Prayer for Recruits

We encourage recruits to immerse each day's reading in prayer as we focus on the reflection questions. Also, take time to contemplate the weekly Word, Theme and Scripture verse. We recommend bringing your Bible to all classes and to have it handy when doing your daily reading. We have also added a chronological New Testament daily reading plan for the four gospels, and believe reading the story of Jesus's ministry as he taught about the Christian life and prayer will reinforce the daily lessons

ORIENTATION CLASS

WEEK 1

Opening- The goal of these lessons and this course is to help us develop a stronger prayer life. We have chosen E.M. Bounds book, *The Necessity of Prayer* and Andrew Murray's book *With Christ in the School of Prayer* to help increase our faith and add power to our prayer life. Over the next nine weeks we have all committed to reading one chapter a day, answering the reflection questions at the end of each lesson and spending time with the Lord in prayer.

We will meet as a class weekly to discuss our readings and prayer needs. The class leader will facilitate discussion about the week's reading as we go over the reflection questions before reciting the weekly memory verse.

Introductions- Each recruit should be prepared to tell the class a little bit about themselves.

1. Name_____

2. How long have you been a Christian? _____

3. Were you raised in Church? _____

4. Who is your favorite Bible character? _____

Take a few minutes to answer these questions. (The class leader will ask these questions and recruits can answer out loud if they choose. These are personal questions for each student to contemplate.)

1. How often do you pray each day? _____

2. Do you have a quiet time alone with God each day? _____

3. How many times did you pray for the lost last week? _____

4. How often do you pray for laborers for the harvest? _____

5. Have you ever read through the Bible? _____

6. How much of your prayer time is spent on praying for other's needs? (circle one) 10% - 20% - 30%- 40%- 50%- 60%- 70%- 80%- 90%- 100%

7. How much of your prayer time is spent praying for your personal requests? (circle one) 10% - 20% - 30%- 40%- 50%- 60%- 70%- 80%- 90%- 100%?

8. Do you ask God to deliver you from the evil one each day? _____

9. How often are your prayers answered? (circle one) 10% - 20% - 30%- 40%- 50%- 60%- 70%- 80%- 90%- 100%?

10. Do you ask for specific or general requests? _____

11. What is your biggest prayer that has been answered? _____

_____

_____

12. What is the last prayer you had answered? _____

_____

_____

13. What do you hope to learn from this class? _____

_____

_____

Next Class 1 Preview-

Word- Faith

Theme – Prayer is Faith in God

Verse- *Therefore I say unto you, what things soever ye desire, when ye pray, believe that ye receive them, and ye shall have them. -Mark 11:24*

Prayer for Recruits-

- Time to Pray Each Day
- A Desire for Prayer
- A Clear Mind During Prayer

THE NESSESITY OF PRAYER

BY

E.M. BOUNDS

FOREWORD

EDWARD McKENDREE BOUNDS did not merely pray well that he might write well about prayer. He prayed because the needs of the world were upon him. He prayed, for long years, upon subjects which the easy-going Christian rarely gives a thought, and for objects which men of less thought and faith are always ready to call impossible. From his solitary prayer-vigils, year by year, there arose teaching equaled by few men in modern Christian history. He wrote transcendently about prayer, because he was himself, transcendent in its practice.

As breathing is a physical reality to us so prayer was a reality for Bounds. He took the command, "Pray without ceasing" almost as literally as animate nature takes the law of the reflex nervous system, which controls our breathing.

Prayer-books -- real text-books, not forms of prayer -- were the fruit of this daily spiritual exercise. Not brief articles for the religious press came from his pen -- though he had been experienced in that field for years -- not pamphlets, but books were the product and result. He was hindered by poverty, obscurity, loss of prestige, yet his victory was not wholly reserved until his death.

In 1907, he gave to the world two small editions. One of these was widely circulated in Great Britain. The years following up to his death in 1913 were filled with constant labor and he went home to God leaving a collection of manuscripts. His letters carry the request that the present editor should publish these products of his gifted pen.

The preservation of the Bounds manuscripts to the present time has clearly been providential. The work of preparing them for the press has been a labor of love, consuming years of effort.

These books are unfailing wells for a lifetime of spiritual water-drawing. They are hidden treasures, wrought in the darkness of the dawn and the heat of the noon, on the anvil of experience, and beaten into wondrous form by the mighty stroke of the Divine. They are living voices whereby he, being dead, yet speaketh.

Claude Chilton, Jr

DAY 1

I. PRAYER AND FAITH

In any study of the principles, and procedure of prayer, of its activities and enterprises, first place, must, of necessity, be given to faith. It is the initial quality in the heart of any man who essays to talk to the Unseen. He must, out of sheer helplessness, stretch forth hands of faith. He *must* believe, where he cannot prove.

In the ultimate issue, prayer is simply faith, claiming its natural yet marvelous prerogatives -- faith taking possession of its illimitable inheritance. True godliness is just as true, steady, and persevering in the realm of faith as it is in the province of prayer. Moreover: when faith ceases to pray, it ceases to live.

In the ultimate issue, prayer is simply faith, claiming its natural yet marvelous prerogatives

Faith does the impossible because it brings God to undertake for us, and nothing is impossible with God. How great -- without qualification or limitation -- is the power of faith! If doubt be banished from the heart, and unbelief made stranger there, what we ask of God shall surely come to pass, and a believer hath vouchsafed to him "whatsoever he saith."

Prayer projects faith on God, and God on the world. Only God can move mountains, but faith and prayer move God. In His cursing of the fig-tree our Lord demonstrated His power. Following that, He proceeded to declare, that large powers were committed to faith and prayer, not in order to kill but to make alive, not to blast but to bless.

At this point in our study, we turn to a saying of our Lord, which there is need to emphasize, since it is the very keystone of the arch of faith and prayer.

"Therefore I say unto you, What things soever ye desire when ye pray, believe that ye receive them, and ye shall have them."

We should ponder well that statement -- "Believe that ye receive them, and ye shall have them." Here is described a faith which realizes, which appropriates, which *takes*. Such faith is a consciousness of the Divine, an experienced communion, a realized certainty.

Is faith growing or declining as the years go by? Does faith stand strong and four square, these days, as iniquity abounds and the love of many grows cold? Does faith maintain its hold, as religion tends to become a mere formality and worldliness increasingly prevails? The enquiry of our Lord, may, with great appropriateness, be ours. "When the Son of Man cometh," He asks, "shall He find faith on the earth?" We believe that He will, and it is ours, in this our day, to see to it that the lamp of faith is trimmed and burning, lest He come who *shall* come, and that right early.

Faith is the foundation of Christian character and the security of the soul. When Jesus was looking forward to Peter's denial, and cautioning him against it, He said unto His disciple:

"Simon, Simon, behold, Satan hath desired to have you, to sift you as wheat; but I have prayed for thee, that thy faith fail not."

Our Lord was declaring a central truth; it was Peter's faith He was seeking to guard; for well He knew that when faith is broken down, the foundations of spiritual life give way, and the entire structure of religious experience falls. It was Peter's faith which needed guarding. Hence Christ's solicitude for the welfare of His disciple's soul and His determination to fortify Peter's faith by His own all-prevailing prayer.

In his *Second Epistle*, Peter has this idea in mind when speaking of growth in grace as a measure of safety in the Christian life, and as implying fruitfulness.

"And besides this," he declares, "giving diligence, add to your faith virtue; and to virtue knowledge; and to knowledge temperance; and to temperance patience; and to patience godliness."

Of this additioning process, faith was the starting-point -- the basis of the other graces of the Spirit. Faith was the foundation on which other things were to be built. Peter does not enjoin his readers to add to works or gifts or virtues but to *faith*. Much depends on starting right in this business of growing in grace. There is a Divine order, of which Peter was aware; and so he goes on to declare that we are to give diligence to making our calling and election sure, which election is rendered certain adding to faith which, in turn, is done by constant, earnest praying. Thus faith is kept alive by prayer, and every step taken, in this adding of grace to grace, is accompanied by prayer.

The faith which creates powerful praying is the faith which centers itself on a powerful Person. Faith in Christ's ability to *do* and to *do greatly*, is the faith which prays greatly. Thus the leper lay hold upon the power of Christ. "Lord, if Thou wilt," he cried, "Thou canst make me clean." In this instance, we are shown how faith centered in Christ's ability to *do*, and how it secured the healing power.

It was concerning this very point, that Jesus questioned the blind men who came to Him for healing:

"Believe ye that I am able to do this?" He asks. "They said unto Him, Yea, Lord. Then touched He their eyes, saying, According to your faith be it unto you."

It was to inspire faith in His ability to *do* that Jesus left behind Him, that last, great statement, which, in the final analysis, is a ringing challenge to faith. "All power," He declared, "is given unto Me in heaven and in earth."

Again: faith is obedient; it goes when commanded, as did the nobleman, who came to Jesus, in the day of His flesh, and whose son was grievously sick.

Moreover: such faith acts. Like the man who was born blind, it goes to wash in the pool of Siloam when *told* to wash. Like Peter on Gennesaret it casts the net where Jesus commands, instantly, without question or doubt. Such faith takes away the stone from the grave of Lazarus promptly. A praying faith keeps the commandments of God and does those things which are well pleasing in His sight. It asks, "Lord, what wilt Thou have me to do?" and answers quickly, "Speak, Lord, Thy servant heareth." Obedience helps faith, and faith, in turn, helps obedience. To do God's will is essential to true faith, and faith is necessary to implicit obedience.

 howe

To do God's will is essential to true faith, and faith is necessary to implicit obedience.

howe

Yet faith is called upon, and that right often to wait in patience before God, and is prepared for God's seeming delays in answering prayer. Faith does not grow disheartened because prayer is not immediately honored; it takes God at His Word, and lets Him take what time He chooses in fulfilling His purposes, and in carrying on His work. There is bound to be much delay and long days of waiting for true faith, but faith accepts the conditions -- knows there will be delays in answering prayer, and regards such delays as times of testing, in the which, it is privileged to show its mettle, and the stern stuff of which it is made.

The case of Lazarus was an instance of where there was delay, where the faith of two good women was sorely tried: Lazarus was critically ill, and his sisters sent for Jesus. But, without any known reason, our Lord delayed His going to the relief of His sick friend. The plea was urgent and touching -- "Lord, behold, he whom Thou lovest is sick," -- but the Master is not moved by it, and the women's earnest request seemed to fall on deaf ears. What a trial to faith! Furthermore: our Lord's tardiness appeared to bring about hopeless disaster. While Jesus tarried, Lazarus died.

But the delay of Jesus was exercised in the interests of a greater good. Finally, He makes His way to the home in Bethany.

"Then said Jesus unto them plainly, Lazarus is dead. And I am glad for your sakes, that I was not there, to the intent ye may believe; nevertheless let us go unto him."

Fear not, O tempted and tried believer, Jesus *will* come, if patience be exercised, and faith hold fast. His delay will serve to make His coming the more richly blessed. Pray on. Wait on. Thou canst not fail. If Christ delay, wait for Him. In His own good time, He *will* come, and will not tarry.

Delay is often the test and the strength of faith. How much patience is required when these times of testing come! Yet faith gathers strength by waiting and praying. Patience has its perfect work in the school of delay. In some instances, delay is of the very essence of the prayer. God has to do many things, antecedent to giving the final answer -- things which are essential to the lasting good of him who is requesting favor at His hands.

Jacob prayed, with point and ardor, to be delivered from Esau. But before that prayer could be answered, there was much to be done with, and for Jacob. He must be changed, as well as Esau. Jacob had to be made into a new man, before Esau could be. Jacob had to be converted to God, before Esau could be converted to Jacob.

Among the large and luminous utterances of Jesus concerning prayer, none is more arresting than this:

"Verily, verily, I say unto you, He that believeth on Me, the works that I do shall he do also; and greater works than these shall he do; because I go unto My Father. And whatsoever ye shall ask in My Name, that will I do, that the Father may be glorified in the Son. If ye shall ask anything in My Name, I will do it."

How wonderful are these statements of what God will do in answer to prayer! Of how great importance these ringing words, prefaced, as they are, with the most solemn verity! Faith in Christ is the basis of all working, and of all praying. All wonderful works depend on wonderful praying, and all praying is done in the Name of Jesus Christ. Amazing lesson, of wondrous simplicity, is this praying in the name of the Lord Jesus! All other conditions are depreciated, everything else is renounced, save Jesus only. The name of Christ -- the Person of our Lord and Savior Jesus Christ -- must be supremely sovereign, in the hour and article of prayer.

If Jesus dwell at the fountain of my life; if the currents of His life have displaced and superseded all self-currents; if implicit obedience to Him be the inspiration and force of every movement of my life, then He can safely commit the praying to my will, and pledge Himself, by an obligation as profound as His own nature, that whatsoever is asked shall be granted. Nothing can be clearer, more distinct, more unlimited both in application and extent, than the exhortation and urgency of Christ, "Have faith in God."

Faith covers temporal as well as spiritual needs. Faith dispels all undue anxiety and needless care about what shall be eaten, what shall be drunk, what shall be worn. Faith lives in the present, and regards the day as being sufficient unto the evil thereof. It lives day by day, and dispels all fears for the morrow. Faith brings great ease of mind and perfect peace of heart.

Faith brings great ease of mind and perfect peace of heart.

"Thou wilt keep him in perfect peace whose mind is stayed on Thee: because he trusted in Thee."

When we pray, "Give us this day our daily bread," we are, in a measure, shutting tomorrow out of our prayer. We do not live in tomorrow but in today. We do not seek tomorrow's grace or tomorrow's bread. They thrive best, and get most out of life, who live in the living present. They pray best who pray for today's needs, not for tomorrows, which may render our prayers unnecessary and redundant by not existing at all!

True prayers are born of present trials and present needs. Bread, for today, is bread enough. Bread given for today is the strongest sort of pledge that there will be bread tomorrow. Victory today, is the assurance of victory tomorrow. Our prayers need to be focused upon the present, we must trust God today, and leave the morrow entirely with Him. The present is ours; the future belongs to God. Prayer is the task and duty of each recurring day -- daily prayer for daily needs.

As every day demands its bread, so every day demands its prayer. No amount of praying, done today, will suffice for tomorrow's praying. On the other hand, no praying for tomorrow is of any great value to us today. To-day's manna is what we need; tomorrow God will see that our needs are supplied. This is the faith which God seeks to inspire. So leave tomorrow, with its cares, its needs, its troubles, in God's hands. There is no storing tomorrow's grace or tomorrow's praying; neither is there any laying-up of today's grace, to meet tomorrow's necessities. We cannot have tomorrow's grace, we cannot eat tomorrow's bread, we cannot do tomorrow's praying. "Sufficient unto the day is the evil thereof;" and, most assuredly, if we possess faith, sufficient also, will be the good.

DAY 1
REFLECTION QUESTIONS

1. Is it possible to pray without faith in God? (circle one) no   yes

2. Why? _____

    _____

3. Do you have faith that God will answer your prayers? _____

    _____

4. Does your faith falter when God delays in answering your prayers? _____

    _____

5. What are two ways to increase faith?

    1._____ 2._____

6. What is a test of your faith? _____

7. What does faith cause us to think of? _____

8. What is my main takeaway from Day 1 that will improve my prayer life? _____

    _____

Fill in the blanks- Therefore I say unto you, what _____ soever ye desire, when ye pray, _____ that ye receive them, and ye shall have them. -Mark 11:24

Answers

1. No
2. The act of praying shows faith that there is a God and asking Him for anything shows faith
3. Personal response
4. Personal response
5. Pray (ask God) and read His word
6. Delay
7. Today and our needs for the present
8. Personal response

Class 1 Verse- *Therefore I say unto you, what things soever ye desire, when ye pray, believe that ye receive them, and ye shall have them.* -Mark 11:24

Day 1 Bible Reading - Luke 1; John 1:1-14

Day 1 notes

_____

_____

_____

_____

_____

_____

_____

_____

_____

_____

_____

_____

DAY 2

II. PRAYER AND FAITH (CONTINUED)

Genuine, authentic faith must be definite and free of doubt. Not simply general in character; not a mere belief in the being, goodness and power of God, but a faith which believes that the things which "he saith, shall come to pass." As the faith is specific, so the answer likewise will be definite: "He shall have whatsoever he saith." Faith and prayer select the things, and God commits Himself to do the very things which faith and persevering prayer nominate, and petition Him to accomplish.

The American Revised Version renders the twenty-fourth verse of the eleventh chapter of Mark, thus: "Therefore I say unto you, all things whatsoever ye pray and ask for, believe that ye receive them, and ye shall have them." Perfect faith has always in its keeping what perfect prayer asks for. How large and unqualified is the area of operation -- the "All things whatsoever!" How definite and specific the promise -- "Ye shall have them!"

Our chief concern is with our faith, -- the problems of its growth, and the activities of its vigorous maturity. A faith which grasps and holds in its keeping the very things it asks for, without wavering, doubt or fear -- that is the faith we need -- faith, such as is a pearl of great price, in the process and practice of prayer.

The statement of our Lord about faith and prayer quoted above is of supreme importance. Faith must be definite, specific; an unqualified, unmistakable request for the things asked for. It is not to be a vague, indefinite, shadowy thing; it must be something more than an abstract belief in God's willingness and ability to do for us. It is to be a definite, specific, asking for, and expecting the things for which we ask. Note the reading of Mark 11:23:

"And shall not doubt in his heart, but shall believe that those things which he saith shall come to pass; he shall have whatever he saith."

Just so far as the faith and the asking is definite, so also will the answer be. The giving is not to be something other than the things prayed for, but the actual things sought and named. "He shall have whatsoever he saith." It is all imperative, "He shall have." The granting is to be unlimited, both in quality and in quantity.

Faith and prayer select the subjects for petition, thereby determining what God is to do. "He shall have whatsoever he saith." Christ holds Himself ready to supply exactly, and fully, all the demands of faith and prayer. If the order on God be made clear, specific and definite, God will fill it, exactly in accordance with the presented terms.

෨෬

Faith is an operation of God, a Divine illumination, a holy energy implanted by the Word of God and the Spirit in the human soul

෨෬

Faith is not an abstract belief in the Word of God, nor a mere mental credence, nor a simple assent of the understanding and will; nor is it a passive acceptance of facts, however sacred or thorough. Faith is an operation of God, a Divine illumination, a holy energy implanted by the Word of God and the Spirit in the human soul -- a spiritual, divine principle which takes of the Supernatural and makes it a thing apprehendable by the faculties of time and sense.

Faith deals with God, and is conscious of God. It deals with the Lord Jesus Christ and sees in Him a Savior; it deals with God's Word, and lays hold of the truth; it deals with the Spirit of God, and is energized and inspired by its holy fire. God is the great objective of faith; for faith rests its whole weight on His Word. Faith is not an aimless act of the soul, but a looking to God and a resting upon His promises. Just as love and hope have always an objective so, also, has faith. Faith is not believing just *anything*; it is believing God, resting in Him, trusting His Word.

Faith gives birth to prayer, and grows stronger, strikes deeper, rises higher, in the struggles and wrestling's of mighty petitioning. Faith is the substance of things hoped for, the assurance and realization of the inheritance of the saints. Faith, too, is humble and persevering. It can wait and pray; it can stay on its knees, or lie in the dust. It is the one great condition of prayer; the lack of it lies at the root of all poor praying, feeble praying, little praying, unanswered praying.

The nature and meaning of faith is more demonstrable in what it does, than it is by reason of any definition given it. Thus, if we turn to the record of faith given us in that great honor roll, which constitutes the eleventh chapter of Hebrews, we see something of the wonderful results of faith. What a glorious list it is -- that of these men and women of faith! What marvelous achievements are there recorded, and set to the credit of faith! The inspired writer, exhausting his resources in cataloguing the Old Testament saints, who were such notable examples of wonderful faith, finally exclaims:

"And what shall I more say? For the time would fail me to tell of Gideon and Barak, and of Samson, and of Jephthae; of David also, and Samuel, and of the prophets."

And then the writer of *Hebrews* goes on again, in a wonderful strain, telling of the unrecorded exploits wrought through the faith of the men of old, "of whom the world was not worthy." "All these," he says, "obtained a good report through faith."

What an era of glorious achievements would dawn for the Church and the world, if only there could be reproduced a race of saints of like mighty faith, of like wonderful praying! It is not the intellectually great that the Church needs; nor is it men of wealth that the times demand. It is not people of great social influence that this day requires. Above everybody and everything else, it is men of faith, men of mighty prayer, men and women after the fashion of the saints and heroes enumerated in *Hebrews*, who "obtained a good report through faith," that the Church and the whole wide world of humanity needs.

Many men, of this day, obtain a good report because of their money-giving, their great mental gifts and talents, but few there be who obtain a "good report" because of their great faith in God, or because of the wonderful things which are being wrought through their great praying. Today, as much as at any time, we need men of great faith and men who are great in prayer. These are the two cardinal virtues which make men great in the eyes of God, the two things which create conditions of real spiritual success in the life and work of the Church. It is our chief concern to see that we maintain a faith of such quality and texture, as counts before God; which grasps, and holds in its keeping, the things for which it asks, without doubt and without fear.

Doubt and fear are the twin foes of faith.

Doubt and fear are the twin foes of faith. Sometimes, they actually usurp the place of faith, and although we pray, it is a restless, disquieted prayer that we offer, uneasy and often complaining. Peter failed to walk on Gennesaret because he permitted the waves to break over him and swamp the power of his faith. Taking his eyes from the Lord and regarding the water all about him, he began to sink and had to cry for succor -- "Lord, save, or I perish!"

Doubts should never be cherished, nor fears harbored. Let none cherish the delusion that he is a martyr to fear and doubt. It is no credit to any man's mental capacity to cherish doubt of God, and no comfort can possibly derive from such a thought. Our eyes should be taken off self, removed from our own weakness and allowed to rest implicitly upon God's strength. "Cast not away therefore your confidence, which hath great recompense of reward." A simple, confiding faith, living day by day, and casting its burden on the Lord, each hour of the day, will dissipate fear, drive away misgiving and deliver from doubt:

"Be careful for nothing, but in everything, by supplication and prayer, with thanksgiving, let your requests be made known unto God."

That is the Divine cure for all fear, anxiety, and undue concern of soul, all of which are closely akin to doubt and unbelief. This is the Divine prescription for securing the peace which passeth all understanding, and keeps the heart and mind in quietness and peace.

All of us need to mark well and heed the caution given in *Hebrews:* "Take heed, brethren, lest there be in any of you an evil heart of unbelief, in departing from the living God."

We need, also, to guard against unbelief as we would against an enemy. Faith needs to be cultivated. We need to keep on praying, "Lord, increase our faith," for faith is susceptible of increase. Paul's tribute to the Thessalonians was, that their faith grew exceedingly. Faith is increased by exercise, by being put into use. It is nourished by sore trials.

"That the trial of your faith, being much more precious than of gold that perisheth, though it be tried with fire, might be found unto praise and honour and glow at the appearing of Jesus Christ."

Faith grows by reading and meditating upon the Word of God. Most, and best of all, faith thrives in an atmosphere of prayer.

It would be well, if all of us were to stop, and inquire personally of ourselves: "Have I faith in God? Have I *real* faith, -- faith which keeps me in perfect peace, about the things of earth and the things of heaven?" This is the most important question a man can propound and expect to be answered. And there is another question, closely akin to it in significance and importance -- "Do I really pray to God so that He hears me and answers my prayers? And do I truly pray unto God so that I get direct from God the things I ask of Him?"

It was claimed for Augustus Caesar that he found Rome a city of wood, and left it a city of marble. The pastor who succeeds in changing his people from a prayerless to a prayerful people, has done a greater work than did Augustus in changing a city from wood to marble. And after all, this is the prime work of the preacher. Primarily, he is dealing with prayerless people -- with people of whom it is said, "God is not in all their thoughts." Such people he meets everywhere, and all the time. His main business is to turn them from being forgetful of God, from being devoid of faith, from being prayerless, so that they become people who habitually pray, who believe in God, remember Him and do His will. The preacher is not sent to merely induce men to join the Church, nor merely to get them to do better. It is to get them to pray, to trust God, and to keep God ever before their eyes that they may not sin against Him.

The work of the ministry is to change unbelieving sinners into praying and believing saints. The call goes forth by Divine authority, "Believe on the Lord Jesus Christ, and thou shalt be saved." We catch a glimpse of the tremendous importance of faith and of the great value God has set upon it, when we remember that He has made it the one indispensable condition of being saved. "By grace are ye saved, through faith." Thus, when we contemplate the great importance of prayer, we find faith standing immediately by its side. By faith are we saved, and by faith we *stay* saved. Prayer introduces us to a life of faith. Paul declared that the life he lived, he lived by faith in the Son of God, who loved him and gave Himself for him -- that he walked by faith and not by sight. Prayer is absolutely dependent upon faith. Virtually, it has no existence apart from it, and accomplishes nothing unless it be its

We need to keep on praying, "Lord, increase our faith," for faith is susceptible of increase.

The work of the ministry is to change unbelieving sinners into praying and believing saints.

inseparable companion. Faith makes prayer effectual, and in a certain important sense, must precede it.

"For he that cometh to God must believe that He is, and that He is a rewarder of them that diligently seek Him."

Before prayer ever starts toward God; before its petition is preferred, before its requests are made known -- faith must have gone on ahead; must have asserted its belief in the existence of God; must have given its assent to the gracious truth that "God is a rewarder of those that diligently seek His face." This is the primary step in praying. In this regard, while faith does not bring the blessing, yet it puts prayer in a position to ask for it, and leads to another step toward realization, by aiding the petitioner to believe that God is able and willing to bless.

Faith starts prayer to work -- clears the way to the mercy-seat. It gives assurance, first of all, that there is a mercy-seat, and that there the High Priest awaits the prayers and the prayers. Faith opens the way for prayer to approach God. But it does more. It accompanies prayer at every step she takes. It is her inseparable companion and when requests are made unto God, it is faith which turns the asking into obtaining. And faith follows prayer, since the spiritual life into which a believer is led by prayer, is a life of faith. The one prominent characteristic of the experience into which believers are brought through prayer, is not a life of works, but of faith.

Faith makes prayer strong, and gives it patience to wait on God. Faith believes that God is a rewarder. No truth is more clearly revealed in the Scriptures than this, while none is more encouraging. Even the closet has its promised reward, "He that seeth in secret, shall reward thee openly," while the most insignificant service rendered to a disciple in the name of the Lord, surely receives its reward. And to this precious truth faith gives its hearty assent.

Yet faith is narrowed down to one particular thing -- it does not believe that God will reward everybody, nor that He is a rewarder of all who pray, but that He is a rewarder of them that *diligently seek Him.* Faith rests its care on diligence in prayer, and gives assurance and encouragement to diligent seekers after God, for it is they, alone, who are richly rewarded when they pray.

We need constantly to be reminded that faith is the one inseparable condition of successful praying. There are other considerations entering into the exercise, but faith is the final, the one indispensable condition of true praying. As it is written in a familiar, primary declaration: "Without faith, it is impossible to please Him."

James puts this truth very plainly.

"If any of you lack wisdom," he says, "let him ask of God, that giveth to all men liberally, and upbraideth not, and it shall be given him. But let him ask in faith, nothing wavering. For he that wavereth (or doubteth) is like a wave of the sea, driven with the wind and tossed. For let not that man think that he shall receive any thing of the Lord."

Doubting is always put under the ban, because it stands as a foe to faith and hinders effectual praying. In the First Epistle to Timothy Paul gives us an invaluable truth relative to the conditions of successful praying, which he thus lays down: "I will therefore that men pray everywhere, lifting up holy hands, without wrath and doubting."

All questioning must be watched against and eschewed. Fear and peradventure have no place in true praying. Faith must assert itself and bid these foes to prayer depart. Too much authority cannot be attributed to faith; but prayer is the scepter by which it signalizes its power. How much of spiritual wisdom there is in the following advice written by an eminent old divine.

"Would you be freed from the bondage to corruption?" he asks. "Would you grow in grace in general and grow in grace in particular? If you would, your way is plain. Ask of God more faith. Beg of Him morning, and noon and night, while you walk by the way, while you sit in the house, when you lie down and when you rise up; beg of Him simply to impress Divine things more deeply on your heart, to give you more and more of the substance of things hoped for and of the evidence of things not seen."

Great incentives to pray are furnished in Holy Scriptures, and our Lord closes His teaching about prayer, with the assurance and promise of heaven. The presence of Jesus Christ in heaven, the preparation for His saints which He is making there, and the assurance that He will come again to receive them -- how all this helps the weariness of praying, strengthens its conflicts, sweetens its arduous toil! These things are the star of hope to prayer, the wiping away of its tears, the putting of the odor of heaven into the bitterness of its cry. The spirit of a pilgrim greatly facilitates praying. An earth-bound, earth-satisfied spirit cannot pray. In such a heart, the flame of spiritual desire is either gone out or smoldering in faintest glow. The wings of its faith are clipped, its eyes are filmed, its tongue silenced. But they, who in unswerving faith and unceasing prayer, wait continually upon the Lord, *do* renew their strength, *do* mount up with wings as eagles, *do* run, and are not weary, *do* walk, and not faint.

and supplication in the Spirit." Wise, with a great wisdom, would the present generation be if all professors of our faith could be induced to realize this all-important and vital truth, which is so absolutely indispensable to a successful Christian life.

It is just at this point in much present-day Christian profession, that one may find its greatest defect. There is little, or nothing, of the soldier element in it. The discipline, self-denial, spirit of hardship, determination, so prominent in and belonging to the military life, are, one and all, largely wanting. Yet the Christian life is *warfare*, all the way.

How comprehensive, pointed and striking are all Paul's directions to the Christian soldier, who is bent on thwarting the devil and saving his soul alive! First of all, he must possess a clear idea of the character of the life on which he has entered. Then, he must know something of his foes -- the adversaries of his immortal soul -- their strength, their skill, their malignity. Knowing, therefore, something of the character of the enemy, and realizing the need of preparation to overcome them, he is prepared to hear the Apostle's decisive conclusion:

"Finally, my brethren, be strong in the Lord, and in the power of His might. Put on the whole armor of God, that ye may be able to stand against the wiles of the devil. Wherefore, take unto you the whole armor of God, that ye may be able to stand in the evil day, and having done all, to stand."

All these directions end in a climax; and that climax is prayer. How can the brave warrior for Christ be made braver still? How can the strong soldier be made stronger still? How can the victorious battler be made still more victorious? Here are Paul's explicit directions to that end:

"Praying always with all prayer and supplication in the Spirit, and watching thereunto with all perseverance and supplication for all saints."

Prayer, and more prayer, adds to the fighting qualities and the more certain victories of God's good fighting-men. The power of prayer is most forceful on the battle-field amid the din and strife of the conflict. Paul was preeminently a soldier of the Cross. For him, life was no flowery bed of ease. He was no dress-parade, holiday soldier, whose only business was to don a uniform on set occasions. His was a life of intense conflict, the facing of many adversaries, the exercise of unsleeping vigilance and constant effort. And, at its close -- in sight of the end -- we hear him chanting his final song of victory, "I have fought a good fight," Reading between the lines, we see that he is more than conqueror!

℘℩℃℣

Prayer, and more prayer, adds to the fighting qualities and the more certain victories of God's good fighting-men.

℘℩℃℣

In his *Epistle to the Romans*, Paul indicates the nature of his soldier-life, giving us some views of the kind of praying needed for such a career. He writes:

"Now I beseech you, brethren, for the Lord Jesus Christ's sake, and for the love of the Spirit, that ye strive together with me in your prayers to God for me, that I may be delivered from them that do not believe in Judaea."

Paul *had* foes in Judaea -- foes who beset and opposed him in the form of "unbelieving men" and this, added to other weighty reasons, led him to urge the Roman Christians to "strive with him in prayer." That word "strive" indicated wrestling, the putting forth of great effort. This is the kind of effort, and this the sort of spirit, which must possess the Christian soldier.

Here is a great soldier, a captain-general, in the great struggle, faced by malignant forces who seek his ruin. His force is well-nigh spent. What reinforcements can he count on? What can give help and bring success to a warrior in such a pressing emergency? It is a critical moment in the conflict. What force can be added to the energy of his own prayers? The answer is -- in the prayers of others, even the prayers of his brethren who were at Rome. These, he believes, will bring him additional aid, so that he can win his fight, overcome his adversaries, and, ultimately, prevail.

The Christian soldier is to pray at all seasons, and under all circumstances. His praying must be arranged so as to cover his times of peace as well as his hours of active conflict. It must be available in his marching and his fighting. Prayer must diffuse all effort, impregnate all ventures, and decide all issues. The Christian soldier must be as intense in his praying as in his fighting, for his victories will depend very much more on his praying than on his fighting. Fervent supplication must be added to steady resolve, prayer and supplication must supplement the armor of God. The Holy Spirit must aid the supplication with His own strenuous plea. And the soldier must pray in the Spirit. In this, as in other forms of warfare, eternal vigilance is the price of victory; and thus, watchfulness and persistent perseverance, must mark the every activity of the Christian warrior.

ℰᘯᘓ

The Christian soldier must be as intense in his praying as in his fighting, for his victories will depend very much more on his praying than on his fighting.

ℰᘯᘓ

The soldier-prayer must reflect its profound concern for the success and well-being of the whole army. The battle is not altogether a personal matter; victory cannot be achieved for self, alone. There is a sense, in which the entire army of Christ is involved. The cause of God, His saints, their woes and trials, their duties and crosses, all should find a voice and a pleader in the Christian soldier, when he prays. He dare not limit his praying to himself. Nothing dries up spiritual secretions so certainly and completely; nothing poisons the fountain of spiritual life so effectively; nothing acts in such deadly fashion, as selfish praying.

Note carefully that the Christian's armor will avail him nothing, unless prayer be added. This is the pivot, the connecting link of the armor of God. This holds it together, and renders it effective. God's true soldier plans his campaigns, arranges his battle-forces, and conducts his conflicts, with prayer. It is all important and absolutely essential to victory, that prayer should so impregnate the life that every breath will be a petition, every sigh a supplication. The Christian soldier must needs be always fighting. He should, of sheer necessity, be always praying.

The Christian soldier is compelled to constant picket-duty. He must always be on his guard. He is faced by a foe who never sleeps, who is always alert, and ever prepared to take advantage of the fortunes of war. Watchfulness is a cardinal principle with Christ's warrior, "watch and pray," forever sounding in his ears. He cannot dare to be asleep at his post. Such a lapse brings him not only under the displeasure of the Captain of his salvation, but exposes him to added danger. Watchfulness, therefore, imperatively constitutes the duty of the soldier of the Lord.

In the New Testament, there are three different words, which are translated "watch." The first means "absence of sleep," and implies a wakeful frame of mind, as opposed to listlessness; it is an enjoinder to keep awake, circumspect, attentive, constant, and vigilant. The second word means "fully awake," -- a state induced by some rousing effort, which faculty excited to attention and interest, active, cautious, lest through carelessness or indolence, some destructive calamity should suddenly evolve. The third word means "to be calm and collected in spirit," dispassionate, untouched by slumberous or beclouding influences, a wariness against all pitfalls and beguilements.

All three definitions are used by St. Paul. Two of them are employed in connection with prayer. Watchfulness intensified, is a requisite for prayer. Watchfulness must guard and cover the whole spiritual man, and fit him for prayer. Everything resembling unpreparedness or non-vigilance, is death to prayer.

In *Ephesians*, Paul gives prominence to the duty of constant watchfulness, "Watching thereunto with all perseverance and supplication." Watch, he says, *watch*, WATCH! "And what I say unto you, I say unto all, Watch."

Sleepless wakefulness is the price one must pay for victory over his spiritual foes. Rest assured that the devil never falls asleep. He is ever "walking about, seeking whom he may devour." Just as a shepherd must never be careless and unwatchful lest the wolf devour his sheep, so the Christian soldier must ever have his eyes wide open, implying his possession of a spirit which neither slumbers nor grows careless. The inseparable companions and safeguards of prayer are vigilance, watchfulness, and a mounted guard. In writing to the Colossians Paul brackets these inseparable qualities together: "Continue in prayer," he enjoins, "and watch in the same, with thanksgiving."

When will Christians more thoroughly learn the twofold lesson, that they are called to a great warfare, and that in order to get the victory they must give themselves to unsleeping watchfulness and unceasing prayer?

"Be sober, be vigilant," says Peter, "because your adversary, the devil, walketh about seeking whom he may devour."

God's Church is a militant host. Its warfare is with unseen forces of evil. God's people compose an army fighting to establish His kingdom in the earth. Their aim is to destroy the sovereignty of Satan, and over its ruins, erect the Kingdom of God, which is "righteousness and peace and joy in the Holy Ghost." This militant army is composed of individual soldiers of the Cross, and the armor of God is needed for its defense. Prayer must be added as that which crowns the whole.

"Stand then in His great might, With all His strength endued; But take, to arm you for the fight, The panoply of God."

Prayer is too simple, too evident a duty, to need definition. Necessity gives being and shape to prayer. Its importance is so absolute, that the Christian soldier's life, in all the breadth and intensity of it, should be one of prayer. The entire life of a Christian soldier -- its being, intention, implication and action -- are all dependent on its being a life of prayer. Without prayer -- no matter what else he have -- the Christian soldier's life will be feeble, and ineffective, and constitute him an easy prey for his spiritual enemies.

Without prayer -- no matter what else he have -- the Christian soldier's life will be feeble

Christian experience will be sapless, and Christian influence will be dry and arid, unless prayer has a high place in the life. Without prayer the Christian graces will wither and die. Without prayer, we may add, preaching is edgeless and a vain thing, and the Gospel loses its wings and its loins. Christ is the lawgiver of prayer, and Paul is His Apostle of prayer. Both declare its primacy and importance, and demonstrate the fact of its indispensability. Their prayer-directions cover all places, include all times, and comprehend all things. How, then, can the Christian soldier hope or dream of victory, unless he be fortified by its power? How can he fail, if in addition to putting on the armor of God he be, at all times and seasons, "watching unto prayer"?

DAY 11
REFLECTION QUESTIONS

1. Define what vigilance is. _____

   _____

2. When are we instructed to pray? _____

3. What one item did Paul add to the armor of God in Ephesians? _____

4. In our conflict with the enemy what strengthens our prayer petitions? _____

   _____

5. Is there any time we can take a break from the battle against evil? _____

6. Have you taken any breaks in your life?   Yes   No

7. What was the result? _____

   _____

8. What is my main takeaway from Day 11 that will improve my prayer life? _____

   _____

   _____

Fill in the blanks - *The effectual* _____ _____ *of a righteous man*
_____ _____. *- James 5:16*

Answers

1. Keeping careful watch out for danger or difficulties
2. In all seasons
3. Prayer
4. Other Christians joining us in prayer
5. No, the devil never sleeps
6. Personal response
7. Personal response
8. Personal response

Class 2 Verse- *The effectual fervent prayer of a righteous man availeth much. - James 5:16*

Day 11 Bible Reading - Matthew 8:1-13; Luke 7

Day 11 notes

_____

_____

_____

_____

_____

_____

_____

_____

_____

_____

_____

_____

_____

_____

DAY 12

XII. PRAYER AND THE WORD OF GOD

God's Word is a record of prayer -- of praying men and their achievements, of the Divine warrant of prayer and of the encouragement given to those who pray. No one can read the instances, commands, examples, multiform statements which concern themselves with prayer, without realizing that the cause of God, and the success of His work in this world is committed to prayer; that praying men have been God's vicegerents on earth; that prayerless men have never been used of Him.

A reverence for God's holy Name is closely related to a high regard for His Word. This hallowing of God's Name; the ability to do His will on earth, as it is done in heaven; the establishment and glory of God's kingdom, are as much involved in prayer, as when Jesus taught men the Universal Prayer. That "men ought always to pray and not to faint," is as fundamental to God's cause, today, as when Jesus Christ enshrined that great truth in the immortal settings of the Parable of the Importunate Widow.

As God's house is called "the house of prayer," because prayer is the most important of its holy offices; so by the same token, the Bible may be called the Book of Prayer. Prayer is the great theme and content of its message to mankind.

God's Word is the basis, as it is the directory of the prayer of faith. "Let the word of Christ dwell in you richly in all wisdom," says St. Paul, "teaching and admonishing one another in psalms and hymns and spiritual songs, singing with grace in your hearts to the Lord."

As this word of Christ dwelling in us richly is transmuted and assimilated, it issues in praying. Faith is constructed of the Word and the Spirit, and faith is the body and substance of prayer.

In many of its aspects, prayer is dependent upon the Word of God. Jesus says:

"If ye abide in Me, and My words abide in you, ye shall ask what ye will, and it shall be done unto you."

The Word of God is the fulcrum upon which the lever of prayer is placed, and by which things are mightily moved. God has committed Himself, His purpose and His promise to prayer. His Word becomes the basis, the inspiration of our praying, and there are circumstances under which, by importunate prayer, we may obtain an addition, or an enlargement of His promises. It is said of the old saints that they, "through faith obtained promises." There would seem to be in prayer the capacity for going even beyond the Word, of getting even beyond His promise, into the very presence of God, Himself.

Jacob wrestled, not so much with a promise, as with the Promiser. We must take hold of the Promiser, lest the promise prove nugatory. Prayer may well be defined as that force which vitalizes and energizes the Word of God, by taking hold of God, Himself. By taking hold of the Promiser, prayer reissues, and makes personal the promise. "There is none that stirreth up himself to take hold of Me," is God's sad lament. "Let him take hold of My strength, that he may make peace with Me," is God's recipe for prayer.

By Scriptural warrant, prayer may be divided into the petition of faith and that of submission. The prayer of faith is based on the written Word, for "faith cometh by hearing, and hearing by the Word of God." It receives its answer, inevitably -- the very thing for which it prays.

The prayer of submission is without a definite word of promise, so to speak, but takes hold of God with a lowly and contrite spirit, and asks and pleads with Him, for that which the soul desires. Abraham had no definite promise that God would spare Sodom. Moses had no definite promise that God would spare Israel; on the contrary, there was the declaration of His wrath, and of His purpose to destroy. But the devoted leader gained his plea with God, when he interceded for the Israelites with incessant prayers and many tears. Daniel had no definite promise that God would reveal to him the meaning of the king's dream, but he prayed specifically, and God answered definitely.

The Word of God is made effectual and operative, by the process and practice of prayer. The Word of the Lord came to Elijah, "Go show thyself to Ahab, and I will send rain on the earth." Elijah showed himself to Ahab; but the answer to his prayer did not come, until he had pressed his fiery prayer upon the Lord seven times.

Paul had the definite promise from Christ that he "would be delivered from the people and the Gentiles," but we find him exhorting the Romans in the urgent and solemn manner concerning this very matter:

"Now I beseech you, brethren, for the Lord Jesus Christ's sake, and for the love of the Spirit, that ye strive together with me in your prayers to God for me; that I may be delivered from them that do not believe in Judaea, and that my service which I have for Jerusalem may be accepted of the saints."

The Word of God is a great help in prayer. If it be lodged and written in our hearts, it will form an outflowing current of prayer, full and irresistible. Promises, stored in the heart, are to be the fuel from which prayer receives life and warmth, just as the coal, stored in the earth, ministers to our comfort on stormy days and wintry nights. The Word of God is the food, by which prayer is nourished and made strong. Prayer, like man, cannot live by bread alone, "but by every word which proceedeth out of the mouth of the Lord."

Unless the vital forces of prayer are supplied by God's Word, prayer, though earnest, even vociferous, in its urgency, is, in reality, flabby, and vapid, and void. The absence of vital force in praying, can be traced to the absence of a constant supply of God's Word, to repair the waste, and renew the life. He who would learn to pray well, must first study God's Word, and store it in his memory and thought.

When we consult God's Word, we find that no duty is more binding, more exacting, than that of prayer.

When we consult God's Word, we find that no duty is more binding, more exacting, than that of prayer. On the other hand, we discover that no privilege is more exalted, no habit more richly owned of God. No promises are more radiant, more abounding, more explicit, more often reiterated, than those which are attached to prayer. "All things, whatsoever" are received by prayer, because "all things whatsoever" are promised. There is no limit to the provisions, included in the promises to prayer, and no exclusion from its promises. "Every one that asketh, receiveth." The word of our Lord is to this all-embracing effect: "If ye shall ask anything in My Name, I will do it."

Here are some of the comprehensive, and exhaustive statements of the Word of God about prayer, the things to be taken in by prayer, the strong promise made in answer to prayer:

"Pray without ceasing;" "continue in prayer;" "continuing instant in prayer;" "in everything by prayer, let your request be made known unto God;" "pray always, pray and not faint;" "men should pray everywhere;" "praying always, with all prayer and supplication."

What clear and strong statements are those which are put in the Divine record, to furnish us with a sure basis of faith, and to urge, constrain and encourage us to pray! How wide the range of prayer, as given us, in the Divine Revelation! How these Scriptures incite us to seek the God of prayer, with all our wants, with all our burdens!

In addition to these statements left on record for our encouragement, the sacred pages teem with facts, examples, incidents, and observations, stressing the importance and the absolute necessity of prayer, and putting emphasis on its all-prevailing power.

The utmost reach and full benefit of the rich promises of the Word of God, should humbly be received by us, and put to the test. The world will never receive the full benefits of the Gospel until this be done. Neither Christian experience nor Christian living will be what they ought to be till these Divine promises have been fully tested by those who pray. By prayer, we bring these promises of God's holy will into the realm of the actual and the real. Prayer is the philosopher's stone which transmutes them into gold.

If it be asked, what is to be done in order to render God's promises real, the answer is, that we must pray, until the words of the promise are clothed upon with the rich raiment of fulfilment.

God's promises are altogether too large to be mastered by desultory praying. When we examine ourselves, all too often, we discover that our praying does not rise to the demands of the situation; is so limited that it is little more than a mere oasis amid the waste and desert of the world's sin. Who of us, in our praying, measures up to this promise of our Lord:

"Verily, verily, I say unto you, He that believeth on Me, the works that I do shall he do also, and greater works than these shall he do, because I go to My Father."

How comprehensive, how far reaching, how all-embracing! How much is here, for the glory of God, how much for the good of man! How much for the manifestation of Christ's enthroned power, how much for the reward of abundant faith! And how great and gracious are the results which can be made to accrue from the exercise of commensurate, believing prayer!

Prayer, coupled with loving obedience, is the way to put God to the test, and to make prayer answer all ends and all things.

Look, for a moment, at another of God's great promises, and discover how we may be undergirded by the Word as we pray, and on what firm ground we may stand on which to make our petitions to our God:

"If ye abide in Me, and My words abide in you, ye shall ask what ye will, and it shall be done unto you."

In these comprehensive words, God turns Himself over to the will of His people. When Christ becomes our all-in-all, prayer lays God's treasures at our feet. Primitive Christianity had an easy and practical solution of the situation, and got all which God had to give. That simple and terse solution is recorded in John's *First Epistle:*

"Whatsoever we ask, we receive of Him, because we keep His commandments, and do those things which are pleasing in His sight."

Prayer, coupled with loving obedience, is the way to put God to the test, and to make prayer answer all ends and all things. Prayer, joined to the Word of God, hallows and makes sacred all God's gifts. Prayer is not simply to get things from God, but to make those things holy, which already have been received from Him. It is not merely to get a blessing, but also to be able to give a blessing. Prayer makes common things holy and secular things, sacred. It receives things from God with thanksgiving and hallows them with thankful hearts, and devoted service.

In the *First Epistle to Timothy*, Paul gives us these words:

"For every creature of God is good, and nothing to be refused, if it be received with thanksgiving. For it is sanctified by the word of God and prayer."

That is a statement which gives a negative to mere asceticism. God's good gifts are to be holy, not only by God's creative power, but, also, because they are made holy to us by prayer. We receive them, appropriate them and sanctify them by prayer.

Doing God's will, and having His Word abiding in us, is an imperative of effectual praying. But, it may be asked, how are we to know what God's will is? The answer is, by studying His Word, by hiding it in our hearts, and by letting the Word dwell in us richly. "The entrance of Thy word, giveth light."

To know God's will in prayer, we must be filled with God's Spirit, who maketh intercession for the saints, and in the saints, according to the will of God. To be filled with God's Spirit, to be filled with God's Word, is to know God's will. It is to be put in such a frame of mind, to be found in such a state of heart, as will enable us to read and interpret aright the purposes of the Infinite. Such filling of the heart, with the Word and the Spirit, gives us an insight into the will of the Father, and enables us to rightly discern His will, and puts within us, a disposition of mind and heart to make it the guide and compass of our lives.

Epaphras prayed that the Colossians might stand "perfect and complete in all the will of God." This is proof positive that, not only may we know the will of God, but that we may know *all* the will of God. And not only may we know all the will of God, but we may *do* all the will of God. We may, moreover, do all the will of God, not occasionally, or by a mere impulse, but with a settled habit of conduct. Still further, it shows us that we may not only do the will of God externally, but from the heart, doing it cheerfully, without reluctance, or secret disinclination, or any drawing or holding back from the intimate presence of the Lord.

DAY 12
REFLECTION QUESTIONS

1. How does Bounds describe the Bible? _____

2. God's word is the _____ of our praying.

3. How can we improve our prayers? _____

4. God's promises in His Word along with our prayers results in _____

5. How can we know God's will? _____

6. Do you know and understand God's will in your life? _____

   _____

7. How much time do you spend studying God's Word? _____

8. What is my main takeaway from Day 12 that will improve my prayer life? _____

   _____

   _____

Fill in the blanks - _____ *effectual* _____ *prayer* _____ _____ *righteous* _____ *availeth*

much. - *James 5:16*

Answers

1. Record of prayer or Book on prayer

2. Inspiration

3. Study God's Word and store it in our memory and heart

4. Answered prayers

5. Study God's Word

6. Personal response

7. Personal response

8. Personal response

Class 2 Verse- *The effectual fervent prayer of a righteous man availeth much. - James 5:16*

Day 12 Bible Reading - Matthew 11

Day 12 notes

_____

_____

_____

_____

_____

_____

_____

_____

_____

_____

_____

_____

_____

_____

DAY 13

XIII. PRAYER AND THE WORD OF GOD (CONTINUED)

Prayer has all to do with the success of the preaching of the Word. This, Paul clearly teaches in that familiar and pressing request he made to the Thessalonians:

"Finally, brethren, pray for us that the Word of the Lord may have free course, and be glorified."

Prayer opens the way for the Word of God to run without let or hindrance, and creates the atmosphere which is favorable to the word accomplishing its purpose. Prayer puts wheels under God's Word, and gives wings to the angel of the Lord "having the everlasting Gospel to preach unto them that dwell on the earth, and to every nation, and kindred, and tongue, and people." Prayer greatly helps the Word of the Lord.

The Parable of the Sower is a notable study of preaching, showing its differing effects and describing the diversity of hearers. The wayside hearers are legion. The soil lies all unprepared either by previous thought or prayer; as a consequence, the devil easily takes away the seed (which is the Word of God) and dissipating all good impressions, renders the work of the sower futile. No one for a moment believes, that so much of present-day sowing would go fruitless if only the hearers would prepare the ground of their hearts beforehand by prayer and meditation.

> **Prayer invariably begets a love for the Word of God, and sets people to the reading of it.**

Similarly with the stony-ground hearers, and the thorny-ground hearers. Although the word lodges in their hearts and begins to sprout, yet all is lost, chiefly because there is no prayer or watchfulness or cultivation following. The good-ground hearers are profited by the sowing, simply because their minds have been prepared for the reception of the seed, and that, after hearing, they have cultivated the seed sown in their hearts, by the exercise of prayer. All this gives peculiar emphasis to the conclusion of this striking parable: "Take heed, therefore, how ye hear." And in order that *we* may take heed how we hear, it is needful to give ourselves continually to prayer.

We have *got* to believe that underlying God's Word is prayer, and upon prayer, its final success will depend. In the *Book of Isaiah* we read:

"So shall My word be that goeth out of My mouth; it shall not return unto Me void, but it shall accomplish that which I please, and it shall prosper in the thing whereto I sent it."

In Psalm 19, David magnifies the Word of God in six statements concerning it. It converts the soul, makes wise the simple, rejoices the heart, enlightens the eyes, endures eternally, and is true and righteous altogether. The Word of God is perfect, sure, right, pure. It is heart-searching, and at the same time purifying, in its effect. It is no surprise therefore that after considering the deep spirituality of the Word of God, its power to search the inner nature of man, and its deep purity, the Psalmist should close his dissertation with this passage:

"Who can understand his errors?" And then praying after this fashion: "Cleanse Thou me from secret faults. Keep back Thy servant also from presumptuous sins. Let them not have dominion over me. Let the words of my mouth, and the meditations of

my heart be acceptable in Thy sight, O Lord, my strength and my redeemer."

James recognizes the deep spirituality of the Word, and its inherent saving power, in the following exhortation:

"Wherefore, lay apart all filthiness and superfluity of naughtiness, and receive with meekness the engrafted word, which is able to save your souls."

And Peter talks along the same line, when describing the saving power of the Word of God:

"Being born again, not of corruptible seed, but of incorruptible, by the word of God, which liveth and abideth forever."

Not only does Peter speak of being born again, by the incorruptible Word of God, but he informs us that to grow in grace we must be like new-born babes, desiring or feeding upon the "sincere milk of the Word."

That is not to say, however, that the mere form of words as they occur in the Bible have in them any saving efficacy. But the Word of God, be it remembered, is impregnated with the Holy Spirit. And just as there is a Divine element in the words of Scripture, so also is the same Divine element to be found in all true preaching of the Word, which is able to save and convert the soul.

Prayer invariably begets a love for the Word of God, and sets people to the reading of it. Prayer leads people to obey the Word of God, and puts into the heart which obeys a joy unspeakable. Praying people and Bible-reading people are the same sort of folk. The God of the Bible and the God of prayer are one. God speaks to man in the Bible; man speaks to God in prayer. One reads the Bible to discover God's will; he prays in order that he may receive power to do that will. Bible-reading and praying are the distinguishing traits of those who strive to know and please God. And just as prayer begets a love for the Scriptures, and sets people to reading the Bible, so, also, does prayer cause men and women to visit the house of God, to hear the Scriptures expounded. Church-going is closely connected with the Bible, not so much because the Bible cautions us against "forsaking the assembling of ourselves together as the manner of some is," but because in God's house, God's chosen minister declares His Word to dying men, explains the Scriptures, and enforces their teachings upon his hearers. And prayer germinates a resolve, in those who practice it, not to forsake the house of God.

Prayer begets a church-going conscience, a church-loving heart, a church-supporting spirit. It is the praying people, who make it a matter of conscience, to attend the preaching of the Word; who delight in its reading; exposition; who support it with their influence and their means. Prayer exalts the Word of God and gives it preeminence in the estimation of those who faithfully and wholeheartedly call upon the Name of the Lord.

ഇറ

Bible-reading and praying are the distinguishing traits of those who strive to know and please God.

ഇറ

Prayer draws its very life from the Bible, and has no standing ground outside of the warrant of the Scriptures. Its very existence and character is dependent on revelation made by God to man in His holy Word. Prayer, in turn, exalts this same revelation, and turns men toward that Word. The nature, necessity and all-comprehending character of prayer, is based on the Word of God.

Psalm 119 is a directory of God's Word. With three or four exceptions, each verse contains a word which identifies, or locates, the Word of God. Quite often, the writer breaks out into supplication, several times praying, "Teach me Thy statutes." So deeply impressed is he with the wonders of God's Word, and of the need for Divine illumination wherewith to see and understand the wonderful things recorded therein, that he fervently prays:

"Open Thou mine eyes, that I may behold wondrous things out of Thy law."

From the opening of this wonderful Psalm to its close, prayer and God's Word are intertwined. Almost every phase of God's Word is touched upon by this inspired writer. So thoroughly convinced was the Psalmist of the deep spiritual power of the Word of God that he makes this declaration:

"Thy word have I hid in my heart that I might not sin against Thee."

Here the Psalmist found his protection against sinning. By having God's Word hidden in his heart; in having his whole being thoroughly impregnated with that Word; in being brought completely under its benign and gracious influence, he was enabled to walk to and fro in the earth, safe from the attack of the Evil One, and fortified against a proneness to wander out of the way.

We find, furthermore, the power of prayer to create a real love for the Scriptures, and to put within men a nature which will take pleasure in the Word. In holy ecstasy he cries, "O, how I love Thy law! It is my meditation all the day." And again: "How sweet are Thy words to my taste! Yea, sweeter than honey to my taste."

Would we have a relish for God's Word? Then let us give ourselves continually to prayer. He who would have a heart for the reading of the Bible must not -- dare not -- forget to pray. The man of whom it can be said, "His delight is in the law of the Lord," is the man who can truly say, "I delight to visit the place of prayer." No man loves the Bible, who does not love to pray. No man loves to pray, who does not delight in the law of the Lord.

ଛୀଔ

Reading God's Word regularly, and praying habitually in the secret place of the Most High puts one where he is absolutely safe from the attacks of the enemy of souls,

ଛୀଔ

Our Lord was a man of prayer, and He magnified the Word of God, quoting often from the Scriptures. Right through His earthly life Jesus observed Sabbath-keeping, church-going and the reading of the Word of God, and had prayer intermingled with them all:

"And He came to Nazareth where He had been brought up, and as His custom was, He went into the synagogue on the Sabbath Day, and stood up to read."

Here, let it be said, that no two things are more essential to a spirit-filled life than Bible-reading and secret prayer; no two things more helpful to growth in grace; to getting the largest joy out of a Christian life; toward establishing one in the ways of eternal peace. The neglect of these all-important duties, presages leanness of soul, loss of joy, absence of peace, dryness of spirit, decay in all that pertains to spiritual life. Neglecting these things paves the way for apostasy, and gives the Evil One an advantage such as he is not likely to ignore. Reading God's Word regularly, and praying habitually in the secret place of the Most High puts one where he is absolutely safe from the attacks of the enemy of souls, and guarantees him salvation and final victory, through the overcoming power of the Lamb.

DAY 13
REFLECTION QUESTIONS

1. How can a believer cultivate the word in their heart? _____

2. Prayer leads to more _____ _____ _____ and a stronger
   _____ for the Word of God.

3. _____ speaks to _____ in the Bible; _____ speaks to _____ in prayer.

4. Have you ever had a time in your life that you didn't want to read your Bible? _____
   _____

5. Were you praying daily during that time? _____

6. What two things are essential to living a spirit filled life? _____
   and _____

7. What is my main takeaway from Day 13 that will improve my prayer life? _____
   _____
   _____

Fill in the blanks - *The* _____ _____ _____ *of a*
_____ _____ _____ *much. - James 5:16*

Answers

1. Pray
2. Reading God's word, love
3. God, man, man, God
4. Personal response
5. Personal response
6. Bible Reading, secret prayer
7. Personal response

Class 2 Verse- *The effectual fervent prayer of a righteous man availeth much. - James 5:16*

Day 13 Bible Reading - Matthew 12:22-50

Day 13 notes

_____

_____

_____

_____

_____

_____

_____

_____

_____

_____

_____

_____

_____

XIV. PRAYER AND THE HOUSE OF GOD

Prayer stands related to places, times, occasions and circumstances. It has to do with God and with everything which is related to God, and it has an intimate and special relationship to His house. A church is a sacred place, set apart from all unhallowed and secular uses, for the worship of God. As worship is prayer, the house of God is a place set apart for worship. It is no common place; it is where God dwells, where He meets with His people, and He delights in the worship of His saints.

Prayer is always in place in the house of God. When prayer is a stranger there, then it ceases to be God's house at all. Our Lord put peculiar emphasis upon what the Church was when He cast out the buyers and sellers in the Temple, repeating the words from Isaiah, "It is written, My house shall be called the house of prayer." He makes prayer preeminent, that which stands out above all else in the house of God. They, who sidetrack prayer or seek to minify it, and give it a secondary place, pervert the Church of God, and make it something less and other than it is ordained to be.

The life, power and glory of the Church is prayer.

Prayer is perfectly at home in the house of God. It is no stranger, no mere guest; it belongs there. It has a peculiar affinity for the place, and has, moreover, a Divine right there, being set, therein, by Divine appointment and approval.

The inner chamber is a sacred place for personal worship. The house of God is a holy place for united worship. The prayer-closet is for individual prayer. The house of God is for mutual prayer, concerted prayer, united prayer. Yet even in the house of God, there is the element of private worship, since God's people are to worship Him and pray to Him, personally, even in public worship. The Church is for the united prayer of kindred, yet individual believers.

The life, power and glory of the Church is prayer. The life of its members is dependent on prayer and the presence of God is secured and retained by prayer. The very place is made sacred by its ministry. Without it, the Church is lifeless and powerless. Without it, even the building, itself, is nothing, more or other, than any other structure. Prayer converts even the bricks, and mortar, and lumber, into a sanctuary, a holy of holies, where the Shekinah dwells. It separates it, in spirit and in purpose from all other edifices. Prayer gives a peculiar sacredness to the building, sanctifies it, sets it apart for God, conserves it from all common and mundane affairs.

With prayer, though the house of God might be supposed to lack everything else, it becomes a Divine sanctuary. So the Tabernacle, moving about from place to place, became the holy of holies, because prayer was there. Without prayer the building may be costly, perfect in all its appointments, beautiful for situation and attractive to the eye, but it comes down to the human, with nothing Divine in it, and is on a level with all other buildings.

Without prayer, a church is like a body without spirit; it is a dead, inanimate thing. A church with prayer in it, has God in it. When prayer is set aside, God is outlawed. When prayer becomes an unfamiliar exercise, then

God Himself is a stranger there.

As God's house is a house of prayer, the Divine intention is that people should leave their homes and go to meet Him in His own house. The building is set apart for prayer especially, and as God has made special promise to meet His people there, it is their duty to go there, and for that specific end. Prayer should be the chief attraction for all spiritually minded church-goers. While it is conceded that the preaching of the Word has an important place in the house of God, yet prayer is its predominating, distinguishing feature. Not that all other places are sinful, or evil, in themselves or in their uses. But they are secular and human, having no special conception of God in them. The Church is, essentially, religious and Divine. The work belonging to other places is done without special reference to God. He is not specifically recognized, nor called upon. In the Church, however, God is acknowledged, and nothing is done without Him. Prayer is the one distinguishing mark of the house of God. As prayer distinguishes Christian from unchristian people, so prayer distinguishes God's house from all other houses. It is a place where faithful believers meet with their Lord.

ಜ೦ೞ

While it is conceded that the preaching of the Word has an important place in the house of God, yet prayer is its predominating, distinguishing feature.

ಜ೦ೞ

As God's house is, preeminently, a house of prayer, prayer should enter into and underlie everything that is undertaken there. Prayer belongs to every sort of work appertaining to the Church of God. As God's house is a house where the business of praying is carried on, so is it a place where the business of making praying people out of prayerless people is done. The house of God is a Divine workshop, and there the work of prayer goes on. Or the house of God is a Divine schoolhouse, in which the lesson of prayer is taught; where men and women learn to pray, and where they are graduated, in the school of prayer.

Any church calling itself the house of God, and failing to magnify prayer; which does not put prayer in the forefront of its activities; which does not teach the great lesson of prayer, should change its teaching to conform to the Divine pattern or change the name of its building to something other than a house of prayer.

On an earlier page, we made reference to the finding of the Book of the Law of the Lord given to Moses. How long that book had been there, we do not know. But when tidings of its discovery were carried to Josiah, he rent his clothes and was greatly disturbed. He lamented the neglect of God's Word and saw, as a natural result, the iniquity which abounded throughout the land.

And then, Josiah thought of God, and commanded Hilkiah, the priest, to go and make inquiry of the Lord. Such neglect of the Word of the Law was too serious a matter to be treated lightly, and God must be enquired of, and repentance shown, by himself, and the nation:

"Go enquire of the Lord for me, and for them that are left in Israel and in Judah, concerning the words of the book that is found; for great is the wrath of the Lord that is poured out upon us, because our fathers have not kept the word of the Lord, to do after all that is written in this book."

But that was not all. Josiah was bent on promoting a revival of religion in his kingdom, so we find him gathering all the elders of Jerusalem and Judah together, for that purpose. When they had come together, the king went into the house of the Lord, and himself read in all the words of the Book of the Covenant that was found in the house of the Lord.

With this righteous king, God's Word was of great importance. He esteemed it at its proper worth, and counted a knowledge of it to be of such grave importance, as to demand his consulting God in prayer about it, and to warrant the gathering together of the notables of his kingdom, so that they, together with himself, should be instructed out of God's Book concerning God's Law.

When Ezra, returned from Babylon, was seeking the reconstruction of his nation, the people, themselves, were alive to the situation, and, on one occasion, the priests, Levites and people assembled themselves together as one man before the water gate.

"And they spake unto Ezra the scribe, to bring the book of the law of Moses, which the Lord had commanded to Israel. And Ezra the priest brought the law before the congregation, both of men and women, and all that could hear with understanding. And he read therein before the street that was before the water gate from the morning until midday; and the ears of all the people were attentive unto the book of the law."

This was Bible-reading Day in Judah -- a real revival of Scripture-study. The leaders read the law before the people, whose ears were keen to hear what God had to say to them out of the Book of the Law. But it was not only a Bible-reading day. It was a time when real preaching was done, as the following passage indicates:

"So they read in the book in the law of God distinctly and gave the sense, and caused them to understand the reading."

Prayer and preaching: preaching and prayer! They cannot be separated.

Here then is the Scriptural definition of preaching. No better definition can be given. To read the Word of God distinctly -- to read it so that the people could hear and understand the words read; not to mumble out the words, nor read it in an undertone or with indistinctness, but boldly and clearly -- that was the method followed in Jerusalem, on this auspicious day. Moreover: the sense of the words was made clear in the meeting held before the water gate; the people were treated to a high type of expository preaching. That was *true* preaching -- preaching of a sort which is sorely needed, today, in order that God's Word may have due effect on the hearts of the people. This meeting in Jerusalem surely contains a lesson which all present-day preachers should learn and heed.

No one having any knowledge of the existing facts, will deny the comparative lack of expository preaching in the pulpit effort of today. And none, we should, at least, imagine, will do other than lament the lack. Topical preaching, polemical preaching, historical preaching, and other forms of sermonic output have, one supposes, their rightful and opportune uses. But expository preaching -- the prayerful expounding of the Word of God is preaching that *is* preaching -- pulpit effort *par excellence*.

For its successful accomplishment, however, a preacher needs must be a man of prayer. For every hour spent in his study-chair, he will have to spend two upon his knees. For every hour he devotes to wrestling with an obscure passage of Holy Writ, he must have two in which to be found wrestling with God. Prayer and preaching: preaching and prayer! They cannot be separated. The ancient cry was: "To your tents, O Israel!" The modern cry should be: "To your knees, O preachers, to your knees!"

DAY 14
REFLECTION QUESTIONS

1. What did Jesus call God's house? _____

2. What secures and retains God's presence? _____

3. Can your church be called a house of prayer? _____

4. What does your church put the most emphasis on? (circle one) Preaching, singing, bible study, fellowship, or prayer.

5. Does your church teach believers how to pray? _____

6. Bounds says _____ must accompany preaching to be successful.

7. What is my main takeaway from Day 14 that will improve my prayer life? _____

    _____

    _____

Fill in the blanks - _____ _____ _____ _____ _____ _____

_____ *man* _____ _____. - *James 5:16*

Answers

1. A house of prayer
2. United prayer
3. Personal response
4. Personal response
5. Personal response
6. Prayer
7. Personal response

Class 2 Verse- *The effectual fervent prayer of a righteous man availeth much. - James 5:16*

Day 14 Bible Reading - Matthew 13; Luke 8

Day 14 notes

_____

_____

_____

_____

_____

_____

_____

_____

_____

_____

_____

_____

_____

_____

CLASS 2

WEEK 3

Opening Prayer –Lord help us to obey. **Word** - Obedience

Key Questions-

1. Which two things cannot co-exist? _____ and _____

2. _____ _____ is the number one reason our prayers go unanswered.

3. Can a man keep all of God's commands? _____

4. What is a key ingredient of effective prayer? _____

5. How can we know God's will? _____

6. What should be the top priority of a church? _____

Theme- God hears the prayers of an obedient child

Testimonies- What is God doing through your prayer life?

Scripture Memory-

Class 2 Verse- *The effectual fervent prayer of a righteous man availeth much. - James 5:16*

Next Class Preview-

Word- Answer

Theme- Everyone Who Asks Receives

Verse- *Ask, and it shall be given you; seek, and ye shall find; knock, and it shall be opened unto you: For every one that asketh receiveth; and he that seeketh findeth; and to him that knocketh it shall be opened.- Matthew 7:7-8*

Prayer for Students-

- Time to Pray Each Day
- A Desire for Prayer
- A Clear Mind During Prayer
- Show us God's will

Class 2 Answers

1. Prayer and sinning
2. Unholy living
3. Yes
4. Obedience
5. Read Bible
6. Prayer

Class 2 notes

_____

_____

_____

_____

_____

_____

_____

_____

_____

_____

_____

_____

_____

_____

_____

_____

_____

WITH CHRIST IN THE SCHOOL OF PRAYER

BY
ANDREW MURRAY

PREFACE.

Of all the promises connected with the command, 'ABIDE IN ME,' there is none higher, and none that sooner brings the confession, 'not that I have already attained, or am already made perfect,' than this: 'If ye abide in me, ask *whatsoever ye will, and it shall be done unto you.'* Power with God is the highest attainment of the life of full abiding.

And of all the traits of a life LIKE CHRIST there is none higher and more glorious than conformity to Him in the work that now engages Him without ceasing in the Father's presence--His all-prevailing intercession. The more we abide in Him, and grow unto His likeness, will His priestly life work in us mightily, and our life become what His is, a life that ever pleads and prevails for men.

'Thou hast made us kings and priests unto God.' Both in the king and the priest the chief thing is power, influence, and blessing. In the king it is the power coming downward; in the priest, the power rising upward, prevailing with God. In our blessed Priest-King, Jesus Christ, the kingly power is founded on the priestly '*He is able* to save to the uttermost, *because* He ever liveth to make intercession.' In us, His priests and kings, it is no otherwise: it is in intercession that the Church is to find and wield its highest power that each member of the Church is to prove his descent from Israel, who as a prince had power with God and with men, and prevailed.

It is under a deep impression that the place and power of prayer in the Christian life is too little understood, that this book has been written. I feel sure that as long as we look on prayer chiefly as the means of maintaining our own Christian life, we shall not know fully what it is meant to be. But when we learn to regard it as the highest part of the work entrusted to us, the root and strength of all other work, we shall see that there is nothing that we so need to study and practice as the art of praying aright. If I have at all succeeded in pointing out the progressive teaching of our Lord in regard to prayer, and the distinct reference the wonderful promises of the last night (John 14:16) have to the works we are to do in His Name, to the greater works, and to the bearing much fruit, we shall all admit that it is only when the Church gives herself up to this holy work of intercession that we can expect the power of Christ to manifest itself in her behalf. It is my prayer that God may use this little book to make clearer to some of His children the wonderful place of power and influence which He is waiting for them to occupy, and for which a weary world is waiting too

In connection with this there is another truth that has come to me with wonderful clearness as I studied the teaching of Jesus on prayer. It is this: that the Father waits to hear every prayer of faith, to give us whatsoever we will, and whatsoever we ask in Jesus' name. We have become so accustomed to limit the wonderful love and the large promises of our God, that we cannot read the simplest and clearest statements of our Lord without the qualifying clauses by which we guard and expound them. If there is one thing I think the Church needs to learn, it is that God means prayer to have an answer, and that it hath not entered into the heart of man to conceive what God will do for His child who gives himself to believe that his prayer will be heard. *God hears prayer;* this is a truth universally admitted, but of which very few understand the meaning, or experience the power. If what I have written stir my reader to go to the Master's words, and take His wondrous promises simply and literally as they stand, my object has been attained.

And then just one thing more. Thousands have in these last year's found an unspeakable blessing in learning how completely Christ is our life, and how He undertakes to be and to do all in us that we need. I know not if we have yet learned to apply this truth to our prayer-life. Many complain that they have not the power to pray in faith, to pray the effectual prayer that availeth much. The message I would fain bring them is that the blessed Jesus is waiting, is longing, to teach them this. Christ is our life: in heaven He ever liveth to pray; His life in us is an ever-praying life, if we will but trust Him for it. Christ teaches us to pray not only by example, by instruction, by command, by promises, but *by showing us* HIMSELF, *the ever-living Intercessor, as our Life.* It is when we believe this, and go and abide in Him for our prayer-life too, that our fears of not being able to pray aright will vanish, and we shall joyfully and triumphantly trust our Lord to teach us to pray, to be Himself the life and the power of our prayer. May God open our eyes to see what the holy ministry of intercession is to which, as His royal priesthood, we have been set apart. May He give us a large and strong heart to believe what mighty influence our prayers can exert. And may all fear as to our being able to fulfil our vocation vanish as we see Jesus, living ever to pray, living in us to pray, and standing surety for our prayer-life.

ANDREW MURRAY

WELLINGTON, *28th October* 1895

DAY 15

LORD TEACH US TO PRAY OR, THE ONLY TEACHER

'And it came to pass, as He was praying in a certain place, that when He ceased, one of His disciples said to Him, Lord, teach us to pray.'--**LUKE 11:1**

The disciples had been with Christ, and seen Him pray. They had learnt to understand something of the connection between His wondrous life in public, and His secret life of prayer. They had learnt to believe in Him as a Master in the art of prayer--none could pray like Him. And so they came to Him with the request, 'Lord, teach us to pray.' And in after years they would have told us that there were few things more wonderful or blessed that He taught them than His lessons on prayer.

And now still it comes to pass, as He is praying in a certain place, that disciples who see Him thus engaged feel the need of repeating the same request, 'Lord, teach us to pray.' As we grow in the Christian life, the thought and the faith of the Beloved Master in His never-failing intercession becomes ever more precious, and the hope of being *Like Christ* in His intercession gains an attractiveness before unknown. And as we see Him pray, and remember that there is none who can pray like Him, and none who can teach like Him, we feel the petition of the disciples, 'Lord, teach us to pray,' is just what we need. And as we think how all He is and has, how He Himself is our very own, how He is Himself our life, we feel assured that we have but to ask, and He will be delighted to take us up into closer fellowship with Himself, and teach us to pray even as He prays.

Come, my brothers! Shall we not go to the Blessed Master and ask Him to enroll our names too anew in that school which He always keeps open for those who long to continue their studies in the Divine art of prayer and intercession? Yes, let us this very day say to the Master, as they did of old, 'Lord, teach us to pray.' As we meditate, we shall find each word of the petition we bring to be full of meaning

'Lord, teach us *to pray*.' Yes, *to pray*. This is what we need to be taught. Though in its beginnings prayer is so simple that the feeblest child can pray, yet it is at the same time the highest and holiest work to which man can rise. It is fellowship with the Unseen and Most Holy One. The powers of the eternal world have been placed at its disposal. It is the very essence of true religion, the channel of all blessings, the secret of power and life. Not only for ourselves, but for others, for the Church, for the world, it is to prayer that God has given the right to take hold of Him and His strength. It is on prayer that the promises wait for their fulfilment, the kingdom for its coming, the glory of God for its full revelation. And for this blessed work, how slothful and unfit we are. It is only the Spirit of God that can enable us to do it aright. How speedily we are deceived into a resting in the form, while the power is wanting. Our early training, the teaching of the Church, the influence of habit, the stirring of the emotions--how easily these lead to prayer which has no spiritual power, and avails but little. True prayer, that takes hold of God's strength, that availeth much, to which the gates of heaven are really opened wide--who would not cry, Oh for someone to teach me thus to pray?

> ℰℭ
>
> **'Lord, teach us *to pray*.' Yes, *to pray*. This is what we need to be taught.**
>
> ℰℭ

92

Jesus has opened a school, in which He trains His redeemed ones, who specially desire it, to have power in prayer. Shall we not enter it with the petition, Lord! it is just this we need to be taught! O teach us to *pray*.

'Lord, teach *us* to pray.' Yes, *us*, Lord. We have read in They Word with what power Thy believing people of old used to pray, and what mighty wonders were done in answer to their prayers. And if this took place under the Old Covenant, in the time of preparation, how much more wilt Thou not now, in these days of fulfilment, give Thy people this sure sign of Thy presence in their midst. We have heard the promises given to Thine apostles of the power of prayer in Thy name, and have seen how gloriously they experienced their truth: we know for certain, they can become true to us too. We hear continually even in these days what glorious tokens of Thy power Thou dost still give to those who trust Thee fully. Lord! these all are men of like passions with ourselves; teach *us* to pray so too. The promises are for us, the powers and gifts of the heavenly world are for us. O teach *us* to pray so that we may receive abundantly. To us too Thou hast entrusted Thy work, on our prayer too the coming of Thy kingdom depends, in our prayer too Thou canst glorify Thy name; 'Lord teach us to pray.' Yes, us, Lord; we offer ourselves as learners; we would indeed be taught of Thee. 'Lord, teach *us* to pray.'

'Lord, *teach* us to pray.' Yes, we feel the need now of being *taught* to pray. At first there is no work appears so simple; later on, none that is more difficult; and the confession is forced from us: We know not how to pray as we ought. It is true we have God's Word, with its clear and sure promises; but sin has so darkened our mind, that we know not always how to apply the word. In spiritual things we do not always seek the most needful things, or fail in praying according to the law of the sanctuary. In temporal things we are still less able to avail ourselves of the wonderful liberty our Father has given us to ask what we need. And even when we know what to ask, how much there is still needed to make prayer acceptable. It must be to the glory of God, in full surrender to His will, in full assurance of faith, in the name of Jesus, and with a perseverance that, if need be, refuses to be denied. All this must be learned. It can only be learned in the school of much prayer, for practice makes perfect. Amid the painful consciousness of ignorance and unworthiness, in the struggle between believing and doubting, the heavenly art of effectual prayer is learnt. Because, even when we do not remember it, there is One, the Beginner and Finisher of faith and prayer, who watches over our praying, and sees to it that *in all who trust Him for it* their education in the school of prayer shall be carried on to perfection. Let but the deep undertone of all our prayer be the teachableness that comes from a sense of ignorance, and from faith in Him as a perfect teacher, and we may be sure we shall be taught, we shall learn to pray in power. Yes, we may depend upon it, He *teaches* to pray.

> It must be to the glory of God, in full surrender to His will, in full assurance of faith, in the name of Jesus, and with a perseverance that, if need be, refuses to be denied.

'*Lord,* teach us to pray.' None can teach like Jesus, none but Jesus; therefore we call on Him, 'LORD, teach us to pray.' A pupil needs a teacher, who knows his work, who has the gift of teaching, who in patience and love will descend to the pupil's needs. Blessed be God! Jesus is all this and much more. He knows what prayer is. It is Jesus, praying Himself, who teaches to pray. He knows what prayer is. He learned it amid the trials and tears of His earthly life. In heaven it is still His beloved work: His life there is prayer. Nothing delights Him more than to find those whom He can take with Him into the Father's presence, whom He can clothe with power to pray down God's blessing on those around them, whom He can train to be His fellow-workers in the intercession by which the kingdom is to be revealed on earth. He knows how to teach. Now by the urgency of felt need, then by the confidence with which joy inspires. Here by the teaching of the Word, there by the testimony of another believer who knows what it is to have prayer heard. By His Holy Spirit, He has access to our heart, and teaches us to pray by showing us the sin that hinders the prayer, or giving us the assurance that we please God. He teaches, by giving not only thoughts of what to ask or how to ask, but by breathing within us the very spirit of prayer, by living within us as the Great Intercessor. We may indeed and most joyfully say, 'Who teacheth like Him?' Jesus never taught His disciples how to preach, only how to pray. He did not speak much of what was needed to preach well, but much of praying well. To know how to speak to God is more than knowing how to speak to man. Not power with men, but power with God is the first thing. Jesus loves to teach us how to pray.

What think you, my beloved fellow-disciples! would it not be just what we need, to ask the Master for a month to give us a course of special lessons on the art of prayer? As we meditate on the words He spake on earth, let us yield ourselves to His teaching in the fullest confidence that, with such a teacher, we shall make progress. Let us take time not only to meditate, but to pray, to tarry at the foot of the throne, and be trained to the work of intercession. Let us do so in the assurance that amidst our stammerings and fears He is carrying on His work most beautifully. He will breathe His own life, which is all prayer, into us. As He makes us partakers of His righteousness and His life, He will of His intercession too. As the members of His body, as a holy priesthood, we shall take part in His priestly work of pleading and prevailing with God for men. Yes, let us most joyfully say, ignorant and feeble though we be, 'Lord, teach us to pray.'

Day 15 Prayer

'LORD, TEACH US TO PRAY.'

Blessed Lord! whoever livest to pray, Thou canst teach me too to pray, me too to live ever to pray. In this Thou lovest to make me share Thy glory in heaven, that I should pray without ceasing, and ever stand as a priest in the presence of my God.

Lord Jesus! I ask Thee this day to enroll my name among those who confess that they know not how to pray as they ought, and specially ask Thee for a course of teaching in prayer. Lord! teach me to tarry with Thee in the school, and give Thee time to train me. May a deep sense of my ignorance, of the wonderful privilege and power of prayer, of the need of the Holy Spirit as the Spirit of prayer, lead me to cast away my thoughts of what I think I know, and make me kneel before Thee in true teachableness and poverty of spirit.

And fill me, Lord, with the confidence that with such a teacher as Thou art I shall learn to pray. In the assurance that I have as my teacher, Jesus who is ever praying to the Father, and by His prayer rules the destinies of His Church and the world, I will not be afraid. As much as I need to know of the mysteries of the prayer-world, Thou wilt unfold for me. And when I may not know, Thou wilt teach me to be strong in faith, giving glory to God.

Blessed Lord! Thou wilt not put to shame Thy scholar who trusts Thee, nor, by Thy grace, would he Thee either. Amen.

DAY 15
REFLECTION QUESTIONS

1. Why do you want to learn to pray better? _____

2. What are some of the things that Murray says depend on our prayers? _____

    _____; _____; _____

3. Do you believe we can obtain the same results by praying as those in the Bible received from their

    prayers? _____

    _____

4. What are some of the requirements that Murray lists for powerful and answered prayers? _____

    _____

    _____

    _____

    _____

    _____

5. What did Jesus not teach his disciples how to do? _____

6. What is my main takeaway from Day 15 that will improve my prayer life? _____

    _____

    _____

Fill in the blanks- _____, and it shall be given you; _____, and ye shall find; _____, and
it shall be opened unto you: For every one that asketh receiveth; and he that seeketh findeth; and to him that
knocketh it shall be opened.- Matthew 7:7-8

Answers

1. Personal response

2. Promises being fulfilled, God's Kingdom coming, Glory of God to be revealed

3. Yes- John 14:12 greater works than these

4. Must be for God's glory, in full surrender to his will, we must have faith to believe, must ask in Jesus name, must persevere

5. To preach

6. Personal response

Class 3 Verse- *Ask, and it shall be given you; seek, and ye shall find; knock, and it shall be opened unto you: For every one that asketh receiveth; and he that seeketh findeth; and to him that knocketh it shall be opened. - Matthew 7:7-8*

Day 15 Bible Reading - Matthew 8:14-34; Mark 4-5

Day 15 notes

_____

_____

_____

_____

_____

_____

_____

_____

_____

_____

_____

_____

_____

_____

DAY 16

IN SPIRIT AND TRUTH OR, THE TRUE WORSHIPPERS

'The hour cometh, and now is, when the true worshippers shall worship the Father in spirit and truth: for such doth the Father seek to be His worshippers. God is a Spirit: and they that worship Him must worship Him in spirit and truth.'--**JOHN 4:23-24**

These words of Jesus to the woman of Samaria are His first recorded teaching on the subject of prayer. They give us some wonderful first glimpses into the world of prayer. The Father *seeks* worshippers: our worship satisfies His loving heart and is a joy to Him. He seeks *true worshippers,* but finds many not such as He would have them. True worship is that which is *in spirit and truth. The Son has come* to open the way for this worship in spirit and in truth, and to teach it us. And so one of our first lessons in the school of prayer must be to understand what it is to pray in spirit and in truth, and to know how we can attain to it.

To the woman of Samaria our Lord spoke of a threefold worship. There is first, the ignorant worship of the Samaritans: 'Ye worship that which ye know not.' The second, the intelligent worship of the Jew, having the true knowledge of God: 'We worship that which we know; for salvation is of the Jews.' And then the new, the spiritual worship which He Himself has come to introduce: 'The hour is coming, and is now, when the true worshippers shall worship the Father in spirit and truth.' From the connection it is evident that the words 'in spirit and truth' do not mean, as if often thought, earnestly, from the heart, in sincerity. The Samaritans had the five books of Moses and some knowledge of God; there was doubtless more than one among them who honestly and earnestly sought God in prayer. The Jews had the true full revelation of God in His word, as thus far given; there were among them godly men, who called upon God with their whole heart. And yet not 'in spirit and truth,' in the full meaning of the words. Jesus says, '*The hour is coming, and now is;'* it is only in and through Him that the worship of God will be in spirit and truth.

We must be taught of Him how to worship in spirit and truth

Among Christians one still finds the three classes of worshippers. Some who in their ignorance hardly know what they ask: they pray earnestly, and yet receive but little. Others there are, who have more correct knowledge, who try to pray with all their mind and heart, and often pray most earnestly, and yet do not attain to the full blessedness of worship in spirit and truth. It is into this third class we must ask our Lord Jesus to take us; we must be taught of Him how to worship in spirit and truth. This alone is spiritual worship; this makes us worshippers such as the Father seeks. In prayer everything will depend on our understanding well and practicing the worship in spirit and truth.

'God is *a Spirit*, and they that worship Him, must worship Him *in spirit* and truth.' The first thought suggested here by the Master is that there must be harmony between God and His worshippers; such as God is, must His worship be. This is according to a principle which prevails throughout the universe: we look for correspondence between an object and the organ to which it reveals or yields itself. The eye has an inner fitness for the light, the ear for sound. The man who would truly worship God, would find and know and possess and enjoy God, must be in harmony with Him, must have the capacity for receiving Him. Because God *is Spirit*, we must worship *in spirit*. As God is, so His worshipper.

And what does this mean? The woman had asked our Lord whether Samaria or Jerusalem was the true place of worship. He answers that henceforth worship is no longer to be limited to a certain place: 'Woman, believe Me, *the hour cometh*, when neither in this mountain, nor in Jerusalem, shall ye worship the Father.' As God is Spirit, not bound by space or time, but in His infinite perfection always and everywhere the same, so His worship would henceforth no longer be confined by place or form, but spiritual as God Himself is spiritual. A lesson of deep importance. How much our Christianity suffers from this, that it is confined to certain times and places. A man, who seeks to pray earnestly in the church or in the closet, spends the greater part of the week or the day in a spirit entirely at variance with that in which he prayed. His worship was the work of a fixed place or hour, not of his whole being. God is a Spirit: He is the Everlasting and Unchangeable One; what He is, He is always and in truth. Our worship must even so be in spirit and truth: His worship must be the spirit of our life; our life must be worship in spirit as God is Spirit.

'God is a Spirit: and they that worship Him must worship Him in spirit and truth.' The second thought that comes to us is that the worship in the spirit must come from God Himself. God is Spirit: He alone has Spirit to give. It was for this He sent His Son, to fit us for such spiritual worship, by giving us the Holy Spirit. It is of His own work that Jesus speaks when He says twice, 'The hour cometh,' and then adds, 'and is now.' He came to baptize with the Holy Spirit; the Spirit could not stream forth till He was glorified (John 1:33, 7:37 & 38, 16:7). It was when He had made an end of sin, and entering into the Holiest of all

> **His worship must be the spirit of our life; our life must be worship in spirit as God is Spirit.**

with His blood, had there on our behalf *received* the Holy Spirit (Acts 2:33), that He could send Him down to us as the Spirit of the Father. It was when Christ had redeemed us, and we in Him had received the position of children, that the Father sent forth the Spirit of His Son into our hearts to cry, 'Abba, Father.' The worship in spirit is the worship of the Father in the Spirit of Christ, the Spirit of Sonship.

This is the reason why Jesus here uses the name of Father. We never find one of the Old Testament saints personally appropriate the name of child or call God his Father. The worship *of the Father* is only possible to those to whom the Spirit of the Son has been given. The worship *in spirit* is only possible to those to whom the Son has revealed the Father, and who have received the spirit of Sonship. It is only Christ who opens the way and teaches the worship in spirit.

And *in truth*. That does not only mean, *in sincerity*. Nor does it only signify, in accordance with the truth of God's Word. The expression is one of deep and Divine meaning. Jesus is 'the only-begotten of the Father, *full of* grace and *truth*.' 'The law was given by Moses; grace and *truth came* by Jesus Christ.' Jesus says, 'I am the *truth* and the life.' In the Old Testament all was shadow and promise; Jesus brought and gives the reality, *the substance,* of things hoped for. In Him the blessings and powers of the eternal life are our actual possession and experience. Jesus is full of grace and truth; the Holy Spirit is the Spirit of truth; through Him the grace that is in Jesus is ours in deed and truth, a positive communication out of the Divine life. And so worship in spirit is worship *in truth*; actual living fellowship with God, a real correspondence and harmony between the Father, who is a Spirit, and the child praying in the spirit.

What Jesus said to the woman of Samaria, she could not at once understand. Pentecost was needed to reveal its full meaning. We are hardly prepared at our first entrance into the school of prayer to grasp such teaching. We shall understand it better later on. Let us only begin and take the lesson as He gives it. We are carnal and cannot bring God the worship He seeks. But Jesus came to give the Spirit: He has given Him to us. Let the disposition in which we set ourselves to pray be what Christ's words have taught us. Let there be the deep confession of our inability to bring God the worship that is pleasing to Him; the childlike teachableness that waits on Him to instruct us; the simple faith that yields itself to the breathing of the Spirit. Above all, let us hold fast the blessed truth--we shall find that the Lord has more to say to us about it-

-that the knowledge of the Fatherhood of God, the revelation of His infinite Fatherliness in our hearts, the faith in the infinite love that gives us His Son and His Spirit to make us children, is indeed the secret of prayer in spirit and truth. This is the new and living way Christ opened up for us. To have Christ the Son, and *the Spirit of the Son*, dwelling within us, and revealing the Father, this makes us true, spiritual worshippers.

Day 16 Prayer

'LORD, TEACH US TO PRAY.'

Blessed Lord! I adore the love with which Thou didst teach a woman, who had refused Thee a cup of water, what the worship of God must be. I rejoice in the assurance that Thou wilt no less now instruct Thy disciple, who comes to Thee with a heart that longs to pray in spirit and in truth. O my Holy Master! do teach me this blessed secret.

Teach me that the worship in spirit and truth is not of man, but only comes from Thee; that it is not only a thing of times and seasons, but the outflowing of a life in Thee. Teach me to draw near to God in prayer under the deep impression of my ignorance and my having nothing in myself to offer Him, and at the same time of the provision Thou, my Saviour, makest for the Spirit's breathing in my childlike stammerings. I do bless Thee that in Thee I am a child, and have a child's liberty of access; that in Thee I have the spirit of Sonship and of worship in truth. Teach me, above all, Blessed Son of the Father, how it is the revelation of the Father that gives confidence in prayer; and let the infinite Fatherliness of God's Heart be my joy and strength for a life of prayer and of worship. Amen.

DAY 16
REFLECTION QUESTIONS

1. Of the three kinds of prayer worship identified by Murray which one have you done the most in the past? _____

2. What is one way to bring us into harmony with God? _____

3. Is your worship confined to certain times and places? _____

4. What does worshipping "in truth" mean? _____

5. Can we worship in spirit and truth by ourselves? _____

6. Have you ever tried? Yes   No   What was the result? _____

7. How much of your prayer and worship is in your own power? _____

8. How close is your harmony with Jesus today? _____

9. What is my main takeaway from Day 16 that will improve my prayer life? _____

_____

_____

Fill in the blanks- Ask, and it shall be _____ you; seek, and ye shall _____; knock, and it shall be _____ unto you: For every one that asketh receiveth; and he that seeketh findeth; and to him that knocketh it shall be opened. - Matthew 7:7-8

Answers

1. Personal response- 1-Earnest Ignorance, 2-pray harder with more knowledge but not in full harmony, 3-in spirit and truth

2. Confess all our sins

3. Personal response

4. To go through Jesus and use the Holy Spirit

5. No

6. Personal response

7. Personal response

8. Personal response

9. Personal response

Class 3 Verse- *Ask, and it shall be given you; seek, and ye shall find; knock, and it shall be opened unto you: For every one that asketh receiveth; and he that seeketh findeth; and to him that knocketh it shall be opened. - Matthew 7:7-8*

Day 16 Bible Reading - Matthew 9-10

Day 16 notes

_____

_____

_____

_____

_____

_____

_____

_____

_____

_____

_____

_____

DAY 17

PRAY TO THE FATHER, WHICH IS IN SECRET OR, ALONE WITH GOD

`But thou, when thou prayest, enter into thine inner chamber, and having shut thy door, pray to thy Father which is in secret, and thy Father which seeth in secret shall recompense thee'--**MATT. 6:6**

After Jesus had called His first disciples, He gave them their first public teaching in the Sermon on the Mount. He there expounded to them the kingdom of God, its laws and its life. In that kingdom God is not only King, but Father, He not only gives all, but is Himself all. In the knowledge and fellowship of Him alone is its blessedness. Hence it came as a matter of course that the revelation of prayer and the prayer-life was a part of His teaching concerning the New Kingdom He came to set up. Moses gave neither command nor regulation with regard to prayer: even the prophets say little directly of the duty of prayer; it is Christ who teaches to pray.

And the first thing the Lord teaches His disciples is that they must have a secret place for prayer; everyone must have some solitary spot where he can be alone with his God. Every teacher must have a schoolroom. We have learnt to know and accept Jesus as our only teacher in the school of prayer. He has already taught us at Samaria that worship is no longer confined to times and places; that worship, spiritual true worship, is a thing of the spirit and the life; the whole man must in his whole life be worship in spirit and truth. And yet He wants each one to choose for himself the fixed spot where He can daily meet him. That inner chamber, that solitary place, is Jesus' schoolroom. That spot may be anywhere; that spot may change from day to day if we have to change our abode; but that secret place there must be, with the quiet time in which the pupil places himself in the Master's presence, to be by Him prepared to worship the Father. There alone, but there most surely, Jesus comes to us to teach us to pray.

Everyone must have some solitary spot where he can be alone with his God

A teacher is always anxious that his schoolroom should be bright and attractive, filled with the light and air of heaven, a place where pupils long to come, and love to stay. In His first words on prayer in the Sermon on the Mount, Jesus seeks to set the inner chamber before us in its most attractive light. If we listen carefully, we soon notice what the chief thing is He has to tell us of our tarrying there. Three times He uses the name of Father: 'Pray to *thy Father*;' '*Thy Father* shall recompense thee;' '*Your Father* knoweth what things ye have need of.' The first thing in closet-prayer is: I must meet my Father. The light that shines in the closet must be: the light of the Father's countenance. The fresh air from heaven with which Jesus would have it filled, the atmosphere in which I am to breathe and pray, is: God's Father-love, God's infinite Fatherliness. Thus each thought or petition we breathe out will be simple, hearty, childlike trust in the Father. This is how the Master teaches us to pray: He brings us into the Father's living presence. What we pray there must avail. Let us listen carefully to hear what the Lord has to say to us.

First, '*Pray to thy Father which is in secret.*' God is a God who hides Himself to the carnal eye. As long as in our worship of God we are chiefly occupied with our own thoughts and exercises, we shall not meet Him who is a Spirit, the unseen One. But to the man who withdraws himself from all that is of the world and man, and prepares to wait upon God alone, the Father will reveal Himself. As he forsakes and gives up and shuts out the world, and the life of the world, and surrenders himself to be led of Christ into the secret of God's presence, the light of the Father's love will rise upon him. The secrecy of the inner chamber and the closed door, the entire separation from all around us, is an image of, and so a help to that inner spiritual sanctuary, the secret of God's tabernacle, within the veil, where our spirit truly comes into contact with the Invisible One. And so we are taught, at the very outset of our search after the secret of effectual prayer, to remember that it is in the inner chamber, where we are alone with the Father, that we shall learn to pray aright. The Father is in secret: in these words Jesus teaches us where He is waiting for us, where He is always to be found. Christians often complain that private prayer is not what it should be. They feel weak and sinful, the heart is cold and dark; it is as if they have so little to pray, and in that little no faith or joy. They are discouraged and kept from prayer by the thought that they cannot come to the Father as they ought or as they wish. Child of God! listen to your Teacher. He tells you that when you go to private prayer your first thought must be: The Father is in secret, the Father waits me there. Just because your heart is cold and prayerless, get you into the presence of the loving Father. As a father pitieth his children, so the Lord pitieth you. Do not be thinking of how little you have to bring God, but of how much He wants to give you. Just place yourself before, and look up into, His face; think of His love, His wonderful, tender, pitying love. Just tell Him how sinful and cold and dark all is: it is the Father's loving heart will give light and warmth to yours. O do what Jesus says: Just shut the door, and pray to thy Father which is in secret. Is it not wonderful? to be able to go alone with God, the infinite God. And then to look up and say: My Father!

ଛ୬ଓଷ

When you go to private prayer your first thought must be: The Father is in secret, the Father waits me there.

ଛ୬ଓଷ

'*And thy Father, which seeth in secret, will recompense thee.*' Here Jesus assures us that secret prayer cannot be fruitless: its blessing will show itself in our life. We have but in secret, alone with God, to entrust our life before men to Him; He will reward us openly; He will see to it that the answer to prayer be made manifest in His blessing upon us. Our Lord would thus teach us that as infinite Fatherliness and Faithfulness is that with which God meets us in secret, so on our part there should be the childlike simplicity of faith, the confidence that our prayer does bring down a blessing. 'He that cometh to God must believe that *He is a rewarder* of them that seek Him.' Not on the strong or the fervent feeling with which I pray does the blessing of the closet depend, but upon the love and the power of the Father to whom I there entrust my needs. And therefore the Master has but one desire: Remember your Father is, and sees and hears in secret; go there and stay there, and go again from there in the confidence: He will recompense. Trust Him for it; depend upon Him: prayer to the Father cannot be vain; He will reward you openly.

Still further to confirm this faith in the Father-love of God, Christ speaks a third word: '*Your Father knoweth what things ye have need of before ye ask Him.*' At first sight it might appear as if this thought made prayer less needful: God knows far better than we what we need. But as we get a deeper insight into what prayer really is, this truth will help much to strengthen our faith. It will teach us that we do not need, as the heathen, with the multitude and urgency of our words, to compel an unwilling God to listen to us. It will lead to a holy thoughtfulness and silence in prayer as it suggests the question: Does my Father really know that I need this? It will, when once we have been led by the Spirit to the certainty that our request is indeed something that, according to the Word, we do need for God's glory, give us wonderful confidence to say, My Father knows I need it and must have it. And if there be any delay in the answer, it will teach us in quiet perseverance to hold on: FATHER! THOU KNOWEST I need it. O the blessed liberty and simplicity of a child that Christ our Teacher would fain cultivate in us, as we draw near to God: let us look up to the Father until His Spirit works it in us. Let us sometimes in our prayers, when we are in danger of being so occupied with our fervent, urgent petitions, as to forget that the Father knows and hears, let us hold still and just quietly say: My Father sees, my Father hears, my Father knows; it will help our faith to take the answer, and to say: We know that we have the petitions we have asked of Him

And now, all ye who have anew entered the school of Christ to be taught to pray, take these lessons, practice them, and trust Him to perfect you in them. Dwell much in the inner chamber, with the door shut--shut in from men, shut up with God; it is there the Father waits you, it is there Jesus will teach you to pray. To be alone in secret with THE FATHER: this be your highest joy. To be assured that THE FATHER will openly reward the secret prayer, so that it cannot remain unblessed: this be your strength day by day. And to know that THE FATHER knows that you need what you ask; this be your liberty to bring every need, in the assurance that your God will supply it according to His riches in Glory in Christ Jesus.

Day 17 Prayer

'LORD, TEACH US TO PRAY.'

Blessed Saviour! with my whole heart I do bless Thee for the appointment of the inner chamber, as the school where Thou meetest each of Thy pupils alone, and revealest to him the Father. O my Lord! strengthen my faith so in the Father's tender love and kindness, that as often as I feel sinful or troubled, the first instinctive thought may be to go where I know the Father waits me, and where prayer never can go unblessed. Let the thought that He knows my need before I ask, bring me, in great restfulness of faith, to trust that He will give what His child requires. O let the place of secret prayer become to me the most beloved spot of earth

And, Lord! hear me as I pray that Thou wouldest everywhere bless the closets of Thy believing people. Let Thy wonderful revelation of a Father's tenderness free all young Christians from every thought of secret prayer as a duty or a burden, and lead them to regard it as the highest privilege of their life, a joy and a blessing. Bring back all who are discouraged, because they cannot find ought to bring Thee in prayer. O give them to understand that they have only to come with their emptiness to Him who has all to give, and delights to do it. Not, what they have to bring the Father, but what the Father waits to give them, be their one thought.

And bless especially the inner chamber of all Thy servants who are working for Thee, as the place where God's truth and God's grace is revealed to them, where they are daily anointed with fresh oil, where their strength is renewed, and the blessings are received in faith, with which they are to bless their fellow-men. Lord, draw us all in the closet nearer to Thyself and the Father. Amen.

DAY 17
REFLECTION QUESTIONS

1. Do you have a secret place for prayer? _____ Where? _____

2. What is the first thing we must have for our prayer time to be effectual? _____
_____

3. What are the benefits of praying in secret behind a shut door? _____
_____

4. How often is your prayer time dominated by your own thoughts and plans? _____
_____

5. Instead of fearing that we have nothing to offer God in your prayer time, what should we be thinking?
_____

6. What does God promise us if we will go to the secret place and pray to Him? _____
_____

7. How can we know our request is God's will? _____
_____

8. What is my main takeaway from Day 17 that will improve my prayer life? _____
_____
_____

Fill in the blanks- Ask, and it _____ be given you; seek, and ye shall find; knock, and it shall be opened unto you: For every one that _____ receiveth; and he that _____ findeth; and to him that _____ it shall be opened.- Matthew 7:7-8

Answers

1. Personal response
2. The Father's presence
3. The world is shut out and we can wait on God
4. Personal response
5. About what the Father has to give us
6. He will reward us- Hebrews 11:6
7. Read the word, will the request bring glory to God
8. Personal response

Class 3 Verse- *Ask, and it shall be given you; seek, and ye shall find; knock, and it shall be opened unto you: For every one that asketh receiveth; and he that seeketh findeth; and to him that knocketh it shall be opened.- Matthew 7:7-8*

Day 17 Bible Reading - Matthew 14; Mark 6; Luke 9:1-17

Day 17 notes

_____

_____

_____

_____

_____

_____

_____

_____

_____

_____

_____

_____

_____

DAY 18

AFTER THIS MANNER PRAY OR THE MODEL PRAYER

`After this manner therefore pray ye:  Our Father which art in heaven.'-`**Matt. 6:9**

Every teacher knows the power of example. He not only tells the child what to do and how to do it, but shows him how it really can be done. In condescension to our weakness, our heavenly Teacher has given us the very words we are to take with us as we draw near to our Father. We have in them a form of prayer in which there breathe the freshness and fullness of the Eternal Life. So simple that the child can lisp it, so divinely rich that it comprehends all that God can give. A form of prayer that becomes the model and inspiration for all other prayer, and yet always draws us back to itself as the deepest utterance of our souls before our God.

'*Our Father which art in heaven!*' To appreciate this word of adoration aright, I must remember that none of the saints had in Scripture ever ventured to address God as their Father. The invocation places us at once in the center of the wonderful revelation the Son came to make of His Father as our Father too. It comprehends the mystery of redemption--Christ delivering us from the curse that we might become the children of God. The mystery of regeneration--the Spirit in the new birth giving us the new life. And the mystery of faith--ere yet the redemption is accomplished or understood, the word is given on the lips of the disciples to prepare them for the blessed experience still to come. The words are the key to the whole prayer, to all prayer. It takes time, it takes life to study them; it will take eternity to understand them fully. The knowledge of God's Father-love is the first and simplest, but also the last and highest lesson in the school of prayer. It is in the personal relation to the living God, and the personal conscious fellowship of love with Himself, that prayer begins. It is in the knowledge of God's Fatherliness, revealed by the Holy Spirit, that the power of prayer will be found to root and grow. In the infinite tenderness and pity and patience of the infinite Father, in His loving readiness to hear and to help, the life of prayer has its joy. O let us take time, until the Spirit has made these words to us spirit and truth, filling heart and life: 'Our Father which art in heaven.' Then we are indeed within the veil, in the secret place of power where prayer always prevails.

ಬಿಛ

While we ordinarily first bring our own needs to God in prayer, and then think of what belongs to God and His interests, the Master reverses the order.

ಬಿಛ

'*Hallowed be Thy name.*' There is something here that strikes us at once. While we ordinarily first bring our own needs to God in prayer, and then think of what belongs to God and His interests, the Master reverses the order. First, *Thy* name, *Thy* kingdom, *Thy* will; then, give *us*, forgive *us*, lead *us*, deliver *us*. The lesson is of more importance than we think. In true worship the Father must be first, must be all. The sooner I learn to forget myself in the desire that HE may be glorified, the richer will the blessing be that prayer will bring to myself. No one ever loses by what he sacrifices for the Father.

This must influence all our prayer. There are two sorts of prayer: personal and intercessory. The latter ordinarily occupies the lesser part of our time and energy. This may not be. Christ has opened the school of prayer specially to train intercessors for the great work of bringing down, by their faith and prayer, the blessings of His work and love on the world around. There can be no deep growth in prayer unless this be made our aim. The little child may ask of the father only what it needs for itself; and yet it soon learns to say, Give some for sister too. But the grown-up son, who only lives for the father's interest and takes charge of the father's business, asks more largely, and gets all that is asked. And Jesus would train us to the blessed life of consecration and service, in which our interests are all subordinate to the Name, and the Kingdom, and the Will of the Father. O let us live for this, and let, on each act of adoration, Our Father! there follow in the same breath *Thy* Name, *Thy* Kingdom, *Thy* Will;--for this we look up and long.

'*Hallowed be Thy name.*' What name? This new name of Father. The word *Holy* is the central word of the Old Testament; the *name* Father of the New. In this name of Love all the holiness and glory of God are now to be revealed. And how is the name to be hallowed? By God Himself: '*I will hallow* My great name which ye have profaned.' Our prayer must be that in ourselves, in all God's children, in presence of the world, God Himself would reveal the holiness, the Divine power, the hidden glory of the name of Father. The Spirit of the Father is the *Holy* Spirit: it is only when we yield ourselves to be led *of Him,* that the name will be *hallowed* in our prayers and our lives. Let us learn the prayer: 'Our Father, hallowed be Thy name.'

'*Thy kingdom come.*' The Father is a King and has a kingdom. The son and heir of a king has no higher ambition than the glory of his father's kingdom. In time of war or danger this becomes his passion; he can think of nothing else. The children of the Father are here in the enemy's territory, where the kingdom, which is in heaven, is not yet fully manifested. What more natural than that, when they learn to hallow the Father-name, they should long and cry with deep enthusiasm: 'Thy kingdom come.' The coming of the kingdom is the one great event on which the revelation of the Father's glory, the blessedness of His children, the salvation of the world depends. On our prayers too, the coming of the kingdom waits. Shall we not join in the deep longing cry of the redeemed: 'Thy kingdom come'? Let us learn it in the school of Jesus.

৪০୧୪

Let us beware of the prayer for forgiveness becoming a formality: only what is really confessed is really forgiven.

৪০୧୪

'*Thy will be done, as in heaven, so on earth.*' This petition is too frequently applied alone to the *suffering* of the will of God. In heaven God's will is *done*, and the Master teaches the child to ask that the will may be done on earth just as in heaven: in the spirit of adoring submission and ready obedience. Because the will of God is the glory of heaven, the doing of it is the blessedness of heaven. As the will is done, the kingdom of heaven comes into the heart. And wherever faith has accepted the Father's love, obedience accepts the Father's will. The surrender to, and the prayer for a life of heaven-like obedience, is the spirit of childlike prayer.

'*Give us this day our daily bread.*' When first the child has yielded himself to the Father in the care for His Name, His Kingdom, and His Will, he has full liberty to ask for his daily bread. A master cares for the food of his servant, a general of his soldiers, a father of his child. And will not the Father in heaven care for the child who has in prayer given himself up to His interests? We may indeed in full confidence say: Father, I live for Thy honor and Thy work; I know Thou carest for me. Consecration to God and His will gives wonderful liberty in prayer for temporal things: the whole earthly life is given to the Father's loving care.

'*And forgive us our debts, as we also have forgiven our debtors.*' As bread is the first need of the body, so forgiveness for the soul. And the provision for the one is as sure as for the other. We are children but sinners too; our right of access to the Father's presence we owe to the precious blood and the forgiveness it has won for us. Let us beware of the prayer for forgiveness becoming a formality: only what is really confessed is really forgiven. Let us in faith accept the forgiveness as promised: as a spiritual reality, an actual transaction between God and us, it is the entrance into all the Father's love and all the privileges of children. Such forgiveness, as a living experience, is impossible without a forgiving spirit to others: as *forgiven* expresses the heavenward, so *forgiving* the earthward, relation of God's child. In each prayer to the Father I must be able to say that I know of no one whom I do not heartily love.

'*And lead us not into temptation, but deliver us from the evil one.*' Our daily bread, the pardon of our sins, and then our being kept from all sin and the power of the evil one, in these three petitions all our personal need is comprehended. The prayer for bread and pardon must be accompanied by the surrender to live in all things in holy obedience to the Father's will, and the believing prayer in everything to be kept by the power of the indwelling Spirit from the power of the evil one.

Children of God! it is thus Jesus would have us to pray to the Father in heaven. O let His Name, and Kingdom, and Will, have the first place in our love; His providing, and pardoning, and keeping love will be our sure portion. So the prayer will lead us up to the true child-life: the Father all to the child, the Father all for the child. We shall understand how Father and child, the *Thine* and the *Our*, are all one, and how the heart that begins its prayer with the God-devoted THINK, will have the power in faith to speak out the OUR too. Such prayer will, indeed, be the fellowship and interchange of love, always bringing us back in trust and worship to Him who is not only the Beginning but the End: 'FOR THINE IS THE KINGDOM, AND THE POWER, AND THE GLORY, FOR EVER, AMEN.' Son of the Father, teach us to pray, 'OUR FATHER.'

In each prayer to the Father I must be able to say that I know of no one whom I do not heartily love.

Day 18 Prayer

'LORD, TEACH US TO PRAY.'

O Thou who art the only-begotten Son, teach us, we beseech Thee, to pray, 'OUR FATHER.' We thank Thee, Lord, for these Living Blessed Words which Thou has given us. We thank Thee for the millions who in them have learnt to know and worship the Father, and for what they have been to us. Lord! it is as if we needed days and weeks in Thy school with each separate petition; so deep and full are they. But we look to Thee to lead us deeper into their meaning: do it, we pray Thee, for Thy Name's sake; Thy name is Son of the Father.

Lord! Thou didst once say: 'No man knoweth the Father save the Son, and he to whom the Son willeth to reveal Him.' And again: 'I made known unto them Thy name, and will make it known, that the love wherewith Thou hast loved Me may be in them.' Lord Jesus! reveal to us the Father. Let His name, His infinite Father-love, the love with which He loved Thee, according to Thy prayer, BE IN US. Then shall we say aright, 'OUR FATHER!' Then shall we apprehend Thy teaching, and the first spontaneous breathing of our heart will be: 'Our Father, Thy Name, Thy Kingdom, Thy Will.' And we shall bring our needs and our sins and our temptations to Him in the confidence that the love of such a Father care for all.

Blessed Lord! we are Thy scholars, we trust Thee; do teach us to pray, 'OUR FATHER.' Amen.

DAY 18
REFLECTION QUESTIONS

1. Is the Father first in your prayers? _____

2. What are the two kinds of prayers Murray identified? _____
   _____

3. Which do you spend the most time on? _____

4. How can we Hallow God's name? _____
   _____

5. Do you have the faith to accept and obey the Father's will? _____

6. What must we do before expecting him to grant our physical requests? _____
   _____

7. Do you have anyone you have un-forgiveness toward? _____

8. What are the three areas of personal need identified in the Lord's Prayer? _____
   _____; _____

9. The Lord's prayer closes with _____

10. What is my main takeaway from Day 18 that will improve my prayer life? _____
    _____
    _____

Fill in the blanks- _____, and it shall be _____ you; _____, and ye shall _____; _____, and it shall be _____ unto you: For every one that _____ _____; and he that _____ _____; and to him that _____ it shall be _____.- Matthew 7:7-8

Answers

1. Personal response

2. Personal needs and intercessory

3. Personal response

4. By allowing the Holy Spirit to direct our lives

5. Personal response

6. Yield ourselves to the Father and the care of His will in work.

7. Personal response

8. Daily bread, pardon of our sins & kept from power of the evil one

9. Praise to God

10. Personal response

Class 3 Verse- *Ask, and it shall be given you; seek, and ye shall find; knock, and it shall be opened unto you: For every one that asketh receiveth; and he that seeketh findeth; and to him that knocketh it shall be opened. - Matthew 7:7-8*

Day 18 Bible Reading - John 6

Day 18 notes

_____

_____

_____

_____

_____

_____

_____

_____

_____

_____

_____

_____

DAY 19

ASK, AND IT SHALL BE GIVEN YOU
OR, THE CERTAINTY OF THE ANSWER TO PRAYER

'Ask, and it shall be given you; seek, and ye shall find; knock, and it shall be opened unto you: for every one that asketh receiveth, and he that seeketh findeth; and to him that knocketh it shall be opened,'--**Matthew 7:7- 8**

'Ye ask, and receive not, because ye ask amiss.'--**James. 4:3**

ur Lord returns here in the Sermon on the Mount a second time to speak of prayer. The first time He had spoken of the Father who is to be found in secret, and rewards openly, and had given us the pattern prayer (Matt. vi. 5-15). Here He wants to teach us what in all Scripture is considered the chief thing in prayer: the assurance that prayer will be heard and answered. Observe how He uses words which mean almost the same thing, and each time repeats the promise so distinctly: 'Ye *shall* receive, ye *shall* find, it *shall* be opened unto you;' and then gives as ground for such assurance the law of the kingdom: 'He that asketh, *receiveth*; he that seeketh, *findeth*; to him that knocketh, *it shall be opened*.' We cannot but feel how in this sixfold repetition He wants to impress deep on our minds this one truth, that we may and must most confidently expect an answer to our prayer. Next to the revelation of the Father's love, there is, in the whole course of the school of prayer, not a more important lesson than this: Every one that asketh, receiveth.

> He knows our heart, how doubt and distrust toward God are natural to us, and how easily we are inclined to rest in prayer as a religious work without an answer

In the three words the Lord uses, *ask, seek, knock,* a difference in meaning has been sought. If such was indeed His purpose, then the first, ASK, refers to the gifts we pray for. But I may ask and receive the gift without the Giver. SEEK is the word Scripture uses of God Himself; Christ assures me that I can find Him. But it is not enough to find God in time of need, without coming to abiding fellowship: KNOCK speaks of admission to dwell with Him and in Him. Asking and receiving the gift would thus lead to seeking and finding the Giver, and this again to the knocking and opening of the door of the Father's home and love. One thing is sure: the Lord does want us to count most certainly on it that asking, seeking, knocking, cannot be in vain: receiving an answer, finding God, the opened heart and home of God, are the certain fruit of prayer.

That the Lord should have thought it needful in so many forms to repeat the truth, is a lesson of deep import. It proves that He knows our heart, how doubt and distrust toward God are natural to us, and how easily we are inclined to rest in prayer as a religious work without an answer. He knows too how, even when we believe that God is the Hearer of prayer, believing prayer that lays hold of the promise, is something spiritual, too high and difficult for the half-hearted disciple. He therefore at the very outset of His instruction to those who would learn to pray, seeks to lodge this truth deep into their hearts: prayer does avail much; ask and ye *shall* receive; *every one* that asketh, receiveth. This is the fixed eternal law of the kingdom: if you ask and receive not, it must be because there is something amiss or wanting in the prayer. Hold on; let the Word and the Spirit teach you to pray aright, but do not let go the confidence He seeks to waken: Every one that asketh, receiveth.

'*Ask, and it shall be given you.*' Christ has no mightier stimulus to persevering prayer in His school than this. As a child has to prove a sum to be correct, so the proof that we have prayed aright is, *the answer.* If we ask and receive not, it is because we have not learned to pray aright. Let every learner in the school of Christ therefore take the Master's word in all simplicity: Every one that asketh, receiveth. He had good reasons for speaking so unconditionally. Let us beware of weakening the Word with our human wisdom. When He tells us heavenly things, let us believe Him: His Word will explain itself to him who believes it fully. If questions and difficulties arise, let us not seek to have them settled before we accept the Word. No; let us entrust them all to Him: it is His to solve them: our work is first and fully to accept and hold fast His promise. Let in our inner chamber, in the inner chamber of our heart too, the Word be inscribed in letters of light: Every one that asketh, receiveth.

It is far easier to the flesh to submit without the answer than to yield itself to be searched and purified by the Spirit

According to this teaching of the Master, prayer consists of two parts, has two sides, a human and a Divine. The human is the asking, the Divine is the giving. Or, to look at both from the human side, there is the asking and the receiving--the two halves that make up a whole. It is as if He would tell us that we are not to rest without an answer, because it is the will of God, the rule in the Father's family: every childlike believing petition is granted. If no answer comes, we are not to sit down in the sloth that calls itself resignation, and suppose that it is not God's will to give an answer. No; there must be something in the prayer that is not as God would have it, childlike and believing; we must seek for grace to pray so that the answer may come. It is far easier to the flesh to submit without the answer than to yield itself to be searched and purified by the Spirit, until it has learnt to pray the prayer of faith.

It is one of the terrible marks of the diseased state of Christian life in these days, that there are so many who rest content without the distinct experience of answer to prayer. They pray daily, they ask many things, and trust that some of them will be heard, but know little of direct definite answer to prayer as the rule of daily life. And it is this the Father wills: He seeks daily intercourse with His children in listening to and granting their petitions. He wills that I should come to Him day by day with distinct requests; He wills day by day to do for me what I ask. It was in His answer to prayer that the saints of old learned to know God as the Living One, and were stirred to praise and love (Ps. 34:1,16:19, 116:1). Our Teacher waits to imprint this upon our minds: prayer and its answer, the child asking and the father giving, belong to each other.

There may be cases in which the answer is a refusal, because the request is not according to God's Word, as when Moses asked to enter Canaan. But still, there was an answer: God did not leave His servant in uncertainty as to His will. The gods of the heathen are dumb and cannot speak. Our Father lets His child know when He cannot give him what he asks, and he withdraws his petition, even as the Son did in Gethsemane. Both Moses the servant and Christ the Son knew that what they asked was not according to what the Lord had spoken: their prayer was the humble supplication whether it was not possible for the decision to be changed. God will teach those who are teachable and give Him time, by His Word and Spirit, whether their request be according to His will or not. Let us withdraw the request, if it be not according to God's mind, or persevere till the answer come. Prayer is appointed to obtain the answer. It is in prayer and its answer that the interchange of love between the Father and His child takes place.

How deep the estrangement of our heart from God must be, that we find it so difficult to grasp such promises. Even while we accept the words and believe their truth, the faith of the heart, that fully has them and rejoices in them, comes so slowly. It is because our spiritual life is still so weak, and the capacity for taking God's thoughts is so feeble. But let us look to Jesus to teach us as none but He can teach. If we take His words in simplicity, and trust Him by His Spirit to make them within us life and power, they will so enter into our inner being, that the spiritual Divine reality of the truth they contain will indeed take possession of us, and we shall not rest content until every petition we offer is borne heavenward on Jesus' own words: 'Ask, and it shall be given you.'

Beloved fellow-disciples in the school of Jesus! Let us set ourselves to learn this lesson well. Let us take these words just as they were spoken. Let us not suffer human reason to weaken their force. Let us take them as Jesus gives them, and believe them. He will teach us in due time how to understand them fully: let us begin by implicitly believing them. Let us take time, as often as we pray, to listen to His voice: Every one that asketh, receiveth. Let us not make the feeble experiences of our unbelief the measure of what our faith may expect. Let us seek, not only just in our seasons of prayer, but at all times, to hold fast the joyful assurance: man's prayer on earth and God's answer in heaven are meant for each other. Let us trust Jesus to teach us so to pray that the answer can come. He will do it, if we hold fast the word He gives today: 'Ask, and ye shall receive.'

Day 19 Prayer

'LORD, TEACH US TO PRAY.'

O Lord Jesus! teach me to understand and believe what Thou hast now promised me. It is not hid from Thee, O my Lord, with what reasonings my heart seeks to satisfy itself, when no answer comes. There is the thought that my prayer is not in harmony with the Father's secret counsel; that there is perhaps something better Thou wouldest give me; or that prayer as fellowship with God is blessing enough without an answer. And yet, my blessed Lord, I find in Thy teaching on prayer that Thou didst not speak of these things, but didst say so plainly, that prayer may and must expect an answer. Thou dost assure us that this is the fellowship of a child with the Father: the child asks and the Father gives.

Blessed Lord! Thy words are faithful and true. It must be, because I pray amiss, that my experience of answered prayer is not clearer. It must be, because I live too little in the Spirit, that my prayer is too little in the Spirit, and that the power for the prayer of faith is wanting.

Lord! teach me to pray. Lord Jesus! I trust Thee for it; teach me to pray in faith. Lord! teach me this lesson of today: Every one that asketh receiveth. Amen.

DAY 19
REFLECTION QUESTIONS

1. What is the chief thing scripture is telling us about prayer? _____

2. Do you believe that all who ask receive? _____

3. What does Murray say is the fruit of prayer? _____

_____

4. Are your prayers just religious work without any answers? _____

5. What does Murray say are the two parts or sides of prayer? _____ and

_____, one _____ and one _____

6. How often do you resign a lack of answers to your prayers as, 'Not God's will?' _____

_____

7. Do you give time to praying about God's will for your prayers and reading the word? _____

_____

8. What is my main takeaway from Day 19 that will improve my prayer life? _____

_____

_____

Fill in the blanks- _____, and it_____ be _____ you; _____, and ye
shall _____; _____, and it shall be _____ unto you: For every one that
_____ _____; and he that _____ _____; and to
_____that _____ it _____ be _____.- Matthew 7:7-8 b

Answers

1. Assurance that prayer will be heard and answered
2. Personal response
3. Receiving an answer, finding God, the opened heart and home of God
4. Personal response
5. Human and Divine – asking and giving
6. Personal response
7. Personal response
8. Personal response

Class 3 Verse- *Ask, and it shall be given you; seek, and ye shall find; knock, and it shall be opened unto you: For every one that asketh receiveth; and he that seeketh findeth; and to him that knocketh it shall be opened.- Matthew 7:7-8*

Day 19 Bible Reading - Matthew 15; Mark 7

Day 19 notes

_____

_____

_____

_____

_____

_____

_____

_____

_____

_____

_____

_____

_____

DAY 20

HOW MUCH MORE? OR, THE INFINITE FATHERLINESS OF GOD

'Or what man is there of you, who, if his son ask him for a loaf, will give him a stone; or if he shall ask for a fish, will give him a serpent? If ye then, being evil, know how to give good gifts unto your children, how much more shall your Father which is in heaven give good things to them that ask Him?' - **Matthew 7:9-11**

In these words our Lord proceeds further to confirm what He had said of the certainty of an answer to prayer. To remove all doubt, and show us on what sure ground His promise rests, He appeals to what everyone has seen and experienced here on earth. We are all children, and know what we expected of our fathers. We are fathers, or continually see them; and everywhere we look upon it as the most natural thing there can be, for a father to hear his child. And the Lord asks us to look up from earthly parents, of whom the best are but evil, and to calculate HOW MUCH MORE the heavenly Father will give good gifts to them that ask Him. Jesus would lead us up to see, that as much greater as God is than sinful man, *so much greater* our assurance ought to be that He will more surely, than any earthly father, grant our childlike petitions. As much greater as God is than man, *so much surer* is it that prayer will be heard with the Father in heaven than with a father on earth.

As simple and intelligible as this parable is, so deep and spiritual is the teaching it contains. The Lord would remind us that the prayer of a child owes its influence entirely to the relation in which he stands to the parent. The prayer can exert that influence only when the child is really living in that relationship, in the home, in the love, in the service of the Father. The power of the promise, 'Ask, and it shall be given you,' lies in the loving relationship between us as children and the Father in heaven; when we live and walk in that relationship, the prayer of faith and its answer will be the natural result. And so the lesson we have today in the school of prayer is this: live as a child of God, then you will be able to pray as a child, and as a child you will most assuredly be heard.

> **Live as a child of God, then you will be able to pray as a child, and as a child you will most assuredly be heard**

And what is the true child-life? The answer can be found in any home. The child that by preference forsakes the father's house, that finds no pleasure in the presence and love and obedience of the father, and still thinks to ask and obtain what he will, will surely be disappointed. On the contrary, he to whom the intercourse and will and honor and love of the father are the joy of his life, will find that it is the father's joy to grant his requests. Scripture says, 'as many as are *led* by the Spirit of God, they are the children of God:' the childlike privilege of asking all is inseparable from the childlike life under the leading of the Spirit. He that gives himself to be led by the Spirit in his life, will be led by Him in his prayers too. And he will find that Fatherlike giving is the Divine response to childlike living.

To see what this childlike living is, in which childlike asking and believing have their ground, we have only to notice what our Lord teaches in the Sermon on the Mount of the Father and His children. In it the prayer-promises are imbedded in the life-precepts; the two are inseparable. They form one whole; and He alone can count on the fulfilment of the promise, who accepts too all that the Lord has connected with it. It is as if in speaking the word, 'Ask, and ye shall receive,' He says: I give these promises to those whom in the beatitudes I have pictured in their childlike poverty and purity, and of whom I have said, 'They shall be called the children of God' (Matt. 5:3-9): to children, who 'let your light shine before men, so that they may glorify your Father in heaven:' to those who walk in love, 'that ye may be children of your Father which is in heaven,' and who seek to be perfect 'even as your Father in heaven is perfect' (5: 45): to those whose fasting and praying and almsgiving (6:1-18) is not before men, but 'before your Father which seeth in secret;' who forgive 'even as your Father forgiveth you' (6:15); who trust the heavenly Father in all earthly need, seeking first the kingdom of God and His righteousness (6:26-32); who not only say, Lord, Lord, but do the will of my Father which is in heaven (7:21). Such are the children of the Father, and such is the life in the Father's love and service; in such a child-life answered prayers are certain and abundant.

But will not such teaching discourage the feeble one? If we are first to answer to this portrait of a child, must not many give up all hope of answers to prayer? The difficulty is removed if we think again of the blessed name of father and child. A child is weak; there is a great difference among children in age and gift. The Lord does not demand of us a perfect fulfilment of the law; no, but only the childlike and whole-hearted surrender to live as a child with Him in obedience and truth. Nothing more. But also, nothing less. The Father must have the whole heart. When this is given, and He sees the child with honest purpose and steady will seeking in everything to be and live as a child, then our prayer will count with Him as the prayer of a child. Let anyone simply and honestly begin to study the Sermon on the Mount and take it as his guide in life, and he will find, notwithstanding weakness and failure, an ever-growing liberty to claim the fulfilment of its promises in regard to prayer. In the names of father and child he has the pledge that his petitions will be granted.

This is the one chief thought on which Jesus dwells here, and which He would have all His scholars take in. He would have us see that the secret of effectual prayer is: to have the heart filled with the Father-love of God. It is not enough for us to know that God is a Father: He would have us take time to come under the full impression of what that name implies. We must take the best earthly father we know; we must think of the tenderness and love with which he regards the request of his child, the love and joy with which he grants every reasonable desire; we must then, as we think in adoring worship of the infinite Love and Fatherliness of God, consider with *how much more* tenderness and joy *He* sees us come to Him, and gives us what we ask aright. And then, when we see how much this Divine arithmetic is beyond our comprehension, and feel how impossible it is for us to apprehend God's readiness to hear us, then He would have us come and open our heart for the Holy Spirit to shed abroad God's Father-love there. Let us do this not only when we want to pray, but let us yield heart and life to dwell in that love. The child who only wants to know the love of the father when he has something to ask, will be disappointed. But he who lets God be Father always and in everything, who would fain live his whole life in the Father's presence and love, who allows God in all the greatness of His love to be a Father to him, oh, he will experience most gloriously that a life in God's infinite Fatherliness and continual answers to prayer are inseparable.

The child who only wants to know the love of the father when he has something to ask, will be disappointed

Beloved fellow-disciple! We begin to see what the reason is that we know so little of daily answers to prayer, and what the chief lesson is which the Lord has for us in His school. It is all in the name of Father. We thought of new and deeper insight into some of the mysteries of the prayer-world as what we should get in Christ's school; He tells us the first is the highest lesson; we must learn to say well, 'Abba, Father!' 'Our Father which art in heaven.' He that can say this, has the key to all prayer. In all the compassion with which a father listens to his weak or sickly child, in all the joy with which he hears his stammering child, in all the gentle patience with which he bears with a thoughtless child, we must, as in so many mirrors, study the heart of our Father, until every prayer be borne upward on the faith of this Divine word: 'How *much more* shall your heavenly Father give good gifts to them that ask Him.'

Day 20 Prayer

'LORD, TEACH US TO PRAY.'

Blessed Lord! Thou knowest that this, though it be one of the first and simplest and most glorious lessons in Thy school, is to our hearts one of the hardest to learn: we know so little of the love of the Father. Lord! teach us so to live with the Father that His love may be to us nearer, clearer, dearer, than the love of any earthly father. And let the assurance of His hearing our prayer be as much greater than the confidence in an earthly parent, as the heavens are higher than earth, as God is infinitely greater than man. Lord! show us that it is only our unchildlike distance from the Father that hinders the answer to prayer, and lead us on to the true life of God's children. Lord Jesus! it is fatherlike love that wakens childlike trust. O reveal to us the Father, and His tender, pitying love, that we may become childlike, and experience how in the child-life lies the power of prayer.

Blessed Son of God! the Father loveth Thee and hath given Thee all things. And Thou lovest the Father, and hast done all things He commanded Thee, and therefore hast the power to ask all things. Lord! give us Thine own Spirit, the Spirit of the Son. Make us childlike, as Thou wert on earth. And let every prayer be breathed in the faith that as the heaven is higher than the earth, so God's Father-love, and His readiness to give us what we ask, surpasses all we can think or conceive. Amen.

NOTE.1

'*Your Father which is in heaven.*' Alas! we speak of it only as the utterance of a reverential homage. We think of it as a figure borrowed from an earthly life, and only in some faint and shallow meaning to be used of God. We are afraid to take God as our own tender and pitiful father. He is a schoolmaster, or almost farther off than that, and knowing less about us--an inspector, who knows nothing of us except through our lessons. His eyes are not on the scholar, but on the book, and all alike must come up to the standard.

Now open the ears of the heart, timid child of God; let it go sinking right down into the inner most depths of the soul. Here is the starting-point of holiness, in the love and patience and pity of our heavenly Father. We have not to learn to be holy as a hard lesson at school, that we may make God think well of us; we are to learn it at home with the Father to help us. God loves you not because you are clever not because you are good, but because He is *your Father*. The Cross of Christ does not make God love us; it is the outcome and measure of His love to us. He loves all His children, the clumsiest, the dullest, the worst of His children. His love lies at the back of everything, and we must get upon that as the solid foundation of our religious life, not growing up into that, but growing up *out if it*. We must begin there or our beginning will come to nothing. Do take hold of this mightily. We must go out of ourselves for any hope, or any strength, or any confidence. And what hope, what strength, what confidence may be ours now that we begin here, *your Father which is in heaven*!

We need to get in at the tenderness and helpfulness which lie in these words, and to rest upon it--*your Father*. Speak them over to yourself until something of the wonderful truth is felt by us. It means that I am bound to God by the closest and tenderest relationship; that I have a right to His love and His power and His blessing, such as nothing else could give me. O the boldness with which we can draw near! O the great things we have a right to ask for! *Your Father*. It means that all His infinite love and patience and wisdom bend over *me* to help *me*. In this relationship lies not only the possibility of holiness; there is infinitely more than that.

Here we are to begin, in the patient love of our Father. Think how He knows us apart and by ourselves, in all our peculiarities, and in all our weaknesses and difficulties. The master judges by the result, but our Father judges by the effort. Failure does not always mean fault. He knows how much things cost, and weighs them where others only measure. YOUR FATHER. Think how great store His love sets by the poor beginnings of the little ones, clumsy and unmeaning as they may be to others. All this lies in this blessed relationship and infinitely more. Do not fear to take it all as your own.

1 From *Thoughts on Holiness*, by Mark Guy Pearse. What is so beautifully said of the knowledge of God's Fatherliness as the starting-point of holiness is no less true of prayer.

DAY 20
REFLECTION QUESTIONS

1. What does Murray say the answers to a child's prayers depend on? _____ _____

2. Are you living as a child of God? _____

3. The Lord does not demand of us _____ _____ of the law; but only the childlike and whole-hearted surrender to live as His child.

4. What does Murray say the secret of effectual prayer is? _____ _____

5. What can a child expect who only wants to know the love of the Father when he has something to ask? _____

6. What does Murray point out as Christ's first and highest lesson in the school of payer _____ _____

7. Are you allowing God to be a Father to you in all areas of your life? _____

8. What is my main takeaway from Day 20 that will improve my prayer life? _____ _____ _____

Fill in the blanks- _____, and it _____ be _____ you; _____, and ye shall _____; _____, and it shall be _____ unto you: For _____ _____ that _____ _____; and he that _____ _____; and to _____ that _____ it _____ be _____.- Matthew 7:7-8

Answers

1. The relation in which he stands to the parent
2. Personal response
3. Perfect fulfillment
4. To have your heart filled with the Father-love of God
5. To be disappointed
6. Learning to say, Abba, Father
7. Personal response
8. Personal response

Class 3 Verse- *Ask, and it shall be given you; seek, and ye shall find; knock, and it shall be opened unto you: For every one that asketh receiveth; and he that seeketh findeth; and to him that knocketh it shall be opened.- Matthew 7:7-8*

Day 20 Bible Reading - Matthew 16; Mark 8; Luke 9:18-27

Day 20 notes

_____

_____

_____

_____

_____

_____

_____

_____

_____

_____

_____

_____

DAY 21

HOW MUCH MORE THE HOLY SPIRIT
OR, THE ALL-COMPREHENSIVE GIFT

'If ye then, being evil, know how to give good gifts unto your children, how much more shall the heavenly Father give the Holy Spirit to them that ask Him?'--**Luke 11:13**

In the Sermon on the Mount, the Lord had already given utterance to His wonderful HOW MUCH MORE? Here in Luke, where He repeats the question, there is a difference. Instead of speaking, as then of giving *good gifts*, He says, 'How much more shall the heavenly Father give THE HOLY SPIRIT?' He thus teaches us that the chief and the best of these gifts is the Holy Spirit, or rather, that in this gift all others are comprised. The Holy Spirit is the first of the Father's gifts, and the one He delights most to bestow. The Holy Spirit is therefore the gift we ought first and chiefly to seek.

The unspeakable worth of this gift we can easily understand. Jesus spoke of the Spirit as '*the* promise of the Father;' the one promise in which God's Fatherhood revealed itself. The best gift a good and wise father can bestow on a child on earth is his own spirit. This is the great object of a father in education--to reproduce in his child his own disposition and character. If the child is to know and understand his father; if, as he grows up, he is to enter into all his will and plans; if he is to have his highest joy in the father, and the father in him,--he must be of one mind and spirit with him. And so it is impossible to conceive of God bestowing any higher gift on His child than this, His own Spirit. God is what He is through His Spirit; the Spirit is the very life of God. Just think what it means--God giving His own Spirit to His child on earth.

The Holy Spirit is the gift we ought to first and chiefly seek

Or was not this the glory of Jesus as a Son upon earth that the Spirit of the Father was in Him? At His baptism in Jordan the two things were united,--the voice, proclaiming Him the Beloved Son, and the Spirit, descending upon Him. And so the apostle says of us, 'because ye are sons, God sent forth the Spirit of His Son into your hearts, crying, Abba, Father.' A king seeks in the whole education of his son to call forth in him a kingly spirit. Our Father in heaven desires to educate us as His children for the holy, heavenly life in which He dwells, and for this gives us, from the depths of His heart, His own Spirit. It was this which was the whole aim of Jesus when, after having made atonement with His own blood, He entered for us into God's presence, that He might obtain for us, and send down to dwell in us, the Holy Spirit. As the Spirit of the Father, and of the Son, the whole life and love of the Father and the Son are in Him; and, coming down into us, He lifts us up into their fellowship. As Spirit of the Father, He sheds abroad the Father's love, with which He loved the Son, in our hearts, and teaches us to live in it. As Spirit of the Son, He breathes in us the childlike liberty, and devotion, and obedience in which the Son lived upon earth. The Father can bestow no higher or more wonderful gift than this: His own Holy Spirit, the Spirit of sonship.

This truth naturally suggests the thought that this first and chief gift of God must be the first and chief object of all prayer. For every need of the spiritual life this is the one thing needful, the Holy Spirit. All the fullness

123

is in Jesus; the fullness of grace and truth, out of which we receive grace for grace. The Holy Spirit is the appointed conveyancer, whose special work it is to make Jesus and all there is in Him for us, ours in personal appropriation, in blessed experience. He is the Spirit of life in Christ Jesus; as wonderful as the life is, so wonderful is the provision by which such an agent is provided to communicate it to us. If we but yield ourselves entirely to the disposal of the Spirit, and let Him have His way with us, He will manifest the life of Christ within us. He will do this with a Divine power, maintaining the life of Christ in us in uninterrupted continuity. Surely, if there is one prayer that should draw us to the Father's throne and keep us there, it is this: for the Holy Spirit, whom we as children have received, to stream into us and out from us in greater fullness.

In the variety of the gifts which the Spirit has to dispense, He meets the believer's every need. Just think of the names He bears. The Spirit of grace, to reveal and impart all of grace there is in Jesus. The Spirit of faith, teaching us to begin and go on and increase in ever believing. The Spirit of adoption and assurance, who witnesses that we are God's children, and inspires the confiding and confident Abba, Father! The Spirit of truth, to lead into all truth, to make each word of God ours in deed and in truth. The Spirit of prayer, through whom we speak with the Father; prayer that must be heard. The Spirit of judgment and burning, to search the heart, and convince of sin. The Spirit of holiness, manifesting and communicating the Father's holy presence within us. The Spirit of power, through whom we are strong to testify boldly and work effectually in the Father's service. The Spirit of glory, the pledge of our inheritance, the preparation and the foretaste of the glory to come. Surely the child of God needs but one thing to be able really to live as a child: it is, to be filled with this Spirit

But we still need to ask and pray for His special gifts and operations as we require them

And now, the lesson Jesus teaches us today in His school is this: That the Father is just longing to give Him to us if we will but ask in the childlike dependence on what He says: 'If ye know to give good gifts unto your children, HOW MUCH MORE shall your heavenly Father give the Holy Spirit to them that ask Him.' In the words of God's promise, 'I will pour out my Spirit *abundantly*;' and of His command, 'Be ye *filled* with the Spirit' we have the measure of what God is ready to give, and what we may obtain. As God's children, we have already received the Spirit. But we still need to ask and pray for His special gifts and operations as we require them. And not only this, but for Himself to take complete and entire possession; for His unceasing momentary guidance. Just as the branch, already filled with the sap of the vine, is ever crying for the continued and increasing flow of that sap that it may bring its fruit to perfection, so the believer, rejoicing in the possession of the Spirit, ever thirsts and cries for more. And what the great Teacher would have us learn is, that nothing less than God's promise and God's command may be the measure of our expectation and our prayer; we must be filled abundantly. He would have us ask this in the assurance that the wonderful HOW MUCH MORE of God's Father-love is the pledge that, when we ask, we do most certainly receive.

Let us now believe this. As we pray to be filled with the Spirit, let us not seek for the answer in our feelings. All spiritual blessings must be received, that is, accepted or taken in faith

1. Let me believe, the Father *gives* the Holy Spirit to His praying child. Even now, while I pray, I must say in faith: I have what I ask, the fullness of the Spirit is mine. Let us continue steadfast in this faith. On the strength of God's Word we know that we have what we ask. Let us, with thanksgiving that we have been heard, with thanksgiving for what we have received and taken and now hold as ours, continue steadfast in believing prayer that the blessing, *which has already been given* us, and which we hold in faith, may break through and fill our whole being. It is in such believing thanksgiving and prayer, that our soul opens up for the Spirit to take entire and undisturbed possession. It is such prayer that not only asks and hopes, but takes and holds, that inherits the full blessing. In all our prayer let us remember the lesson the Savior would teach us this day, that, *if there is one thing on earth we can be sure of, it is this, that the Father desires to have us filled with His Spirit, that He delights to give us His Spirit.*

And when once we have learned thus to believe for ourselves, and each day to take out of the treasure we hold in heaven, what liberty and power to pray for the outpouring of the Spirit on the Church of God, on all flesh, on individuals, or on special efforts! He that has once learned to know the Father in prayer for himself, learns to pray most confidently for others too. The Father gives the

Holy Spirit to them that ask Him, not least, but most, when they ask for others.

Day 21 Prayer

'LORD, TEACH US TO PRAY.'

Father in heaven! Thou didst send Thy Son to reveal Thyself to us, Thy Father-love, and all that that love has for us. And He has taught us, that the gift above all gifts which Thou wouldst bestow in answer to prayer is, the Holy Spirit.

O my Father! I come to Thee with this prayer; there is nothing I would--may I not say, I do--desire so much as to be filled with the Spirit, the Holy Spirit. The blessings He brings are so unspeakable, and just what I need. He sheds abroad Thy love in the heart, and fills it with Thy self. I long for this. He breathes the mind and life of Christ in me, so that I live as He did, in and for the Father's love. I long for this. He endues with power from on high for all my walk and work. I long for this. O Father! I beseech Thee, give me this day the fulness of Thy Spirit.

Father! I ask this, resting on the words of my Lord: 'HOW MUCH MORE THE HOLY SPIRIT.' I do believe that Thou hearest my prayer; I receive now what I ask; Father! I claim and I take it: the fulness of Thy Spirit is mine. I receive the gift this day again as a faith gift; in faith I reckon my Father works through the Spirit all He has promised. The Father delights to breathe His Spirit into His waiting child as He tarries in fellowship with Himself. Amen.

1The Greek word for receiving and taking is the same. When Jesus said, 'Everyone that asketh *receiveth*,' He used the same verb as at the Supper, '*Take*, eat,' or on the resurrection morning, '*Receive*,' accept, take, 'the Holy Spirit.' Receiving not only implies God's bestowment, but our acceptance.

DAY 21
REFLECTION QUESTIONS

1. What is the best gift we can receive from the Father? _____

2. What two things did God do to Jesus at His baptism? _____
   _____& _____

3. After Jesus' death and resurrection what did He enter back into God's presence so believers could obtain? _____

4. What is another name Murray uses for the Holy Spirit _____

5. Murray says, the first and chief object of prayer should be? _____

6. Is having the indwelling Holy Spirt in your life a part of your daily prayer? _____

7. Are you yielding entirely to the disposal of the Spirit, letting Him have His way with you? _____
   _____

8. What is the one thing you need to be able to live as a child of God? _____
   _____
   _____

9. As a Christian are you, 'ever-thirsting and crying' for more of God's Spirit?_____
   _____

10. What is my main takeaway from Day 21 that will improve my prayer life? _____
    _____
    _____

Fill in the blanks- _____, and it_____ be _____ _____; _____,
and ye shall _____; _____, and it _____ be _____ unto _____: For
_____ _____ that _____ _____; and he that _____
_____; and to _____that _____ it _____ be
_____.- Matthew 7:7-8

Answers

1. Holy Spirit

2. Proclaimed Him the Beloved Son with His voice & the Holy Spirit descended on Him

3. A heart filled with the Father-love of God

4. Spirit of Sonship

5. The indwelling of the Holy Spirit

6. Personal response

7. Personal response

8. To be filled with the Holy Spirit

9. Personal response

10. Personal response

Class 3 Verse- *Ask, and it shall be given you; seek, and ye shall find; knock, and it shall be opened unto you: For every one that asketh receiveth; and he that seeketh findeth; and to him that knocketh it shall be opened.- Matthew 7:7-8*

Day 21 Bible Reading - Matthew 17; Mark 9; Luke 9:28-62

Day 21 notes

_____

_____

_____

_____

_____

_____

_____

_____

_____

_____

_____

_____

_____

CLASS 3

WEEK 4

Opening Prayer –Thank God for answering our prayers. **Word** – Answer

Key Questions-

1. Do you believe we can obtain the same results by praying today that those in the bible received from their prayers? _____

2. What is one way to bring us into harmony with God? _____

3. Instead of fearing that we have nothing to offer God in your prayer time we should be thinking? _____

4. What are the benefits of praying in secret behind a shut door? _____

5. What are the three areas of personal need identified in the Lord's Prayer? _____, _____, _____

6. What is the chief thing scripture is telling us about prayer? _____

7. What can a child expect who only wants to know the love of the father when he has something to ask? _____

8. Murray says, the first and chief object of prayer should be? _____

Theme – Everyone Who Asks Receives

Testimonies- What is God doing through your prayer life?

Scripture Memory-

Class 3 Verse- *Ask, and it shall be given you; seek, and ye shall find; knock, and it shall be opened unto you: For every one that asketh receiveth; and he that seeketh findeth; and to him that knocketh it shall be opened. - Matthew 7:7-8*

Next Class Preview-

Word- Belief

Theme- Have faith in the promisor

Verse- *And Jesus answering saith unto them, Have faith in God. For verily I say unto you, That whosoever shall say unto this mountain, Be thou removed, and be thou cast into the sea; and shall not doubt in his heart, but shall believe that those things which he saith shall come to pass; he shall have whatsoever he saith.- Mark 11:22-23*

Prayer for Students-

- Time to Pray Each Day
- A Desire for Prayer

- A Clear Mind During Prayer
- Show us God's will

Class 3 Answers

1. Yes –greater works than these John 14:12
2. Confess our sins
3. About what the father has to give us
4. Daily bread, pardon of our sins & kept from power of the evil one
5. Assurance that prayer will be heard and answered
6. To be disappointed
7. The indwelling of the Holy Spirit

Class 3 notes

_____

_____

_____

_____

_____

_____

_____

_____

_____

_____

_____

_____

_____

_____

DAY 22

BECAUSE OF HIS IMPORTUNITY
OR, THE BOLDNESS OF GOD'S FRIENDS

'And He said unto them, Which of you shall have a friend, and shall go to him at midnight, and say to him, Friend, lend me three loaves; for a friend of mine is come to me from a journey, and I have nothing to set before him' and he from within shall answer and say, Trouble me not: the door is now shut, and my children are with me in bed; I cannot rise and give thee. I say unto you, though he will not rise and give him because he is his friend, yet because of his importunity he will rise and give him as many as he needeth.'--**Luke 11:5-8**

The first teaching to His disciples was given by our Lord in the Sermon on the Mount. It was near a year later that the disciples asked Jesus to teach them to pray. In answer He gave them a second time the Lord's Prayer, so teaching them *what* to pray. He then speaks of *how* they ought to pray, and repeats what he formerly said of God's Fatherliness and the certainty of an answer. But in between He adds the beautiful parable of the friend at midnight, to teach them the two fold lesson, that God does not only want us to pray for ourselves, but for the perishing around us, and that in such intercession great boldness of entreaty is often needful, and always lawful, yea, pleasing to God.

God does not only want us to pray for ourselves, but for the perishing around us

The parable is a perfect storehouse of instruction in regard to true intercession. There is, first, *the love* which seeks to help the needy around us: '*my friend* is come to me.' Then *the need* which urges to the cry 'I *have nothing* to set before him.' Then follows *the confidence* that help is to be had: 'which of you shall have a *friend*, and say, *Friend*, lend me three loaves.' Then comes the unexpected *refusal*: 'I *cannot* rise and give thee.' Then again the *perseverance* that takes no refusal: 'because of his *importunity*.' And lastly, the reward of such prayer: 'he will give him *as many as he needeth*.' A wonderful setting forth of the way of prayer and faith in which the blessing of God has so often been sought and found.

Let us confine ourselves to the chief thought: prayer as an appeal to the friendship of God; and we shall find that two lessons are specially suggested. The one, that if we are God's friends, and come as such to Him, we must prove ourselves the friends of the needy; God's friendship to us and ours to others go hand in hand. The other, that when we come thus we may use the utmost liberty in claiming an answer.

There is a twofold use of prayer: the one, to obtain strength and blessing for our own life; the other, the higher, the true glory of prayer, for which Christ has taken us into His fellowship and teaching, is intercession, where prayer is the royal power a child of God exercises in heaven on behalf of others and even of the kingdom. We see it in Scripture, how it was in intercession for others that Abraham and Moses, Samuel and Elijah, with all the holy men of old, proved that they had power with God and prevailed. It is when we give ourselves to be a blessing that we can specially count on the blessing of God. It is when we draw near to God as the friend of the poor and the perishing that we may count on His friendliness; the righteous man who is the friend of the poor is very specially the friend of God. This gives wonderful liberty in prayer. Lord! I have a needy friend whom I must help. As a friend I have undertaken to help him. In Thee I have a Friend, whose kindness and riches I know to be infinite: I am sure Thou wilt give me what I ask. If I, being evil, am ready to do for my friend what I can, how much more wilt Thou, O my heavenly Friend, now do for Thy friend what he asks?

The question might suggest itself, whether the Fatherhood of God does not give such confidence in prayer, that the thought of His Friendship can hardly teach us anything more: a father is more than a friend. And yet, if we consider it, this pleading the friendship of God opens new wonders to us. That a child obtains what he asks of his father looks so perfectly natural, we almost count it the father's duty to give. But with a friend it is as if the kindness is more free, dependent, not on nature, but on sympathy and character. And then the relation of a child is more that of perfect dependence; two friends are more nearly on a level. And so our Lord, in seeking to unfold to us the spiritual mystery of prayer, would fain have us approach God in this relation too, as those whom He has acknowledged as His friends, whose mind and life are in sympathy with His.

But then we must be living as His friends. I am still a child even when a wanderer; but friendship depends upon the conduct. 'Ye are my friends if ye do whatsoever I command you.' 'Thou seest that faith wrought with his works, and by works was faith made perfect; and the scripture was fulfilled which saith, And Abraham believed God, and he was called *the friend of God*.' It is the Spirit, '*the same* Spirit,' that leads us that also bears witness to our acceptance with God; '*likewise*, also,' the same Spirit helpeth us in prayer. It is a life as the friend of God that gives the wonderful liberty to say: I have a friend to whom I can go even at midnight. And how much more when I go in the very spirit of that friendliness, manifesting myself the very kindness I look for in God, seeking to help my friend as I want God to help me. When I come to God in prayer, He always looks to what the aim is of my petition. If it be merely for my own comfort or joy I seek His grace, I do not receive. But if I can say that it is that He may be glorified in my dispensing His blessings to others, I shall not ask in vain. Or if I ask for others, but want to wait until God has made me so rich, that it is no sacrifice or act of faith to aid them, I shall not obtain. But if I can say that I have already undertaken for my needy friend, that in my poverty I have already begun the work of love, because I know I had a friend Who would help me, my prayer will be heard. Oh, we know not how much the plea avails: the friendship of earth looking in its need to the friendship of heaven: 'He will give him as much as he needeth.'

If it is that He may be glorified in my dispensing His blessings to others, I shall not ask in vain.

But not always at once. The one thing by which man can honor and enjoy his God is *faith*. Intercession is part of faith's training-school. There our friendship with men and with God is tested. There it is seen whether my friendship with the needy is so real, that I will take time and sacrifice my rest, will go even at midnight and not cease until I have obtained for them what I need. There it is seen whether my friendship with God is so clear, that I can depend on Him not to turn me away and therefore pray on until He gives.

O what a deep heavenly mystery this is of persevering prayer. The God who has promised, who longs, whose fixed purpose it is to give the blessing, holds it back. It is to Him a matter of such deep importance that His friends on earth should know and fully trust their rich Friend in heaven, that He trains them, in the school of answer delayed, to find out how their perseverance really does prevail, and what the mighty power is they can wield in heaven, if they do but set themselves to it. There is a faith that sees the promise, and embraces it, and yet does not receive it (Heb. xi. 13, 39). It is when the answer to prayer does not come, and the promise we are most firmly trusting appears to be of none effect, that the trial of faith, more precious than of gold, takes place. It is in this trial that the faith that has embraced the promise is purified and strengthened and prepared in personal, holy fellowship with the living God, to see the glory of God. It takes and holds the promise until it has received the fulfilment of what it had claimed in a living truth in the unseen but living

God.

Let each child of God who is seeking to work the work of love in his Father's service take courage. The parent with his child, the teacher with his class, the visitor with his district, the Bible reader with his circle, the preacher with his hearers, each one who, in his little circle, has accepted and is bearing the burden of hungry, perishing souls,--let them all take courage. Nothing is at first so strange to us as that God should really require persevering prayer, that there should be a real spiritual needs-be for importunity. To teach it us, the Master uses this almost strange parable. If the unfriendliness of a selfish earthly friend can be conquered by importunity, how much more will it avail with the heavenly Friend, who does so love to give, but is held back by our spiritual unfitness, our incapacity to possess what He has to give. O let us thank Him that in delaying His answer He is educating us up to our true position and the exercise of all our power with Him, training us to live with Him in the fellowship of undoubting faith and trust, to be indeed the friends of God. And let us hold fast the threefold cord that cannot be broken: the hungry friend needing the help, and the praying friend seeking the help, and the Mighty Friend, loving to give as much as he needeth.

Day 22 Prayer

'LORD, TEACH US TO PRAY.'

O my Blessed Lord and Teacher! I must come to Thee in prayer. Thy teaching is so glorious, and yet too high for me to grasp. I must confess that my heart is too little to take in these thoughts of the wonderful boldness I may use with Thy Father as my Friend. Lord Jesus! I trust Thee to give me Thy Spirit with Thy Word, and to make the Word quick and powerful in my heart. I desire to keep Thy Word of this day: 'Because of his importunity he will give him as many as he needeth.'

Lord! teach me more to know the power of persevering prayer. I know that in it the Father suits Himself to our need of time for the inner life to attain its growth and ripeness, so that His grace may indeed be assimilated and made our very own. I know that He would fain thus train us to the exercise of that strong faith that does not let Him go even in the face of seeming disappointment. I know He wants to lift us to that wonderful liberty, in which we understand how really He has made the dispensing of His gift dependent on our prayer. Lord! I know this: O teach me to see it in spirit and truth.

And may it now be the joy of my life to become the almoner of my Rich Friend in heaven, to care for all the hungry and perishing, even at midnight, because I know MY FRIEND, who always gives to him who perseveres, because of his importunity, as many as he needeth. Amen.

DAY 22
REFLECTION QUESTIONS

1. What does Murray say the chief thought of prayer is? _____

2. God's friendship with _____ and our friendship with _____ go hand in hand.

3. What is required to be a 'friend of God'? _____

4. What does Murray say is higher, and the true glory of prayer? _____

5. When we give ourselves to be a_____ we can specifically count on the _____ of God.

6. How much time and sacrifice do you put into prayer for those in need? _____
   _____

7. Does your perseverance prevail through delayed answer to prayer? _____
   _____

8. What is the threefold cord Murray references from today's scripture? 1._____
   _____ 2. _____

   3._____

9. What is my main takeaway from Day 22 that will improve my prayer life? _____
   _____
   _____

Fill in the blanks- And Jesus answering saith unto them, Have _____ in God. For verily I say unto you, That whosoever shall say unto this mountain, Be thou _____, and be thou cast into the sea; and shall not _____ in his heart, but shall believe that those things which he saith shall come to pass; he shall have _____ he saith.- Mark 11:22-23

Answers

1. Prayer as an appeal to the friendship of God

2. Us & others

3. Keep His commands- John 15:14 & James 2:22-23

4. Intercession

5. Blessing, blessings

6. Personal response

7. Personal response- Hebrews 11:13-39

8. The hungry friend needing the help, the praying friend seeking help, the Mighty Friend loving to give as much as he need

9. Personal response

Class 4 Verse- *And Jesus answering saith unto them, Have faith in God. For verily I say unto you, That whosoever shall say unto this mountain, Be thou removed, and be thou cast into the sea; and shall not doubt in his heart, but shall believe that those things which he saith shall come to pass; he shall have whatsoever he saith.- Mark 11:22-23*

Day 22 Bible Reading - Matthew 18

Day 22 notes

_____

_____

_____

_____

_____

_____

_____

_____

_____

_____

_____

DAY 23

PRAY THE LORD OF THE HARVEST
OR, PRAYER PROVIDES LABORERS

'Then saith He unto His disciples, The harvest truly is plenteous, but the laborers are few. Pray ye therefore the Lord of the harvest, that He will send forth laborers into His harvest.'--**Matthew 9:37-38**

ℰ𝒪ℭℬ

The Lord frequently taught His disciples *that* they must pray, and *how*; but seldom *what* to pray

ℰ𝒪ℭℬ

The Lord frequently taught His disciples *that* they must pray, and *how*; but seldom *what* to pray. This he left to their sense of need, and the leading of the Spirit. But here we have one thing He expressly enjoins them to remember: in view of the plenteous harvest, and the need of reapers, they must cry to the Lord of the harvest to send forth laborers. Just as in the parable of the friend at midnight, He would have them understand that prayer is not to be selfish; so here it is the power through which blessing can come to others. The Father is Lord of the harvest; when we pray for the Holy Spirit, we must pray for Him to prepare and send forth laborers for the work.

Strange, is it not, that He should ask His disciples to pray for this? And could He not pray Himself? And would not one prayer of His avail more than a thousand of theirs? And God, the Lord of the harvest, did He not see the need? And would not He, in His own good time, send forth laborers without their prayer? Such questions lead us up to the deepest mysteries of prayer, and its power in the Kingdom of God. The answer to such questions will convince us that prayer is indeed a power, on which the ingathering of the harvest and the coming of the Kingdom do in very truth depend.

Prayer is no form or show. The Lord Jesus was Himself the truth; everything He spake was the deepest truth. It was when (see ver. 36) 'He saw the multitude, and was moved with compassion on them, because they were scattered abroad, as sheep having no shepherd,' that He called on the disciples to pray for laborers to be sent among them. He did so because He really believed that their prayer was needed, and would help. The veil which so hides the invisible world from us was wonderfully transparent to the holy human soul of Jesus. He had looked long and deep and far into the hidden connection of cause and effect in the spirit world. He had marked in God's Word how, when God called men like Abraham and Moses, Joshua and Samuel and Daniel, and given them authority over men in His name, He had at the same time given them authority and right to call in the powers of heaven to their aid as they needed them. He knew that as to these men of old, and to Himself for a time, here upon earth, the work of God had been entrusted, so it was now about to pass over into the hands of His disciples. He knew that when this work should be given in charge to them, it would not be a mere matter of form or show, but that on them, and their being faithful or unfaithful, the success of the work would actually depend. As a single individual, within the limitations of

ℰ𝒪ℭℬ

On them, and their being faithful or unfaithful, the success of the work would actually depend

ℰ𝒪ℭℬ

135

a human body and a human life, Jesus feels how little a short visit can accomplish among these wandering sheep He sees around Him, and He longs for help to have them properly cared for. And so He tells His disciples now to begin and pray, and, when they have taken over the work from Him on earth, to make this one of the chief petitions in their prayer: That the Lord of the harvest Himself would send forth labourers into His harvest. The God who entrusted them with the work, and made it to so large extent dependent on them, gives them authority to apply to Him for laborers to help, and makes the supply dependent on their prayer.

How little Christians really feel and mourn the need of laborers in the fields of the world so white to the harvest. And how little they believe that our labor-supply depends on prayer, that prayer will really provide 'as many as he needeth.' Not that the dearth of labor is not known or discussed. Not that efforts are not sometimes put forth to supply the want. But how little the burden of the sheep wandering without a Shepherd is really borne in the faith that the Lord of the harvest *will*, in answer to prayer, send forth the laborers, and in the solemn conviction that without this prayer fields ready for reaping will be left to perish. And yet it is so. So wonderful is the surrender of His work into the hands of His Church, so dependent has the Lord made Himself on them as His body, through whom alone His work can be done, so real is the power which the Lord gives His people to exercise in heaven and earth, that the number of the laborers and the measure of the harvest does actually depend upon their prayer.

Solemn thought! O why is it that we do not obey the injunction of the Master more heartily, and cry more earnestly for laborers? There are two reasons for this. The one is: We miss the compassion of Jesus, which gave rise to this request for prayer. When believers learn that to love their neighbors as themselves, that to live entirely for God's glory in their fellow-men, is the Father's first commandment to His redeemed ones, they will accept of the perishing ones as the charge entrusted to them by their Lord. And, accepting them not only as a field of labor, but as the objects of loving care and interest, it will not be long before compassion towards the hopelessly perishing will touch their heart, and the cry ascend with an earnestness till then unknown: Lord, send laborers. The other reason for the neglect of the command, the want of faith, will then make itself felt, but will be overcome as our pity pleads for help. We believe too little in the power of prayer to bring about definite results. We do not live close enough to God, and are not enough entirely given up to His service and Kingdom, to be capable of the confidence that He will give it in answer to our prayer. O let us pray for a life so one with Christ that His compassion may stream into us and His Spirit be able to assure us that our prayer avails.

> So real is the power which the Lord gives His people to exercise in heaven and earth, that the number of the laborers and the measure of the harvest does actually depend upon their prayer.

Such prayer will ask and obtain a twofold blessing. There will first be the desire for the increase of men entirely given up to the service of God. It is a terrible blot upon the Church of Christ that there are times when actually men cannot be found for the service of the Master as ministers, missionaries, or teachers of God's Word. As God's children make this a matter of supplication for their own circle or Church, it will be given. The Lord Jesus is now Lord of the harvest. He has been exalted to bestow gifts--the gifts of the Spirit. His chief gifts are men filled with the Spirit. But the supply and distribution of the gifts depend on the co-operation of Head and members. It is just prayer will lead to such co-operation; the believing suppliants will be stirred to find the men and the means for the work.

The other blessing to be asked will not be less. Every believer is a laborer; not one of God's children who has not been redeemed for service, and has not his work waiting. It must be our prayer that the Lord would so fill all His people with the spirit of devotion, that not one may be found standing idle in the vineyard. Wherever there is a complaint of the want of helpers, or of fit helpers in God's work, prayer has the promise of a supply. There is no Sunday school or district visiting, no Bible reading or rescue work, where

God is not ready and able to provide. It may take time and importunity, but the command of Christ to ask the Lord of the harvest is the pledge that the prayer will be heard: 'I say unto you, he will arise and give him as many as he needeth.'

Solemn, blessed thought, this power has been given us in prayer to provide in the need of the world, to secure the servants for God's work. The Lord of the harvest will hear. Christ, who called us so specially to pray thus, will support our prayers offered in His name and interest. Let us set apart time and give ourselves to this part of our intercessory work. It will lead us into the fellowship of that compassionate heart of His that led Him to call for our prayers. It will elevate us to the insight of our regal position, as those whose will counts for something with the great God in the advancement of His Kingdom. It will make us feel how really we are God's fellow-workers on earth, to whom a share in His work has in downright earnest been entrusted. It will make us partakers in the soul travail, but also in the soul satisfaction of Jesus, as we know how, in answer to our prayer, blessing has been given that otherwise would not have come.

Day 23 Prayer

'LORD, TEACH US TO PRAY.'

Blessed Lord! Thou hast this day again given us another of Thy wondrous lessons to learn. We humbly ask Thee, O give us to see aright the spiritual realities of which Thou hast been speaking. There is the harvest which is so large, and perishing, as it waits for sleepy disciples to give the signal for laborers to come. Lord, teach us to look out upon it with a heart moved with compassion and pity. There are the laborers, so few. Lord, show us how terrible the sin of the want of prayer and faith, of which this is the token. And there is the Lord of the harvest, so able and ready to send them forth. Lord, show us how He does indeed wait for the prayer to which He has bound His answer. And there are the disciples, to whom the commission to pray has been given: Lord, show us how Thou canst pour down Thy Spirit and breathe upon them, so that Thy compassion and the faith in Thy promise shall rouse them to unceasing, prevailing prayer.

O our Lord! we cannot understand how Thou canst entrust such work and give such power to men so slothful and unfaithful. We thank Thee for all whom Thou art teaching to cry day and night for laborers to be sent forth. Lord, breathe Thine own Spirit on all Thy children that they may learn to live for this one thing alone--the Kingdom and glory of their Lord--and become fully awake to the faith of what their prayer can accomplish. And let all our hearts in this, as in every petition, be filled with the assurance that prayer, offered in loving faith in the living God, will bring certain and abundant answer. Amen.

DAY 23
REFLECTION QUESTIONS

1. What does Matthew 9:37-38 say the gathering of the harvest and the coming of the Kingdom depend on? _____

2. Murray points out that Jesus seldom taught His disciples what to pray for. What is one of the chief things Jesus taught his disciples to pray for? _____

3. Do you mourn the need for laborers in the fields? _____

4. Do you really believe the number of laborers and the size of the harvest depends on our prayers?
   _____

5. What does Murray say are the two reason we do not obey the command to pray for labors?
   1._____
   2._____

6. Is there a shortage of ministers, missionaries, or teachers of God's Word in your community?
   _____

7. What two blessings result from praying for laborers? 1. _____
   _____ 2._____

8. Giving your time to pray for laborers for the harvest will lead to what in your life? _____
   _____

9. What is my main takeaway from Day 23 that will improve my prayer life? _____
   _____
   _____

Fill in the blanks- And Jesus answering saith unto them, Have faith in _____. For verily I say unto you, That _____ shall say unto this _____ , Be thou removed, and be thou _____ into the _____; and shall not doubt in his _____, but shall believe that those _____ which he saith shall come to pass; he _____ have whatsoever he saith.- Mark 11:22-23

Answers

1. Prayer

2. Laborers for the harvest

3. Personal response

4. Personal response

5. We don't have Christ's compassion for the lost, lack of faith

6. Personal response

7. A desire for more believers given up to God's service, every believer is a laborer

8. A compassionate heart like Christ's

9. Personal response

Class 4 Verse- *And Jesus answering saith unto them, Have faith in God. For verily I say unto you, That whosoever shall say unto this mountain, Be thou removed, and be thou cast into the sea; and shall not doubt in his heart, but shall believe that those things which he saith shall come to pass; he shall have whatsoever he saith.- Mark 11:22-23*

Day 23 Bible Reading - John 7-8

Day 23 notes

_____

_____

_____

_____

_____

_____

_____

_____

_____

_____

_____

DAY 24

WHAT WILL THOU? OR, PRAYER MUST BE DEFINITE

"And Jesus answered him, and said, 'What wilt thou that I should do unto thee'--**Mark 10:51**

"Saying, What wilt thou that I shall do unto thee? And he said, Lord, that I may receive my sight." - **Luke 18:41**

𝕿he blind man had been crying out aloud, and that a great deal, 'Thou Son of David, have mercy on me.' The cry had reached the ear of the Lord; He knew what he wanted, and was ready to grant it him. But ere He does it, He asks him: 'What wilt thou that I should do unto thee?' He wants to hear from his own lips, not only the general petition for mercy, but the distinct expression of what his desire was. Until he speaks it out, he is not healed.

There is now still many a suppliant to whom the Lord puts the same question, and who cannot, until it has been answered, get the aid he asks. Our prayers must not be a vague appeal to His mercy, an indefinite cry for blessing, but the distinct expression of definite need. Not that His loving heart does not understand our cry, or is not ready to hear. But He desires it for our own sakes. Such definite prayer teaches us to know our own needs better. It demands time, and thought, and self-scrutiny to find out what really is our greatest need. It searches us and puts us to the test as to whether our desires are honest and real, such as we are ready to persevere in. It leads us to judge whether our desires are according to God's Word, and whether we really believe that we shall receive the things we ask. It helps us to wait for the special answer, and to mark it when it comes.

> **It demands time, and thought, and self-scrutiny to find out what really is our greatest need.**

And yet how much of our prayer is vague and pointless. Some cry for mercy, but take not the trouble to know what mercy must do for them. Others ask, perhaps, to be delivered from sin, but do not begin by bringing any sin by name from which the deliverance may be claimed. Still others pray for God's blessing on those around them, for the outpouring of God's Spirit on their land or the world, and yet have no special field where they wait and expect to see the answer. To all the Lord says: And what is it now you really want and expect Me to do? Every Christian has but limited powers, and as he must have his own special field of labor in which he works, so with his prayers too. Each believer has his own circle, his family, his friends, his neighbors. If he were to take one or more of these by name, he would find that this really brings him into the training-school of faith, and leads to personal and pointed dealing with his God. It is when in such distinct matters we have in faith claimed and received answers, that our more general prayers will be believing and effectual.

We all know with what surprise the whole civilized world heard of the way in which trained troops were repulsed by the Transvaal Boers at Majuba. And to what did they owe their success? In the armies of

Europe the soldier fires upon the enemy standing in large masses, and never thinks of seeking an aim for every bullet. In hunting game the Boer had learnt a different lesson: his practiced eye knew to send every bullet on its special message, to seek and find its man. Such aiming must gain the day in the spiritual world too. As long as in prayer we just pour out our hearts in a multitude of petitions, without taking time to see whether every petition is sent with the purpose and expectation of getting an answer, not many will reach the mark. But if, as in silence of soul we bow before the Lord, we were to ask such questions as these: What is now really my desire? Do I desire it in faith, expecting to receive? Am I now ready to place and leave it in the Father's bosom? Is it a settled thing between God and me that I am to have the answer? We should learn so to pray that God would see and we would know what we really expect.

ഇൻ

As long as in prayer we just pour out our hearts in a multitude of petitions, without taking time to see whether every petition is sent with the purpose and expectation of getting an answer, not many will reach the mark.

ഇൻ

It is for this, among other reasons, that the Lord warns us against the vain repetitions of the Gentiles, who think to be heard for their much praying. We often hear prayers of great earnestness and fervor, in which a multitude of petitions are poured forth, but to which the Savior would undoubtedly answer 'What wilt thou that I should do unto thee?' If I am in a strange land, in the interests of the business which my father owns, I would certainly write two different sorts of letters. There will be family letters giving expression to all the intercourse to which affection prompts; and there will be business letters, containing orders for what I need. And there may be letters in which both are found. The answers will correspond to the letters. To each sentence of the letters containing the family news I do not expect a special answer. But for each order I send I am confident of an answer whether the desired article has been forwarded. In our dealings with God the business element must not be wanting. With our expression of need and sin, of love and faith and consecration, there must be the pointed statement of what we ask and expect to receive; it is in the answer that the Father loves to give us the token of His approval and acceptance.

But the word of the Master teaches us more. He does not say, what dost thou wish? But, what does thou will? One often wishes for a thing without willing it. I wish to have a certain article, but I find the price too high; I resolve not to take it; I wish, but do not will to have it. The sluggard wishes to be rich, but does not will it. Many a one wishes to be saved, but perishes because he does not will it. The will rules the whole heart and life; if I really will to have anything that is within my reach, I do not rest till I have it. And so, when Jesus says to us, 'What wilt thou?' He asks whether it is indeed our purpose to have what we ask at any price, however great the sacrifice. Dost thou indeed so will to have it that, though He delay it long, thou dost not hold thy peace till He hear thee? Alas, how many prayers are wishes, sent up for a short time and then forgotten, or sent up year after year as matter of duty, while we rest content with the prayer without the answer?

ഇൻ

How many prayers are wishes, sent up for a short time and then forgotten, or sent up year after year as matter of duty, while we rest content with the prayer without the answer?

ഇൻ

But, it may be asked, is it not best to make our wishes known to God, and then to leave it to Him to decide what is best, without seeking to assert our will? By no means. This is the very essence of the prayer of faith, to which Jesus sought to train His disciples, that it does not only make known its desire and then leave the decision to God. That would be the prayer of submission, for cases in which we cannot know God's will. But the prayer of faith, finding God's will in some promise of the Word, pleads for that till it come. In Matthew (9: 28) we read Jesus said to the blind man: 'Believe ye that I can do this?' Here, in Mark, He says: 'What wilt thou that I should do?' In both cases He said that faith had saved them. And so He said to the Syrophenician woman, too: 'Great is thy faith: be it unto thee even as thou wilt.' Faith is nothing but the purpose of the will resting on God's word, and saying: I must have it. To believe truly is to will firmly.

But is not such a will at variance with our dependence on God and our submission to Him? By no means; it is much rather the true submission that honors God. It is only when the child has yielded his own will in entire surrender to the Father, that he receives from the Father liberty and power to will what he would have. But, when once the believer has accepted the will of God, as revealed through the Word and Spirit, as his will, too, then it is the will of God that His child should use this renewed will in His service. The will is the highest power in the soul; grace wants above everything to sanctify and restore this will, one of the chief traits of God's image, to full and free exercise. As a son, who only lives for his father's interests, who seeks not his own but his father's will is trusted by the father with his business, so God speaks to His child in all truth, 'What wilt thou?' It is often spiritual sloth that, under the appearance of humility, professes to have no will, because it fears the trouble of searching out the will of God, or, when found, the struggle of claiming it in faith. True humility is ever in company with strong faith, which only seeks to know what is according to the will of God, and then boldly claims the fulfilment of the promise: 'Ye shall ask what ye will, and it shall be done unto you.'

It is often spiritual sloth that, under the appearance of humility, professes to have no will,

Day 24 Prayer

`LORD, TEACH US TO PRAY.'

Lord Jesus! teach me to pray with all my heart and strength, that there may be no doubt with Thee or with me as to what I have asked. May I so know what I desire that, even as my petitions are recorded in heaven, I can record them on earth too, and note each answer as it comes. And may my faith in what Thy Word has promised be so clear that the Spirit may indeed work in me the liberty to will that it shall come. Lord! renew, strengthen, sanctify wholly my will for the work of effectual prayer.

Blessed Saviour! I do beseech Thee to reveal to me the wonderful condescension Thou showest us, thus asking us to say what we will that Thou shouldest do, and promising to do whatever we will. Son of God! I cannot understand it; I can only believe that Thou hast indeed redeemed us wholly for Thyself, and dost seek to make the will, as our noblest part, Thy most efficient servant. Lord! I do most unreservedly yield my will to Thee, as the power through which Thy Spirit is to rule my whole being. Let Him take possession of it, lead it into the truth of Thy promises, and make it so strong in prayer that I may ever hear Thy voice saying: 'Great is thy faith: be it unto thee even as thou wilt.' Amen.

DAY 24
REFLECTION QUESTIONS

1. What did the blind man have to do before he was healed? _____

2. Our prayers must not be an _____ appeal to His mercy, or an_____ cry for blessing, but the _____ expression of a _____ need.

3. What are three things Murray says we need to identify our needs? 1._____

    _____2._____

    3._____

4. What is the difference between wishing and willing in our prayers? _____

    _____

    _____

    _____

5. Are your prayers filled with your wishes or your will? _____

6. When is a prayer of submission appropriate? _____

7. Have you gone to the trouble of searching out God's will? _____

8. What is my main takeaway from Day 24 that will improve my prayer life? _____

    _____

    _____

Fill in the blanks- And _____ answering saith unto _____, Have faith in _____. For verily I say unto _____, That whosoever shall _____ unto this mountain, Be _____ removed, and be thou cast into the sea; and _____ not doubt in _____ heart, but _____ believe that those things which he saith _____ come to pass; he _____ have whatsoever he saith.- Mark 11:22-23

143

Answers

1. Speak his specific request

2. Vague, indefinite, distinct, definite

3. Time, thought, self-scrutiny

4. Wishing is a hope or dream, while will is the follow through or actions required to attain the wish.

5. Personal response

6. When we do not know God's will

7. Personal response

8. Personal response

Class 4 Verse- *And Jesus answering saith unto them, Have faith in God. For verily I say unto you, That whosoever shall say unto this mountain, Be thou removed, and be thou cast into the sea; and shall not doubt in his heart, but shall believe that those things which he saith shall come to pass; he shall have whatsoever he saith.- Mark 11:22-23*

Day 24 Bible Reading - John 9:1-10:21

Day 24 notes

_____

_____

_____

_____

_____

_____

_____

_____

_____

_____

_____

_____

DAY 25

BELIEVE THAT YE HAVE RECEIVED OR, THE FAITH THAT TAKES

'Therefore I say unto you, All things whatsoever ye pray and ask for, believe that ye have received them, and ye shall have them.'--**Mark 11:24**

What a promise! So large, so divine, that our little hearts cannot take it in, and in every possible way seek to limit it to what we think safe or probable; instead of allowing it, in its quickening power and energy, just as He gave it, to enter in, and to enlarge our hearts to the measure of what His love and power are really ready to do for us. Faith is very far from being a mere conviction of the truth of God's word, or a conclusion drawn from certain premises. It is the ear which has heard God say what He will do, the eye which has seen Him doing it, and, therefore, where there is true faith, it is impossible but the answer must come. If we only see to it that we do the one thing that He asks of us as we pray: BELIEVE *that ye have received*; He will see to it that He does the thing He has promised: 'Ye shall have them.' The key-note of Solomon's prayer (2 Chron. 6:4), 'Blessed be the Lord God of Israel, who hath *with His hands fulfilled* that which *He spake with His mouth* to my father David,' is the key-note of all true prayer: the joyful adoration of a God whose *hand* always secures the fulfilment of what His *mouth* hath spoken. Let us in this spirit listen to the promise Jesus gives; each part of it has its Divine message.

'All things whatsoever.' At this first word our human wisdom at once begins to doubt and ask: This surely cannot be literally true? But if it be not, why did the Master speak it, using the very strongest expression He could find: 'All things whatsoever.' And it is not as if this were the only time He spoke thus; is it not He who also said, 'If thou canst believe, ALL THINGS are possible to him that believeth;' 'If ye have faith, NOTHING shall be impossible to you.' Faith is so wholly the work of God's Spirit through His word in the prepared heart of the believing disciple that it is impossible that the fulfilment should not come; faith is the pledge and forerunner of the coming answer. Yes, 'ALL THINGS WHATSOEVER ye shall ask in prayer *believing, ye receive*.' The tendency of human reason is to interpose here, and with certain qualifying clauses, 'if expedient,' 'if according to God's will,' to break the force of a statement which appears dangerous. O let us beware of dealing thus with the Master's words. His promise is most literally true. He wants His oft repeated 'ALL THINGS' to enter into our hearts, and reveal to us how mighty the power of faith is, how truly the Head calls the members to share with Him in His power, how wholly our Father places His power at the disposal of the child that wholly trusts Him. In this 'all things' faith is to have its food and strength: as we weaken it we weaken faith. The WHATSOEVER is unconditional: the only condition is what is implied in the believing. Ere we can believe we must find out and know what God's will is' believing is the exercise of a soul surrendered and given up to the influence of the Word and the Spirit; but when once we do believe nothing shall be impossible. God forbid that we should try and bring down His ALL THINGS to the level of what we think possible. Let us now simply take Christ's 'WHATSOEVER' as

> **God forbid that we should try and bring down His ALL THINGS to the level of what we think possible**

the measure and the hope of our faith: it is a seed-word which, if taken just as He gives it, and kept in the heart, will unfold itself and strike root, fill our life with its fullness, and bring forth fruit abundantly.

'All things whatsoever *ye pray and ask for*.' It is in prayer that these 'all things' are to be brought to God, to be asked and received of Him. The faith that receives them is the fruit of the prayer. In one aspect there must be faith before there can be prayer; in another the faith is the outcome and the growth of prayer. It is in the personal presence of the Savior, in intercourse with Him, that faith rises to grasp what at first appeared too high. It is in prayer that we hold up our desire to the light of God's Holy Will, that our motives are tested, and proof given whether we ask indeed in the name of Jesus, and only for the glory of God. It is in prayer that we wait for the leading of the Spirit to show us whether we are asking the right thing and in the right spirit. It is in prayer that we become conscious of our want of faith, that we are led on to say to the Father that we do believe, and that we prove the reality of our faith by the confidence with which we persevere. It is in prayer that Jesus teaches and inspires faith. He that waits to pray, or loses heart in prayer, because he does not yet feel the faith needed to get the answer, will never learn to believe. He who begins to pray and ask will find the Spirit of faith is given nowhere so surely as at the foot of the Throne.

'*Believe* that ye have received.' It is clear that what we are to believe is, that we receive the very things we ask. The Savior does not hint that because the Father knows what is best, He may give us something else. The very mountain faith bids depart is cast into the sea. There is a prayer in which, in everything, we make known our requests with prayer and supplication, and the reward is the sweet peace of God keeping heart and mind. This is the prayer of trust. It has reference to things of which we cannot find out if God is going to give them. As children we make known our desires in the countless things of daily life, and leave it to the Father to give or not as He thinks best. But the prayer of faith of which Jesus speaks is something different, something higher. When, whether in the greater interests of the Master's work, or in the lesser concerns of our daily life, the soul is led to see how there is nothing that so honours the Father as the faith that is assured that He will do what He has said in giving us whatsoever we ask for, and takes its stand on the promise as brought home by the Spirit, it may know most certainly that it does receive exactly what it asks. Just see how clearly the Lord sets this before us in verse 23: 'Whosoever shall not doubt in his heart, but shall believe that *what he saith* cometh to pass, he shall have it.' This is the blessing of the prayer of faith of which Jesus speaks.

> He that waits to pray, or loses heart in prayer, because he does not yet feel the faith needed to get the answer, will never learn to believe.

'Believe that ye *have received*.' This is the word of central importance, of which the meaning is too often misunderstood. Believe that you have received! now, while praying, the thing you ask for. It may only be later that you shall have it in personal experience, that you shall see what you believe; but now, without seeing, you are to believe that it has been given you of the Father in heaven. The receiving or accepting of an answer to prayer is just like the receiving or accepting of Jesus or of pardon, a spiritual thing, an act of faith apart from all feeling. When I come as a supplicant for pardon, I believe that Jesus in heaven is for me, and so I receive or take Him. When I come as a supplicant for any special gift, which is according to God's word, I believe that what I ask is given me: I believe that I have it, I hold it in faith; I thank God that it is mine. 'If we know that He heareth us, whatsoever we ask, we know that we have the petitions which we have asked of Him.'

'*And ye shall have them.*' That is, the gift which we first hold in faith as bestowed upon us in heaven will also become ours in personal experience. But will it be needful to pray longer if once we know we have been heard and have received what we asked? There are cases in which such prayer will not be needful, in which the blessing is ready to break through at once, if we but hold fast our confidence, and prove our faith by praising for what we have received, in the face of our not yet having it in experience. There are other cases in which the faith that has received needs to be still further tried and strengthened in persevering prayer. God only knows when everything in and around us is fully ripe for the manifestation of the blessing that has been given to faith. Elijah knew for certain that rain would come; God had promised it; and yet he had to pray the seven times. And that prayer was no show or play; an intense spiritual reality in the heart of him who lay pleading there, and in the heaven above where it had its effectual work to do. It is 'through faith *and patience* we inherit the promises.' Faith says most confidently, I have received it. Patience perseveres in prayer until the gift bestowed in heaven is seen on earth. 'Believe that *ye have received*, and *ye shall have*.' Between the *have received* in heaven, and the *shall have* of earth, *believe*: believing praise and prayer is the link.

Through faith *and patience* we inherit the promises

And now, remember one thing more: It is Jesus who said this. As we see heaven thus opened to us, and the Father on the Throne offering to give us whatsoever we ask in faith, our hearts feel full of shame that we have so little availed ourselves of our privilege, and full of fear lest our feeble faith still fail to grasp what is so clearly placed within our reach. There is one thing that must make us strong and full of hope: it is Jesus who has brought us this message from the Father. He Himself, when He was on earth, lived the life of faith and prayer. It was when the disciples expressed their surprise at what He had done to the fig-tree, that He told them that the very same life He led could be theirs; that they could not only command the fig-tree, but the very mountain, and it must obey. And He is our life: all He was on earth He is in us now; all He teaches He really gives. He is Himself the Author and the Perfecter of our faith: He gives the spirit of faith; let us not be afraid that such faith is not meant for us. It is meant for every child of the Father; it is within reach of each one who will but be childlike, yielding himself to the Father's Will and Love, trusting the Father's Word and Power. Dear fellow-Christian, let the thought that this word comes through Jesus, the Son, our Brother, give us courage, and let our answer be: Yea, Blessed Lord, we do believe Thy Word, we do believe that we receive.

Day 25 Prayer

'LORD, TEACH US TO PRAY.'

Blessed Lord! Thou didst come from the Father to show us all His love, and all the treasures of blessing that love is waiting to bestow. Lord! Thou hast this day again flung the gates so wide open, and given us such promises as to our liberty in prayer, that we must blush that our poor hearts have so little taken it in. It has been too large for us to believe.

Lord, we now look up to Thee to teach us to take and keep and use this precious word of Thine: 'All things whatsoever ye ask, believe that ye have received.' Blessed Jesus, it is Thy self in whom our faith must be rooted if it is to grow strong. Thy work has freed us wholly from the power of sin, and opened the way to the Father; Thy Love is ever longing to bring us into the full fellowship of Thy glory and power; Thy Spirit is ever drawing us upward into a life of perfect faith and confidence; we are assured that in Thy teaching we shall learn to pray the prayer of faith. Thou wilt train us to pray so that we believe that we receive, to believe that we really have what we ask. Lord! teach me so to know and trust and love Thee, so to live and abide in Thee, that all my prayers rise up and come before God in Thee, and that my soul may have in Thee the assurance that I am heard. Amen.

DAY 25
REFLECTION QUESTIONS

1. What is the one thing we must do to have true faith that our prayers will be answered?
_____

2. In 2 Chronicles 6:4 Solomon said God had fulfilled the promise He _____
_____?

3. If you qualify your prayers with, "if it is God's will," is this because of a lack of faith?_____
_____
_____
_____

4. What must we know to truly believe our prayers? _____

5. Our faith increases as we are in the _____ _____ of the
Savior, and in _____ with Him.

6. Time in prayer with God increases our _____.

7. How can we be certain that our prayers are God's will and not our own sinful desires?
_____, _____

8. Do you actually believe Jesus's promise that whatever we ask with faith we shall receive? (read the
following verses) Mark 9:23, Matt. 17:20, Matt. 21.22, Mark 11:23 _____
_____

9. What is my main takeaway from Day 25 that will improve my prayer life? _____
_____
_____

Fill in the blanks- And _____ _____ saith unto them, Have _____ in
_____. For verily I say unto you, That _____ _____ say unto this
_____, Be thou removed, and be thou _____ into the _____; and shall
_____ _____ in his heart, but shall _____ _____ those things which he
_____ _____ come to _____; he shall have whatsoever he saith.- Mark 11:22-23

Answers

1. Believe that you receive

2. Spoke with His mouth

3. Personal response

4. God's will

5. Personal presence and communication

6. Faith

7. Spend time reading God's Word and praying in the Holy Spirit

8. Personal response-

    a. Mark 9:23- *Jesus said unto him, if thou canst believe, all things are possible to him that believeth.*

    b. Mark 11:23- *For verily I say unto you, That whosoever shall say unto this mountain, Be thou removed, and be thou cast into the sea; and shall not doubt in his heart, but shall believe that those things which he saith shall come to pass; he shall have whatsoever he saith.*

    c. Matt. 17:20- *And Jesus said unto them, Because of your unbelief: for verily I say unto you, If ye have faith as a grain of mustard seed, ye shall say unto this mountain, Remove hence to yonder place; and it shall remove; and nothing shall be impossible unto you.*

    d. Mat 21:21- *Jesus answered and said unto them, Verily I say unto you, If ye have faith, and doubt not, ye shall not only do this which is done to the fig tree, but also if ye shall say unto this mountain, Be thou removed, and be thou cast into the sea; it shall be done.*

9. Personal response

Class 4 Verse- *And Jesus answering saith unto them, Have faith in God. For verily I say unto you, That whosoever shall say unto this mountain, Be thou removed, and be thou cast into the sea; and shall not doubt in his heart, but shall believe that those things which he saith shall come to pass; he shall have whatsoever he saith.- Mark 11:22-23*

Day 25 Bible Reading - Luke 10-11; John 10:22-42

Day 25 notes

_____

_____

_____

_____

_____

_____

_____

DAY 26

HAVE FAITH IN GOD OR, THE SECRET OF BELIEVING PRAYER

'Jesus, answering, said unto them, Have faith in God. Verily I say unto you, Whosoever shall not doubt in his heart, but shall believe that what He saith cometh to pass; he shall have it. Therefore I say unto you, All things whatsoever ye pray and ask for, believe that ye have received them, and ye shall have them.'--**Mark 11:22-24**

The promise of answer to prayer which formed our yesterday's lesson is one of the most wonderful in all Scripture. In how many hearts it has raised the question: How ever can I attain the faith that knows that it receives all it asks?

It is this question our Lord would answer today. Ere He gave that wonderful promise to His disciples, He spoke another word, in which He points out where the faith in the answer to prayer takes its rise, and ever finds its strength. HAVE FAITH IN GOD: this word precedes the other, Have faith in the promise of an answer to prayer. The power to believe *a promise* depends entirely, but only, on faith in *the promiser.* Trust in the person begets trust in his word. It is only where we live and associate with God in personal, loving intercourse, where GOD HIMSELF is all to us, where our whole being is continually opened up and exposed to the mighty influences that are at work where His Holy Presence is revealed, that the capacity will be developed for believing that He gives whatsoever we ask.

It is on my knowledge of what the promiser is that faith in the promise depends

This connection between faith in God and faith in His promise will become clear to us if we think what faith really is. It is often compared to the hand or the mouth, by which we take and appropriate what is offered to us. But it is of importance that we should understand that faith is also the ear by which I hear what is promised, the eye by which I see what is offered me. On this the power to take depends. I must *hear* the person who gives me the promise: the very tone of his voice gives me courage to believe. I must *see* him: in the light of his eye and countenance all fear as to my right to take passes away. The value of the promise depends on the promiser: it is on my knowledge of what the promiser is that faith in the promise depends.

It is for this reason that Jesus, ere He gives that wonderful prayer-promise, first says, 'HAVE FAITH IN GOD.' That is, let thine eye be open to the Living God, and gaze on Him, seeing Him who is Invisible. It is through the eye that I yield myself to the influence of what is before me; I just allow it to enter, to exert its influence, to leave its impression upon my mind. So believing God is just looking to God and what He is, allowing Him to reveal His presence, giving Him time and yielding the whole being to take in the full impression of what He is as God, the soul opened up to receive and rejoice in the overshadowing of His love. Yes, faith is the eye to which God shows what He is and does: through faith the light of His presence and the workings of His mighty power stream into the soul. As that which I see lives in me, so by faith God lives in me too.

And even so faith is also the ear through which the voice of God is always heard and intercourse with Him kept up. It is through the Holy Spirit the Father speaks to us; the Son is the Word, the substance of what God says; the Spirit is the living voice. This the child of God needs to lead and guide him; the secret voice from heaven must teach him, as it taught Jesus, what to say and what to do. An ear opened towards God, that is, a believing heart waiting on Him, to hear what He says, will hear Him speak. The words of God will not only be the words of a Book, but, proceeding from the mouth of God, they will be spirit and truth, life and power. They will bring in deed and living experience what are otherwise only thoughts. Through this opened ear the soul tarries under the influence of the life and power of God Himself. As the words I hear enter the mind and dwell and work there, so through faith God enters the heart, and dwells and works there.

When faith now is in full exercise as eye and ear, as the faculty of the soul by which we see and hear God, then it will be able to exercise its full power as hand and mouth, by which we appropriate God and His blessing. The power of reception will depend entirely on the power of spiritual perception. For this reason Jesus said, ere He gave the promise that God would answer believing prayer: 'HAVE FAITH IN GOD.' Faith is simply surrender: I yield myself to the impression the tidings I hear make on me. By faith *I yield myself to the living God.* His glory and love fill my heart, and have the mastery over my life. Faith is fellowship; I give myself up to the influence of the friend who makes me a promise, and become linked to him by it. And it is when we enter into this living fellowship *with God Himself,* in a faith that always sees and hears Him, that it becomes easy and natural to believe His promise as to prayer. Faith in the promise is the fruit of faith in the promiser: the prayer of faith is rooted in the life of faith. And in this way the faith that prays effectually is indeed a gift of God. Not as something that He bestows or infuses at once, but in a far deeper and truer sense, as the blessed disposition or habit of soul which is wrought and grows up in us in a life of intercourse with Him. Surely for one who knows his Father well, and lives in constant close intercourse with Him, it is a simple thing to believe the promise that He will do the will of His child who lives in union with Himself.

It is because very many of God's children do not understand this connection between the life of faith and the prayer of faith that their experience of the power of prayer is so limited

It is because very many of God's children do not understand this connection between the life of faith and the prayer of faith that their experience of the power of prayer is so limited. When they desire earnestly to obtain an answer from God, they fix their whole heart upon the promise, and try their utmost to grasp that promise in faith. When they do not succeed, they are ready to give up hope; the promise is true, but it is beyond their power to take hold of it in faith. Listen to the lesson Jesus teaches us this day: HAVE FAITH IN GOD, the Living God: let faith look to God more than the thing promised: it is His love, His power, His living presence will waken and work the faith. A physician would say to one asking for some means to get more strength in his arms and hands to seize and hold, that his whole constitution must be built up and strengthened. So the cure of a feeble faith is alone to be found in the invigoration of our whole spiritual life by intercourse with God. Learn to believe in God, to take hold of God, to let God take possession of thy life, and it will be easy to take hold of the promise. He that knows and trusts God finds it easy to trust the promise too.

Just note how distinctly this comes out in the saints of old. Every special exhibition of the power of faith was the fruit of a special revelation of God. See it in Abraham: 'And *the word of the Lord came* unto Abram, saying, Fear not, Abram; *I am thy shield.* And *He brought him forth* abroad, *and said* . . . AND HE BELIEVED THE LORD.' And later again: 'The Lord *appeared unto him, and said* unto him, I am God Almighty. And Abram fell on his face, and *God talked with him,* saying, As for me, behold my covenant is with thee.' It was the revelation of God Himself that gave the promise its living power to enter the heart and work the faith. Because they knew God, these men of faith could not do anything but trust His promise. God's promise will be to us what God Himself is. It is the man who walks before the Lord, and falls upon his face to listen while the living God speaks to him, who will really receive the promise. Though we have God's promises in the Bible, with full liberty to take them, the spiritual power is wanting, except as *God Himself speaks them to us. And He speaks to those who walk and live with Him.* Therefore, HAVE FAITH IN GOD: let faith be all eye and ear, the surrender to let God make His full impression, and reveal Himself fully in the soul. Count it one of the chief blessings of prayer to exercise faith in God, as the Living Mighty God who waits to fulfil in us all the good pleasure of His will, and the work of faith with power. See in Him the God of Love, whose delight it is to bless and impart Himself. In such worship of faith in God the power will speedily come to believe the promise too: 'ALL THINGS WHATSOEVER YE ASK, BELIEVE THAT YE RECEIVE.' Yes, see that thou dost in faith make God thine own; the promise will be thine too.

We seek God's gifts, but God wants to give us HIMSELF first

Precious lessons that Jesus has to teach us this day. We seek God's gifts: God wants to give us HIMSELF first. We think of prayer as the power to draw down good gifts from heaven; Jesus as the means to draw ourselves up to God. We want to stand at the door and cry; Jesus would have us first enter in and realize that we are friends and children. Let us accept the teaching. Let every experience of the littleness of our faith in prayer urge us first to have and exercise more faith in the living God, and in such faith to yield ourselves to Him. A heart full of God has power for the prayer of faith. Faith in God begets faith in the promise, in the promise too of an answer to prayer.

Therefore, child of God, take time, take time, to bow before *Him,* to wait on *Him* to reveal *Himself.* Take time, and let thy soul in holy awe and worship exercise and express its faith in the Infinite One, and as He imparts Himself and takes possession of thee, the prayer of faith will crown thy faith in God.

Day 26 Prayer

'LORD, TEACH US TO PRAY.'

O my God! I do believe in Thee. I believe in Thee as the Father, Infinite in Thy Love and Power. And as the Son, my Redeemer and my Life. And as the Holy Spirit, Comforter and Guide and Strength. Three-One God, I have faith in Thee. I know and am sure that all that Thou art Thou art to me, that all Thou hast promised Thou wilt perform

Lord Jesus, increase this faith. Teach me to take time, and wait and worship in the Holy Presence until my faith takes in all there is in my God for me. Let it see Him as the Fountain of all Life, working with Almighty Strength to accomplish His will on the world and in me. Let it see Him in His love longing to meet and fulfil my desires. Let it so take possession of my heart and life that through faith God alone may dwell there. Lord Jesus, help me, with my whole heart would I believe in God. Let faith in God each moment fill me.

O my Blessed Savior, how can Thy Church glorify Thee, how can it fulfil that work of intercession through which Thy kingdom must come, unless our whole life be FAITH IN GOD. Blessed Lord, speak Thy Word, 'HAVE FAITH IN GOD,' unto the depths of our souls.

DAY 26
REFLECTION QUESTIONS

1. The power to believe a promise depends on our faith in the _____.

2. What two senses does Murray say help us have faith in the promiser? _____
_____

3. What is one way for us to hear and see more of God? _____

4. Murray says faith is _____ and _____

5. Is your prayer of faith weak because your life of faith is weak? _____

6. Murray points out the cure for weak faith is _____.

7. Who does Murray say God speaks to? _____

8. Before we seek God's gifts in prayer we need to seek _____ first.

9. Murray says our faith increases as God reveals Himself and takes possession of us. What is the key ingredient required to for this to happen? _____

10. What is my main takeaway from Day 26 that will improve my prayer life? _____
_____
_____

Fill in the blanks- And _____ _____ saith unto _____, Have _____ in _____. For verily I say unto you, That _____ _____ say unto this _____, Be thou _____, and be thou _____ into the _____; and shall _____ _____ in his _____, but shall _____ _____ those _____ which he _____ _____ come to _____; he shall have _____ he saith.- Mark 11:22-23

Answers

1. Promisor
2. Hearing, seeing
3. Pray
4. Surrender and fellowship
5. Personal response
6. Fellowship with God-prayer
7. Those who walk and live with Him
8. God
9. Time
10. Personal response

Class 4 Verse- *And Jesus answering saith unto them, Have faith in God. For verily I say unto you, That whosoever shall say unto this mountain, Be thou removed, and be thou cast into the sea; and shall not doubt in his heart, but shall believe that those things which he saith shall come to pass; he shall have whatsoever he saith.- Mark 11:22-23*

Day 26 Bible Reading - Luke 12-13

Day 26 notes

_____

_____

_____

_____

_____

_____

_____

_____

_____

_____

_____

DAY 27

PRAYER AND FASTING OR, THE CURE OF UNBELIEF

'Then came the disciples to Jesus apart, and said, Why could not we cast him out? And Jesus said unto them, Because of your unbelief: for verily I say unto you, If ye have faith as a grain of mustard seed, nothing shall be impossible to you. Howbeit this kind goeth not out but by prayer and fasting'--**Matthew 17:19-21**

When the disciples saw Jesus cast the evil spirit out of the epileptic whom 'they could not cure,' they asked the Master for the cause of their failure. He had given them 'power and authority over all devils, and to cure all diseases.' They had often exercised that power, and joyfully told how the devils were subject to them. And yet now, while He was on the Mount, they had utterly failed. That there had been nothing in the will of God or in the nature of the case to render deliverance impossible, had been proved: at Christ's bidding the evil spirit had gone out. From their expression, 'Why could we not?' it is evident that they had wished and sought to do so; they had probably used the Master's name, and called upon the evil spirit to go out. Their efforts had been vain, and in presence of the multitude, they had been put to shame. 'Why could we not?'

Christ's answer was direct and plain: 'Because of your unbelief.' The cause of His success and their failure, was not owing to His having a special power to which they had no access. No; the reason was not far to seek. He had so often taught them that there is one power, that of faith, to which, in the kingdom of darkness, as in the kingdom of God, everything must bow; in the spiritual world failure has but one cause, the want of faith. Faith is the one condition on which all Divine power can enter into man and work through him. It is the susceptibility of the unseen: man's will yielded up to, and molded by, the will of God. The power they had received to cast out devils, they did not hold in themselves as a permanent gift or possession; the power was in Christ, to be received, and held, and used by faith alone, living faith in Himself. Had they been full of faith *in Him* as Lord and Conqueror in the spirit-world, had they been full of faith *in Him* as having given them authority to cast out in His name, this faith would have given them the victory. 'Because of your unbelief' was, for all time, the Master's explanation and reproof of impotence and failure in His Church.

₧₧₧

In the spiritual world failure has but one cause, the want of faith

₧₧₧

But such want of faith must have a cause too. Well might the disciples have asked: 'And why could we not believe? Our faith has cast out devils before this: why have we now failed in believing? 'The Master proceeds to tell them ere they ask: 'This kind goeth not out but by fasting and prayer.' As faith is the simplest, so it is the highest exercise of the spiritual life, where our spirit yields itself in perfect receptivity to God's Spirit and so is strengthened to its highest activity. This faith depends entirely upon the state of the spiritual life; only when this is strong and in full health, when the Spirit of God has full sway in our life, is there the power of faith to do its mighty deeds. And therefore Jesus adds: 'Howbeit this kind goeth not out but by fasting and prayer.' The faith that can overcome such stubborn resistance as you have just seen in this evil spirit, Jesus tells them, is not possible except to men living in very close fellowship with God, and in very special separation from the world--in prayer and fasting. And so He teaches us two lessons in regard to prayer of deep importance. The one, that faith needs a life of prayer in which to grow and keep strong. The other, that prayer needs fasting for its full and perfect development.

Faith needs a life of prayer for its full growth. In all the different parts of the spiritual life, there is such close union, such unceasing action and re-action, that each may be both cause and effect. Thus it is with faith. There can be no true prayer without faith; some measure of faith must precede prayer. And yet prayer is also the way to more faith; there can be no higher degrees of faith except through much prayer. This is the lesson Jesus teaches here. There is nothing needs so much to grow as our faith. 'Your faith groweth exceedingly,' is said of one Church. When Jesus spoke the words, 'According to your faith be it unto you,' He announced the law of the kingdom, which tells us that all have not equal degrees of faith, that the same person has not always the same degree, and that the measure of faith must always determine the measure of power and of blessing. If we want to know where and how our faith is to grow, the Master points us to the throne of God. It is in prayer, in the exercise of the faith I have, in fellowship with the living God, that faith can increase. Faith can only live by feeding on what is Divine, on God Himself.

There can be no higher degrees of faith except through much prayer.

It is in the adoring worship of God, the waiting on Him and for Him, the deep silence of soul that yields itself for God to reveal Himself, that the capacity for knowing and trusting God will be developed. It is as we take His word from the Blessed Book, and bring it to Himself, asking him to speak it to us with His living loving voice, that the power will come fully to believe and receive the word as God's own word to us. It is in prayer, in living contact with God in living faith, that faith, the power to trust God, and in that trust, to accept everything He says, to accept every possibility He has offered to our faith will become strong in us. Many Christians cannot understand what is meant by the much prayer they sometimes hear spoken of: they can form no conception, nor do they feel the need, of spending hours with God. But what the Master says, the experience of His people has confirmed: men of strong faith are men of much prayer.

This just brings us back again to the lesson we learned when Jesus, before telling us to believe that we receive what we ask, first said, 'Have faith in God.' It is God, the living God, into whom our faith must strike its roots deep and broad; then it will be strong to remove mountains and cast out devils. 'If ye have faith, nothing shall be impossible to you.' Oh! if we do but give ourselves up to the work God has for us in the world, coming into contact with the mountains and the devils there are to be cast away and cast out, we should soon comprehend the need there is of much faith, and of much prayer, as the soil in which alone faith can be cultivated. Christ Jesus is our life, the life of our faith too. It is His life in us that makes us strong, and makes us simple to believe. It is in the dying to self which much prayer implies, in closer union to Jesus, that the spirit of faith will come in power. *Faith needs prayer* for its full growth.

And *prayer needs fasting* for its full growth: this is the second lesson. Prayer is the one hand with which we grasp the invisible; fasting, the other, with which we let loose and cast away the visible. In nothing is man more closely connected with the world of sense than in his need of food, and his enjoyment of it. It was the fruit, good for food, with which man was tempted and fell in Paradise. It was with bread to be made of stones

Men of strong faith are men of much prayer

that Jesus, when an hungered, was tempted in the wilderness, and in fasting that He triumphed. The body has been redeemed to be a temple of the Holy Spirit; it is in body as well as spirit, it is very specially, Scripture says, in eating and drinking, we are to glorify God. It is to be feared that there are many Christians to whom this eating to the glory of God has not yet become a spiritual reality. And the first thought suggested by Jesus' words in regard to fasting and prayer, is, that it is only in a life of moderation and temperance and self-denial that there will be the heart or the strength to pray much.

But then there is also its more literal meaning. Sorrow and anxiety cannot eat: joy celebrates its feasts with eating and drinking. There may come times of intense desire, when it is strongly felt how the body, with its appetites, lawful though they be, still hinder the spirit in its battle with the powers of darkness, and the need is felt of keeping it under. We are creatures of the senses: our mind is helped by what comes to us embodied in concrete form; fasting helps to express, to deepen, and to confirm the resolution that we are ready to sacrifice anything, to sacrifice ourselves, to attain what we seek for the kingdom of God. And He who accepted the fasting and sacrifice of the Son, knows to value and accept and reward with spiritual power the soul that is thus ready to give up all for Christ and His kingdom.

And then follows a still wider application. Prayer is the reaching out after God and the unseen; fasting, the letting go of all that is of the seen and temporal. While ordinary Christians imagine that all that is not positively forbidden and sinful is lawful to them, and seek to retain as much as possible of this world, with its property, its literature, its enjoyments, the truly consecrated soul is as the soldier who carries only what he needs for the warfare. Laying aside every weight, as well as the easily besetting sin, afraid of entangling himself with the affairs of this life, he seeks to lead a Nazarite life, as one specially set apart for the Lord and His service. Without such voluntary separation, even from what is lawful, no one will attain power in prayer: this kind goeth not out but by fasting and prayer.

Disciples of Jesus, who have asked the Master to teach you to pray, come now and accept His lessons. He tells you that prayer is the path to faith, strong faith, that can cast out devils. He tells you: 'If ye have faith, nothing shall be impossible to you;' let this glorious promise encourage you to pray much. Is the prize not worth the price? Shall we not give up all to follow Jesus in the path He opens to us here; shall we not, if need be, fast? Shall we not do anything that neither the body nor the world around hinder us in our great life-work,--having intercourse with our God in prayer, that we may become men of faith, whom He can use in His work of saving the world?

Day 27 Prayer

'LORD, TEACH US TO PRAY.'

O Lord Jesus! how continually Thou hast to reprove us for our unbelief! How strange it must appear to Thee, this terrible incapacity of trusting our Father and His promises. Lord! let Thy reproof, with its searching, 'Because of your unbelief,' sink into the very depths of our hearts, and reveal to us how much of the sin and suffering around us is our blame. And then teach us, Blessed Lord, that there is a place where faith can be learned and gained,--even in the prayer and fasting that brings into living and abiding fellowship with Thyself and the Father.

O Savior! Thou Thyself art the Author and the Perfecter of our faith; teach us what it is to let Thee live in us by Thy Holy Spirit. Lord! our efforts and prayers for grace to believe have been so unavailing. We know why it was: we sought for strength in ourselves to be given from Thee. Holy Jesus! do at length teach us the mystery of Thy life in us, and how Thou, by Thy Spirit, dost undertake to live in us the life of faith, to see to it that our faith shall not fail. O let us see that our faith will just be a part of that wonderful prayer-life which Thou givest in them who expect their training for the ministry of intercession, not in word and thought only, but in the Holy Unction Thou givest, the inflowing of the Spirit of Thine own life. And teach us how, in fasting and prayer, we may grow up to the faith to which nothing shall be impossible. Amen.

NOTE

At the time when Blumhardt was passing through his terrible conflict with the evil spirits in those who were possessed, and seeking to cast them out by prayer, he often wondered what it was that hindered the answer. One day a friend, to whom he had spoken of his trouble, directed his attention to our Lord's words about fasting. Blumhardt resolved to give himself to fasting, sometimes for more than thirty hours. From reflection and experience he gained the conviction that it is of more importance than is generally thought. He says, 'Inasmuch as the fasting is before God, a practical proof that the thing we ask is to us a matter of true and pressing interest, and inasmuch as in a high degree it strengthens the intensity and power of the prayer, and becomes the unceasing practical expression of a prayer without words, I could believe that it would not be without efficacy, especially as the Master's words had reference to a case like the present. I tried it, without telling anyone, and in truth the later conflict was extraordinarily lightened by it. I could speak with much greater restfulness and decision. I did not require to be so long present with the sick one; and I felt that I could influence without being present.'

DAY 27
REFLECTION QUESTIONS

1. What does Murray say the one and only cause of spiritual failure is? _____

2. How many of your unanswered prayers can be attributed to unbelief? _____

3. What are the two lessons Jesus was teaching in Matt. 17: 19-21? _____
   _____,_____

4. One of the best ways to increase faith is to _____.

5. The amount of faith you possess will determine your _____ and
   _____

6. Fasting helps us let go of everything _____.

7. Fasting helps us express and confirm our resolution to _____
   _____ to attain what we seek for the kingdom of God.

8. Is fasting a part of your prayer life? _____

9. What is my main takeaway from Day 27 that will improve my prayer life? _____
   _____
   _____

Fill in the blanks- And _____ _____ saith unto _____, Have _____ in _____. For _____ I say unto _____, That _____ _____ say unto this _____, Be thou _____, and _____ thou _____ into the _____; _____ shall _____ _____ in his _____, but shall _____ _____ those _____ which he _____ _____ come _____ _____; he _____ have _____ he _____.- Mark 11:22-23

159

Answers

1. Lack of faith-unbelief

2. Personal response

3. Faith grows from a life of prayer, and fasting helps fully develop prayer

4. Spend time in prayer

5. Blessings and power

6. Temporal/worldly

7. Sacrifice ourselves

8. Personal response

9. Personal response

Class 4 Verse- *And Jesus answering saith unto them, Have faith in God. For verily I say unto you, That whosoever shall say unto this mountain, Be thou removed, and be thou cast into the sea; and shall not doubt in his heart, but shall believe that those things which he saith shall come to pass; he shall have whatsoever he saith.- Mark 11:22-23*

Day 27 Bible Reading - Luke 14-15

Day 27 notes

_____

_____

_____

_____

_____

_____

_____

_____

_____

_____

_____

DAY 28

WHEN YE STAND PRAYING FORGIVE
OR, PRAYER AND LOVE

'And whensoever ye stand praying, forgive, if ye have aught against any one; that your Father also which is in heaven may forgive you your trespasses.'--**Mark 11:25**

These words follow immediately on the great prayer-promise, 'All things whatsoever ye pray, believe that ye have received them, and ye shall have them.' We have already seen how the words that preceded that promise, 'Have faith in God,' taught us that in prayer all depends upon our relation to God being clear; these words that follow on it remind us that our relation with fellow-men must be clear too. Love to God and love to our neighbor are inseparable: the prayer from a heart, that is either not right with God on the one side, or with men on the other, cannot prevail. Faith and love are essential to each other.

We find that this is a thought to which our Lord frequently gave expression. In the Sermon on the Mount (Matt. 5:23-24), when speaking of the sixth commandment, He taught His disciples how impossible acceptable worship to the Father was if everything were not right with the brother: 'If thou art offering thy gift at the altar, and there rememberest that thy brother hath aught against thee, leave there thy gift before the altar, and go thy way; first be reconciled to thy brother, and then come and offer thy gift.' And so later, when speaking of prayer to God, after having taught us to pray, 'Forgive us our debts, as we also have forgiven our debtors,' He added at the close of the prayer: 'If you forgive not men their trespasses, neither will your Father forgive your trespasses.' At the close of the parable of the unmerciful servant He applies His teaching in the words: 'So shall also my Heavenly Father do unto you, if ye forgive not everyone his brother from your hearts.' And so here, beside the dried-up fig-tree, where He speaks of the wonderful power of faith and the prayer of faith, He all at once, apparently without connection, introduces the thought, 'Whensoever ye stand praying, forgive, if ye have aught against any one; that your Father also which is in heaven may forgive you your trespasses.' It is as if the Lord had learned during His life at Nazareth and afterwards that disobedience to the law of love to men was the great sin even of praying people, and the great cause of the feebleness of their prayer. And it is as if He wanted to lead us into His own blessed experience that nothing gives such liberty of access and such power in believing as the consciousness that we have given ourselves in love and compassion, for those whom God loves.

The deep sure ground of answer to prayer is God's forgiving love

The first lesson taught here is that of a forgiving disposition. We pray, 'Forgive, *even as* we have forgiven.' Scripture says, 'Forgive one another, even as God also in Christ forgave you.' God's full and free forgiveness is to be the rule of ours with men. Otherwise our reluctant, half-hearted forgiveness, which is not forgiveness at all, will be God's rule with us. Every prayer rests upon our faith in God's pardoning grace. If God dealt with us after our sins, not one prayer could be heard. Pardon opens the door to all God's love and blessing: because God has pardoned all our sin, our prayer can prevail to obtain all we need. The deep sure ground of answer to prayer is God's forgiving love. When it has taken possession of the heart, we pray in faith. But also, when it has taken possession of the heart, we live in love. God's forgiving disposition, revealed in His love to us, becomes a disposition in us; as the power of His forgiving love shed abroad and dwelling within us, we forgive even as He forgives. If there be great and grievous injury or injustice done us, we seek first of all to possess a Godlike disposition; to be kept from a sense of wounded honor, from a desire to maintain our rights, or from rewarding the offender as he has deserved. In the little annoyances of daily life, we are watchful not to excuse the hasty temper, the sharp word, the quick judgment, with the thought that we mean no harm, that we do not keep the anger long, or that it would be too much to expect from feeble human nature, that we should really forgive the way God and Christ do. No, we take the command literally, 'Even as Christ forgave, so also do ye.' The blood that cleanses the conscience from dead works, cleanses from selfishness too; the love it reveals is pardoning love that takes possession of us and flows through us to others. Our forgiving love to men is the evidence of the reality of God's forgiving love in us, and so the condition of the prayer of faith.

There is a second, more general lesson: our daily life in the world is made the test of our intercourse with God in prayer. How often the Christian, when he comes to pray, does his utmost to cultivate certain frames of mind which he thinks will be pleasing. He does not understand, or forgets, that life does not consist of so many loose pieces, of which now the one, then the other, can be taken up. Life is a whole, and the pious frame of the hour of prayer is judged of by God from the ordinary frame of the daily life of which the hour of prayer is but a small part. Not the feeling I call up, but the tone of my life during the day, is God's criterion of what I really am and desire. My drawing nigh to God is of one piece with my intercourse with men and earth: failure here will cause failure there. And that not only when there is the distinct consciousness of anything wrong between my neighbor and myself; but the ordinary current of my thinking and judging, the unloving thoughts and words I allow to pass unnoticed, can hinder my prayer. The effectual prayer of faith comes out from a life given up to the will and the love of God. Not according to what I try to be when praying, but what I am when not praying, is my prayer dealt with by God.

We may gather these thoughts into a third lesson: In our life with men the one thing on which everything depends is love. The spirit of forgiveness is the spirit of love. Because God is love, He forgives: it is only when we are dwelling in love that we can forgive as God forgives. In love to the brethren we have the evidence of love to the Father, the ground of confidence before God, and the assurance that our prayer will be heard, (1 John 4:20, 3:18-21, 23.). 'Let us love in deed and truth; *hereby* shall we assure our heart before Him. If our heart condemn us not, we have boldness toward God, and whatever we ask,

The spirit of forgiveness is the spirit of love.

we receive of Him.' Neither faith nor work will profit if we have not love; it is love that unites with God, it is love that proves the reality of faith. As essential as in the word that precedes the great prayer-promise in Mark 11:24, 'Have faith in God,' is this one that follows it, 'Have love to men.' The right relations to the living God above me, and the living men around me, are the conditions of effectual prayer.

This love is of special consequence when we labor for such and pray for them. We sometimes give ourselves to work for Christ, from zeal for His cause, as we call it, or for our own spiritual health, without giving ourselves in personal self-sacrificing love for those whose souls we seek. No wonder that our faith is feeble and does not conquer. To look on each wretched one, however unlovable he be, in the light of the tender love of Jesus the Shepherd seeking the lost; to see Jesus Christ in him, and to take him up, for Jesus' sake, in a heart that really loves, --this, this is the secret of believing prayer and successful effort. Jesus, in speaking of forgiveness, speaks of love as its root. Just as in the Sermon on the Mount He connected His teaching and promises about prayer with the call to be merciful, as the Father in heaven is merciful (Matt. 5:7, 9, 22, 38-48), so we see it here: a loving life is the condition of believing prayer.

It has been said: There is nothing so heart-searching as believing prayer, or even the honest effort to pray in faith. O let us not turn the edge of that self-examination by the thought that God does not hear our prayer for reasons known to Himself alone. By no means. 'Ye ask and receive not, because ye ask amiss.' Let that word of God search us. Let us ask whether our prayer be indeed the expression of a life wholly given over to the will of God and the love of man. Love is the only soil in which faith can strike its roots and thrive. As it throws its arms up, and opens its heart heavenward, the Father always looks to see if it has them opened towards the evil and the unworthy too. In that love, not indeed the love of perfect attainment, but the love of fixed purpose and sincere obedience, faith can alone obtain the blessing. It is he who gives himself to let the love of God dwell in him, and in the practice of daily life to love as God loves, who will have the power to believe in the Love that hears his every prayer. It is *the Lamb*, who is in the midst of the throne: it is suffering and forbearing love that prevails with God in prayer. The merciful shall obtain mercy; the meek shall inherit the earth.

Day 28 Prayer

'LORD, TEACH US TO PRAY.'

Blessed Father! Thou art Love, and only he that abideth in love abideth in Thee and in fellowship with Thee. The Blessed Son hath this day again taught me how deeply true this is of my fellowship with Thee in prayer. O my God! let Thy love, shed abroad in my heart by the Holy Spirit, be in me a fountain of love to all around me, that out of a life in love may spring the power of believing prayer. O my Father! grant by the Holy Spirit that this may be my experience, that a life in love to all around me is the gate to a life in the love of my God. And give me especially to find in the joy with which I forgive day by day whoever might offend me, the proof that Thy forgiveness to me is a power and a life.

 Lord Jesus! my Blessed Teacher! teach Thou me to forgive and to love. Let the power of Thy blood make the pardon of my sins such a reality, that forgiveness, as shown by Thee to me, and by me to others, may be the very joy of heaven. Show me whatever in my intercourse with fellowmen might hinder my fellowship with God, so that my daily life in my own home and in society may be the school in which strength and confidence are gathered for the prayer of faith. Amen.

DAY 28
REFLECTION QUESTIONS

1. For our prayers to be answered our hearts must be right with _____ and with

   _____

2. Murray states that feebleness in our prayers come from _____

   _____.

3. Is there anyone in your life you carry a grudge or resentment against or have not forgiven?

   _____

4. In what manner will God forgive us? _____

5. Do you have a forgiving disposition and do you offer full forgiveness to those who wrong you?

   _____

6. Answer to our prayers rests in God's _____ grace.

7. How is your attitude during your prayer time different from your attitude during your daily interactions

   with others_____

   _____

8. What is the one thing required for us to forgive as God forgives? _____

9. Do you chalk up unanswered prayers to God's unknown will or do you spend time self-examining

   your heart to see if unforgiveness may be the cause?_____

   _____

10. What is my main takeaway from Day 28 that will improve my prayer life? _____

    _____

Fill in the blanks- And _____ _____ saith unto _____, Have _____ in _____. For _____ I say unto _____, That _____ _____ say _____ this _____, Be thou _____, and _____ thou _____ into the _____; _____ shall _____ _____ in his _____, but _____ _____ _____ those _____ which he _____ _____ come _____ _____; _____ _____ have _____ _____ _____.- Mark 11:22-23

164

Answers

1. God and man

2. Disobedience to the law of love to men

3. Personal response –take time to pray and ask the Holy Spirt to reveal this to you

4. In the same manner that we forgive others

5. Personal response

6. Pardoning

7. Personal response - It is not the time you spend dutifully praying to God in your quiet time each day that allows God to judge your character, but your attitude, thoughts, reactions and responses to life's circumstances reveal your true identity and love for Christ.

8. Love

9. Personal response

10. Personal response

Class 4 Verse- *And Jesus answering saith unto them, Have faith in God. For verily I say unto you, That whosoever shall say unto this mountain, Be thou removed, and be thou cast into the sea; and shall not doubt in his heart, but shall believe that those things which he saith shall come to pass; he shall have whatsoever he saith.- Mark 11:22-23*

Day 28 Bible Reading - Luke 16-17:10

Day 28 notes

_____

_____

_____

_____

_____

_____

_____

_____

_____

_____

_____

CLASS 4

WEEK 5

Opening Prayer –Thank God for answering our prayers.

Word- Belief, **Theme**- Have faith in the promisor

Key Questions-

1. What is required to be a 'friend of God'? _____

2. What does Murray say are the two reasons we do not obey the command to pray for labors?

   1._____

   2._____

3. What are three things Murray says we need to identify our needs?

   1._____2._____

   3._____

4. What must we know to truly believe our prayers? _____

5. What is the cure for weak faith? _____

6. What are the two lessons Jesus was teaching in Matt. 17:19-21? _____

   _____, _____

7. For our prayers to be answered our hearts must be right with _____ and with

   _____.

Testimonies- What is God doing through your prayer life?

Scripture Memory-

Class 4 Verse- *And Jesus answering saith unto them, Have faith in God. For verily I say unto you, That whosoever shall say unto this mountain, Be thou removed, and be thou cast into the sea; and shall not doubt in his heart, but shall believe that those things which he saith shall come to pass; he shall have whatsoever he saith.- Mark 11:22-23*

Next Class Preview-

Word- Abide, **Theme**- The chief object of prayer is God's glory.

Verse- *If ye abide in me, and my words abide in you, ye shall ask what ye will, and it shall be done unto you. - John 15:7*

Prayer for Students-

- Time to Pray Each Day
- A Desire for Prayer
- A Clear Mind During Prayer
- Show us God's Will

Class 4 Answers

1. Keep His Commands- John 15:14 & James 2:22-23
2. We do not have compassion for the lost, we lack faith
3. Time, thought, self-scrutiny
4. God's will
5. Fellowship with God-prayer
6. Faith grows from a life of prayer, and fasting helps fully develop prayer
7. God and man

Class 4 notes

_____

_____

_____

_____

_____

_____

_____

_____

_____

_____

_____

_____

_____

_____

_____

_____

DAY 29

IF TWO OR THREE AGREE OR, THE POWER OF UNITED PRAYER

'Again I say unto you, That if two of you shall agree on earth as touching anything that they shall ask, it shall be done for them of my Father which is in heaven. For where two or three are gathered together in my Name, there am I in the midst of them.'-- **Matthew 18:19-20**

One of the first lessons of our Lord in His school of prayer was: Not to be seen of men. Enter thy inner chamber; be alone with the Father. When He has thus taught us that the meaning of prayer is personal individual contact with God, He comes with a second lesson: You have need not only of secret solitary, but also of public united prayer. And He gives us a very special promise for the united prayer of two or three who agree in what they ask. As a tree has its root hidden in the ground and its stem growing up into the sunlight, so prayer needs equally for its full development the hidden secrecy in which the soul meets God alone, and the public fellowship with those who find in the name of Jesus their common meeting-place.

The reason why this must be so is plain. The bond that unites a man to his fellow-men is no less real and close than that which unites him to God: he is one with them. Grace renews not alone our relation to God but to man too. We not only learn to say 'My Father,' but 'Our Father.' Nothing would be more unnatural than that the children of a family should always meet their father separately, but never in the united expression of their desires or their love. Believers are not only members of one family, but even of one body. Just as each member of the body depends on the other, and the full action of the spirit dwelling in the body depends on the union and co-operation of all, so Christians cannot reach the full blessing God is ready to bestow through His Spirit, but as they seek and receive it in fellowship with each other. It is in the union and fellowship of believers that the Spirit can manifest His full power. It was to the hundred and twenty continuing in one place together, and praying with one accord, that the Spirit came from the throne of the glorified Lord.

The marks of true united prayer are given us in these words of our Lord. The first is agreement as to the thing asked. There must not only be generally the consent to agree with anything another may ask: there must be some special thing, matter of distinct united desire; the agreement must be, as all prayer, in spirit and in truth. In such agreement it will become very clear to us what exactly we are asking, whether we may confidently ask according to God's will, and whether we are ready to believe that we have received what we ask.

> **You have need not only of secret solitary, but also of public united prayer**

The second mark is the gathering in, or into, the Name of Jesus. We shall afterwards have much more to learn of the need and the power of the Name of Jesus in prayer; here our Lord teaches us that the Name must be the center of union to which believers gather, the bond of union that makes them one, just as a home contains and unites all who are in it. 'The Name of the Lord is a strong tower; the righteous runneth into it and escape.' That Name is such a reality to those who understand and believe it, that to meet within it is to have Himself present. The love and unity of His disciples have to Jesus infinite attraction: 'Where two or three are gathered in my Name, there am I in the midst of them.' It is the living presence of Jesus, in the fellowship of His loving praying disciples that gives united prayer its power.

The third mark is, the sure answer: 'It shall be done for them of my Father.' A prayer-meeting for maintaining religious fellowship, or seeking our own edification, may have its use; this was not the Savior's view in its appointment. He meant it as a means of securing special answer to prayer. A prayer meeting without recognized answer to prayer ought to be an anomaly. When any of us have distinct desires in regard to which we feel too weak to exercise the needful faith, we ought to seek strength in the help of others. In the unity of faith and of love and of the Spirit, the power of the Name and the Presence of Jesus acts more freely and the answer comes more surely. The mark that there has been true united prayer is the fruit, the answer, the receiving of the thing we have asked: 'I say unto you, It shall be done for them of my Father which is in heaven.'

What an unspeakable privilege this of united prayer is, and what a power it might be. If the believing husband and wife knew that they were joined together in the Name of Jesus to experience His presence and power in united prayer (1 Peter); if friends believed what mighty help two or three praying in concert could give each other; if in every prayer meeting the coming together in the Name, the faith in the Presence, and the expectation of the answer, stood in the foreground; if in every Church united effectual prayer were regarded as one of the chief purposes for which they are banded together, the highest exercise of their power as a Church; if in the Church universal the coming of the kingdom, the coming of the King Himself, first in the mighty outpouring of His Holy Spirit, then in His own glorious person, were really matter of unceasing united crying to God;--O who can say what blessing might come to, and through, those who thus agreed to prove God in the fulfilment of His promise.

The mark that there has been true united prayer is the answer, or the receiving of the thing we have asked

In the Apostle Paul we see very distinctly what a reality his faith in the power of united prayer was. To the Romans he writes (25:30): 'I beseech you, brethren, by the love of the Spirit that ye strive together with me in your prayer to God for me.' He expects in answer to be delivered from his enemies, and to be prospered in his work. To the Corinthians (2 Cor. 1:11), 'God will still deliver us, ye also helping together on our behalf by your supplications;' their prayer is to have a real share in his deliverance. To the Ephesians he writes: 'With all prayer and supplication praying at all seasons in the Spirit for all the saints and on my behalf that utterance may be given unto me.' His power and success in his ministry he makes to depend on their prayers. With the Philippians (1:19) he expects that his trials will turn to his salvation and the progress of the gospel 'through your supplications and the supply of the spirit of Jesus Christ.; To the Colossians (4:3) he adds to the injunction to continue steadfast in prayer: 'Withal praying for us too, that God may open unto us a door for the word.' And to the Thessalonians (2 Thess. 3:1) he writes: 'Finally, brethren, pray for us, that the word of the Lord may run and be glorified, and that we may be delivered from unreasonable men.' It is everywhere evident that Paul felt himself the member of a body, on the sympathy and co-operation of which he was dependent, and that he counted on the prayers of these Churches to gain for him, what otherwise might not be given. The prayers of the Church were to him as real a factor in the work of the kingdom, as the power of God.

Who can say what power a Church could develop and exercise, if it gave itself to the work of prayer day and night for the coming of the kingdom, for God's power on His servants and His word, for the glorifying of God in the salvation of souls? Most Churches think their members are gathered into one simply to take care of and build up each other. They know not that God rules the world by the prayers of His saints; that prayer is the power by which Satan is conquered; that by prayer the Church on earth has disposal of the powers of the heavenly world. They do not remember that Jesus has, by His promise, consecrated every assembly in His Name to be a gate of heaven, where His Presence is to be felt, and His Power experienced in the Father fulfilling their desires.

We cannot sufficiently thank God for the blessed week of united prayer, with which Christendom in our days opens every year. As proof of our unity and our faith in the power of united prayer, as a training-school for the enlargement of our hearts to take in all the needs of the Church universal, as a help to united persevering prayer, it is of unspeakable value. But very especially as a stimulus to continued union in prayer in the smaller circles, its blessing has been great. And it will become even greater, as God's people recognize what it is, all to meet as one in the Name of Jesus to have His presence in the midst of a body all united in the Holy Spirit, and boldly to claim the promise that it shall be done of the Father what they agree to ask.

Day 29 Prayer

'LORD, TEACH US TO PRAY'

Blessed Lord! who didst in Thy high-priestly prayer ask so earnestly for the unity of Thy people, teach us how Thou dost invite and urge us to this unity by Thy precious promise given to united prayer. It is when we are one in love and desire that our faith has Thy presence and the Father's answer.

O Father! we pray for Thy people, and for every smaller circle of those who meet together, that they may be one. Remove, we pray, all selfishness and self-interest, all narrowness of heart and estrangement, by which that unity is hindered. Cast out the spirit of the world and the flesh, through which Thy promise loses all its power. O let the thought of Thy presence and the Father's favor draw us all nearer to each other.

Grant especially Blessed Lord, that Thy Church may believe that it is by the power of united prayer that she can bind and loose in heaven; that Satan can be cast out; that souls can be saved; that mountains can be removed; that the kingdom can be hastened. And grant, good Lord! that in the circle with which I pray, the prayer of the Church may indeed be the power through which Thy Name and Word are glorified. Amen.

DAY 29
REFLECTION QUESTIONS

1. Murray says we need both secret solitary prayer and _____, _____ prayer.

2. When is the Spirit's full power manifested? _____ _____

3. What must a group of believers have when uniting in prayer? _____

4. What gives united prayer its power? _____

5. Murray points out that the focus of our prayer meeting should be _____ _____.

6. What two mistaken reasons some churches hold prayer meeting for? _____ _____, _____

7. Does your church have an organized prayer meeting? _____

8. Why do you attend prayer meetings? _____

9. Murray says God rules the world by _____

10. What is my main takeaway from Day 29 that will improve my prayer life? _____ _____ _____

Fill in the blanks- *If ye _____ in me, and my words abide in you, ye shall _____ what ye will, and it shall be _____ unto you. - John 15:7*

Answers

1. Public, united
2. When believers are united in fellowship
3. Agreement
4. The living presence of Jesus
5. Securing answers to prayer
6. Religious fellowship, personal edification
7. Personal response
8. Personal response
9. Prayers of the saints
10. Personal response

Class 5 Verse- *If ye abide in me, and my words abide in you, ye shall ask what ye will, and it shall be done unto you. - John 15:7*

Day 29 Bible Reading - John 11

Day 29 notes

_____

_____

_____

_____

_____

_____

_____

_____

_____

_____

DAY 30

SPEEDILY, THOUGH BEARING LONG
OR, THE POWER OF PERSERVING PRAYER

*'And He spake a parable unto them to the end that they ought always to pray, and not to faint. . . . And the Lord said, Hear what the unrighteous judge saith. And shall not God avenge His own elect, which cry to Him day and night, and He is long-suffering over them? I say unto you, that He will avenge them speedily.'--***Luke 18:1-8**

Of all the mysteries of the prayer world, the need of persevering prayer is one of the greatest. That the Lord, who is so loving and longing to bless, should have to be supplicated time after time, sometimes year after year, before the answer comes, we cannot easily understand. It is also one of the greatest practical difficulties in the exercise of believing prayer. When, after persevering supplication, our prayer remains unanswered, it is often easiest for our slothful flesh, and it has all the appearance of pious submission, to think that we must now cease praying, because God may have His secret reason for withholding His answer to our request.

It is by faith alone that the difficulty is overcome. When once faith has taken its stand upon God's word, and the Name of Jesus, and has yielded itself to the leading of the Spirit to seek God's will and honour alone in its prayer, it need not be discouraged by delay. It knows from Scripture that the power of believing prayer is simply irresistible; real faith can never be disappointed. It knows how, just as water, to exercise the irresistible power it can have, must be gathered up and accumulated, until the stream can come down in full force, there must often be a heaping up of prayer, until God sees that the measure is full, and the answer comes. It knows how, just as the ploughman has to take his ten thousand steps, and sow his ten thousand seeds, each one a part of the preparation for the final harvest, so there is a need-be for oft-repeated persevering prayer, all working out some desired blessing. It knows for certain that not a single believing prayer can fail of its effect in heaven, but has its influence, and is treasured up to work out an answer in due time to him who persevereth to the end. It knows that it has to do not with human thoughts or possibilities, but with the word of the living God. And so even as Abraham through so many years 'in hope believed against hope,' and then 'through faith *and patience* inherited the promise,' it counts that the long-suffering of the Lord is salvation, *waiting* and *hasting* unto the coming of its Lord to fulfil His promise.

God will not delay one moment longer than is absolutely necessary

To enable us, when the answer to our prayer does not come at once, to combine quiet patience and joyful confidence in our persevering prayer, we must specially try to understand the two words in which our Lord sets forth the character and conduct, not of the unjust judge, but of our God and Father towards those whom He allows to cry day and night to Him: 'He is *long-suffering* over them; He will avenge them *speedily.*'

He will avenge them *speedily*, the Master says. The blessing is all prepared; He is not only willing but most anxious to give them what they ask; everlasting love burns with the longing desire to reveal itself fully to its beloved, and to satisfy their needs. God will not delay one moment longer than is absolutely necessary; He will do all in His power to hasten and speed the answer.

 But why, if this be true and His power be infinite, does it often last so long with the answer to prayer? And why must God's own elect so often, in the midst of suffering and conflict, cry day and night? 'He is *long-suffering* over them.' 'Behold, the husbandman waiteth for the precious fruit of the earth, being *long-suffering* over it, till it receive the early and the latter rain.' The husbandman does indeed long for his harvest, but knows that it must have its full time of sunshine and rain, and has long patience. A child so often wants to pick the half-ripe fruit; the husbandman knows to wait till the proper time. Man, in his spiritual nature too, is under the law of gradual growth that reigns in all created life. It is only in the path of development that he can reach his divine destiny. And it is the Father, in whose hands are the times and seasons, who alone knows the moment when the soul or the Church is ripened to that fullness of faith in which it can really take and keep the blessing. As a father who longs to have his only child home from school, and yet waits patiently till the time of training is completed, so it is with God and His children: He is the long-suffering One, and answers speedily.

Our great danger in this school of the answer delayed, is the temptation to think that, after all, it may not be God's will to give us what we ask

The insight into this truth leads the believer to cultivate the corresponding dispositions: *patience* and *faith, waiting* and *hasting,* are the secret of his perseverance. By faith in the promise of God, we know that we *have* the petitions we have asked of Him. Faith takes and holds the answer in the promise, as an unseen spiritual possession, rejoices in it, and praises for it. But there is a difference between the faith that thus holds the word and knows that it has the answer, and the clearer, fuller, riper faith that obtains the promise as a present experience. It is in persevering, not unbelieving, but confident and praising prayer that the soul grows up into that full union with its Lord in which it can enter upon the possession of the blessing in Him.

There may be in these around us, there may be in that great system of being of which we are part, there may be in God's government, things that have to be put right through our prayer, ere the answer can fully come: the faith that has, according to the command, believed that it has received, can allow God to take His time: it knows it has prevailed and must prevail. In quiet, persistent, and determined perseverance it continues in prayer and thanksgiving until the blessing come. And so we see combined what at first sight appears so contradictory; the faith that rejoices in the answer of the unseen God as a present possession, with the patience that cries day and night until it be revealed. The *speedily* of God's *long-suffering* is met by the triumphant but patient faith of His waiting child.

 Our great danger in this school of the answer delayed, is the temptation to think that, after all, it may not be God's will to give us what we ask. If our prayer be according to God's word, and under the leading of the Spirit, let us not give way to these fears. Let us learn to give God time. God needs time with us. If we only give Him time, that is, time in the daily fellowship with Himself, for Him to exercise the full influence of His presence on us, and time, day by day, in the course of our being kept waiting, for faith to prove its reality and to fill our whole being, He Himself will lead us from faith to vision; we shall see the glory of God. Let no delay shake our faith. Of faith it holds good: first the blade, then the ear, then the full corn in the ear. Each believing prayer brings a step nearer the final victory. Each believing prayer helps to ripen the fruit and bring us nearer to it; it fills up the measure of prayer and faith known to God alone; it conquers the hindrances in the unseen world; it hastens the end. Child of God, give the Father time. He is long-suffering over you. He wants the blessing to be rich, and full, and sure; give Him time, while you cry day and night. Only remember the word: 'I say unto you, He will avenge them speedily.'

The blessing of such persevering prayer is unspeakable. There is nothing as heart-searching as the prayer of faith. It teaches you to discover and confess, and give up everything that hinders the coming of the blessing; everything there may be not in accordance with the Father's will. It leads to closer fellowship with

Him who alone can teach to pray, to a more entire surrender to draw nigh under no covering but that of the blood, and the Spirit. It calls to a closer and more simple abiding in Christ alone. Christian, give God time. He will perfect that which concerneth you. 'Long-suffering--speedily,' this is God's watchword as you enter the gates of prayer: be it yours too.

Let it be thus whether you pray for yourself, or for others. All labor, bodily or mental, needs time and effort: we must give up *ourselves* to it. Nature discovers her secrets and yields her treasures only to diligent and thoughtful labor. However little we can understand it, in the spiritual husbandry it is the same: the seed we sow in the soil of heaven, the efforts we put forth, and the influence we seek to exert in the world above, need our whole being: we must *give ourselves* to prayer. But let us hold fast the great confidence, that in due season we shall reap, if we faint not.

And let us specially learn the lesson as we pray for the Church of Christ. She is indeed as the poor widow, in the absence of her Lord, apparently at the mercy of her adversary, helpless to obtain redress. Let us, when we pray for His Church or any portion of it, under the power of the world, asking Him to visit her with the mighty workings of His Spirit and to prepare her for His coming, let us pray in the assured faith: prayer does help, praying always and not fainting will bring the answer. Only give God time. And then keep crying day and night. 'Hear what the unrighteous judge saith. And shall not God avenge His own elect, which cry to Him day and night, and *He is long-suffering* over them. I say unto you, *He will avenge them speedily.'*

The prayer of faith teaches you to discover and confess, and give up everything that hinders the coming of the blessing

Day 30 Prayer

'LORD, TEACH US TO PRAY.'

O Lord my God! teach me now to know Thy way, and in faith to apprehend what Thy Beloved Son has taught: 'He will avenge them speedily.' Let Thy tender love, and the delight Thou hast in hearing and blessing Thy children, lead me implicitly to accept Thy promise, that we receive what we believe, that we have the petitions we ask, and that the answer will in due time be seen. Lord! we understand the seasons in nature, and know to wait with patience for the fruit we long for--O fill us with the assurance that not one moment longer than is needed wilt Thou delay, and that faith will hasten the answer.

Blessed Master! Thou hast said that it is a sign of God's elect that they cry day and night. O teach us to understand this. Thou knowest how speedily we grow faint and weary. It is as if the Divine Majesty is so much beyond the need or the reach of continued supplication, that it does not become us to be too importunate. O Lord! do teach me how real the labor of prayer is. I know how here on earth, when I have failed in an undertaking, I can often succeed by renewed and more continuing effort, by giving more time and thought: show me how, by giving myself more entirely to prayer, to live in prayer, I shall obtain what I ask. And above all, O my blessed Teacher! Author and perfecter of faith, let by Thy grace my whole life be one of faith in the Son of God who loved me and gave Himself for me--in whom my prayer gains acceptance, in whom I have the assurance of the answer, in whom the answer will be mine. Lord Jesus! in this faith I will pray always and not faint. Amen.

NOTE

The need of persevering importunate prayer appears to some to be at variance with the faith which knows that it has received what it asks (Mark 11:24). One of the mysteries of the Divine life is the harmony between the gradual and the sudden, immediate full possession, and slow imperfect appropriation. And so here persevering prayer appears to be the school in which the soul is strengthened for the boldness of faith. And with the diversity of operations of the Spirit there may be some in whom faith takes more the form of persistent waiting; while to others, triumphant thanksgiving appears the only proper expressions of the assurance of having been heard.

In a remarkable way the need of persevering prayer, and the gradual rising into greater ease in obtaining answer, is illustrated in the life of Blumhardt. Complaints had been lodged against him of neglecting his work as a minister of the gospel, and devoting himself to the healing of the sick; and especially his unauthorized healing of the sick belonging to other congregations. In his defense he writes: 'I simply ventured to do what becomes one who has the charge of souls, and to pray according to the command of the Lord in James 1:6-7. In no way did I trust to my own power, or imagine that I had any gift that others had not. But this is true, I set myself to the work as a minister of the gospel, who has a right to pray. But I speedily discovered that the gates of heaven were not fully opened to me. Often I was inclined to retire in despair. But the sight of the sick ones, who could find help nowhere, gave me no rest. I thought of the word of the Lord: "Ask, and it shall be given you" (Luke 11: 9-10). And farther, I thought that if the Church and her ministers had, through unbelief, sloth, and disobedience lost what was needed for overcoming of the power of Satan, it was just for such times of leanness and famine that the Lord had spoken the parable of the friend at midnight and his three loaves. I felt that I was not worthy thus at midnight, in a time of great darkness, to appear before God as His friend and ask for a member of my congregation what he needed. And yet, to leave him uncared for, I could not either. And so I kept knocking, as the parable directs, or, as some have said, with great presumption and tempting God. Be this as it may, I could not leave my guest unprovided. At this time the parable of the widow became very precious to me. I saw that the Church was the widow, and I was a minister of the Church. I had the right to be her mouthpiece against the adversary; but for a long time the Lord would not. I asked nothing more than the three loaves; what I needed for my guest. At last the Lord listened to the importunate beggar, and helped me. Was it wrong of me to pray thus? The two parables must surely be applicable somewhere, and where was greater need to be conceived?

And what was the fruit of my prayer? The friend who was at first unwilling, did not say, Go now; I will myself give to your friend what he needs; I do not require you; but gave it to me as His friend, to give to my guest. And so I used the three loaves, and had to spare. But the supply was small, and new guests came; because they saw I had a heart to help them, and that I would take the trouble even at midnight to go to my friend. When I asked for them, too, I got the needful again, and there was again to spare. How could I help that the needy continually came to my house? Was I to harden myself, and say, why do you come to me? There are large and better homes in the city, go there. Their answer was, dear sir, we cannot go there. We have been there: they were very sorry to send us away so hungry, but they could not undertake to go and ask a friend for what we wanted. Do go, and get us bread for we suffer great pain. What could I do? They spoke the truth, and their suffering touched my heart. However, much labor it cost me, I went each time again, and got the three loaves. Often I got what I asked much quicker than at first, and also much more abundantly. But all did not care for this bread, so some left my home hungry.'[1]

In his first struggles with the evil spirits, it took him more than eighteen months of prayer and labor before the final victory was gained. Afterwards he had such ease of access to the throne, and stood in such close communication with the unseen world, that often, with letters came asking prayer for sick people, he could, after just looking upward for a single moment, obtain the answer as to whether they would be healed.

[1]From *Johann Christophe Blumhardt, Ein Lebenabild von F. Etindel.*

DAY 30
REFLECTION QUESTIONS

1. The biggest practical difficulty in exercising believing prayer is _____.

2. Persevering prayer has nothing to do with _____

3. Combining _____ _____ and _____ _____ enables us to persevere when the answer to our prayers are delayed.

4. List the four ingredients of successful persevering prayer. _____
_____, _____, _____

5. Delayed answers to prayer cause believers to question if their prayers are according to_____
_____ , _____

6. How often do you blame unanswered prayers on God's secret will? _____
_____

7. We must give God _____ because God wants _____ with us.

8. One of the blessings of persevering prayer is. _____
_____.

9. One thing we cannot do while waiting for the answer to our prayers is. _____.

10. What is my main takeaway from Day 30 that will improve my prayer life? _____
_____

_____

Fill in the blanks- *If ye abide in _____, and my _____ abide in you, ye _____ ask what ye will, and it shall be done _____ you. - John 15:7*

Answers

1. Unanswered prayers

2. Human thoughts

3. Quiet patience and joyful confidence

4. Patience, faith, waiting and praise

5. God's will

6. Personal response

7. Time

8. Teaches us to discover, confess and give up everything that hinders the coming of the answer

9. Lose heart

10. Personal response

Class 5 Verse- *If ye abide in me, and my words abide in you, ye shall ask what ye will, and it shall be done unto you. - John 15:7*

Day 30 Bible Reading - Luke 17:11-18:14

Day 30 notes

_____

_____

_____

_____

_____

_____

_____

_____

_____

_____

DAY 31

I KNOW THAT THOU HEAREST ME ALWAYS OR
PRAYER IN HARMONY WITH THE BEING OF GOD

`Father, I thank Thee that Thou hearest me. And I knew that Thou hearest me always.'--**John 11:41-42**

'Thou art my Son; this day have I begotten Thee. Ask of me, and I shall give Thee.'--**Palms 2:7-8**

In the New Testament we find a distinction made between faith and knowledge. `To one is given, through the Spirit, the word of wisdom; to another the word of *knowledge*, according to the same Spirit; to another *faith*, in the same Spirit.' In a child or a simple-minded Christian there may be much faith with little knowledge. Childlike simplicity accepts the truth without difficulty, and often cares little to give itself or others any reason for its faith but this: God has said. But it is the will of God that we should love and serve Him, not only with all the heart but also with all the mind; that we should grow up into an insight into the Divine wisdom and beauty of all His ways and words and works. It is only thus that the believer will be able fully to approach and rightly to adore the glory of God's grace; and only thus that our heart can intelligently apprehend the treasures of wisdom and knowledge there are in redemption, and be prepared to enter fully into the highest note of the song that rises before the throne: `O the depth of the riches both of the wisdom and knowledge of God!'

In our prayer life this truth has its full application. While prayer and faith are so simple that the new-born convert can pray with power, true Christian science finds in the doctrine of prayer some of its deepest problems. In how far is the power of prayer a reality? If so, how God can grant to prayer such mighty power? How can the action of prayer be harmonized with the will and the decrees of God? How can God's sovereignty and our will, God's liberty and ours, be reconciled?--these and other like questions are fit subjects for Christian meditation and inquiry. The more earnestly and reverently we approach such mysteries, the more shall we in adoring wonder fall down to praise Him who hath in prayer given such power to man.

One of the secret difficulties with regard to prayer,--one which, though not expressed, does often really hinder prayer,--is derived from the perfection of God, in His absolute independence of all that is outside of Himself. Is He not the Infinite Being, who owes what He is to Himself alone, who determines Himself, and whose wise and holy will has determined all that is to be? How can prayer influence Him, or He be moved by prayer to do what otherwise would not be done? Is not the promise of an answer to prayer simply a condescension to our weakness? Is what is said of the power--the much-availing power--of prayer anything more than an accommodation to our mode of thought, because the Deity never can be dependent on any action from without for its doings? And is not the blessing of prayer simply the influence it exercises upon ourselves?

In seeking an answer to such questions, we find the key in the very being of God, in the mystery of the Holy Trinity. If God was only one Person, shut up within Himself, there could be no thought of nearness to Him or influence on Him. But in God there are three Persons. In God we have Father and Son, who have in the

Holy Spirit their living bond of unity and fellowship. When eternal Love begat the Son, and the Father gave the Son as the Second Person a place next Himself as His Equal and His Counsellor, there was a way opened for prayer and its influence in the very inmost life of Deity itself. Just as on earth, so in heaven the whole relation between Father and Son is that of giving and taking. And if that taking is to be as voluntary and self-determined as the giving, there must be on the part of the Son an asking and receiving. In the holy fellowship of the Divine Persons, this asking of the Son was one of the great operations of the Thrice Blessed Life of God. Hence we have it in Psalm 2: `This day I have begotten Thee: ask of me and I will give Thee.' The Father gave the Son the place and the power to act upon Him. The asking of the Son was no mere show or shadow, but one of those life-movements in which the love of the Father and the Son met and completed each other. The Father had determined that He should not be alone in His counsels: there was a Son on whose asking and accepting their fulfilment should depend. And so there was in the very Being and Life of God an asking of which prayer on earth was to be the reflection and the outflow. It was not without including this that Jesus said, "I knew that Thou always hearest me.' Just as the Sonship of Jesus on earth may not be separated from His Sonship in heaven, even so with His prayer on earth, it is the continuation and the counterpart of His asking in heaven. The prayer of the man Christ Jesus is the link between the eternal asking of the only-begotten Son in the bosom of the Father and the prayer of men upon earth. Prayer has its rise and its deepest source in the very Being of God. In the bosom of Deity nothing is ever done without prayer--the asking of the Son and the giving of the Father.1

This may help us somewhat to understand how the prayer of man, coming through the Son, can have effect upon God. The decrees of God are not decisions made by Him without reference to the Son, or His petition, or the petition to be sent up through Him. By no means. The Lord Jesus is the first-begotten, the Head and Heir of all things: all things were created *through Him* and *unto Him*, and all things consist *in Him*. In the counsels of the Father, the Son, as Representative of all creation, had always a voice; in the decrees of the eternal purpose there was always room left for the liberty of the Son as Mediator and Intercessor, and so for the petitions of all who draw nigh to the Father in the Son.

And if the thought come that this liberty and power of the Son to act upon the Father is at variance with the immutability of the Divine decrees, let us not forget that there is not with God as with man, a past by which He is irrevocably bound. God does not live in time with its past and future; the distinctions of time have no reference to Him who inhabits Eternity. And Eternity is an ever-present Now, in which the past is never past, and the future always present. To meet our human weakness, Scripture must speak of past decrees, and a coming future. In reality, the immutability of God's counsel is ever still in perfect harmony with His liberty to do whatsoever He will. Not so were the prayers of the Son and His people taken up into the eternal decrees that their effect should only be an apparent one; but so, that the Father-heart holds itself open and free to listen to every prayer that rises through the Son, and that God does indeed allow Himself to be decided by prayer to do what He otherwise would not have done.

> **God does indeed allow Himself to be decided by prayer to do what He otherwise would not have done**

This perfect harmony and union of Divine Sovereignty and human liberty is to us an unfathomable mystery, because God as THE ETERNAL ONE transcends all our thoughts. But let it be our comfort and strength to be assured that in the eternal fellowship of the Father and the Son, the power of prayer has its origin and certainty, and that through our union with the Son, our prayer is taken up and can have its influence in the inner life of the Blessed Trinity. God's decrees are no iron framework against which man's liberty would vainly seek to struggle. No. God Himself is the Living Love, who in His Son as man has entered into the tenderest relation with all that is human, who through the Holy Spirit takes up all that is human into the Divine life of love, and keeps Himself free to give every human prayer its place in His government of the world.

It is in the daybreak light of such thoughts that the doctrine of the Blessed Trinity no longer is an abstract speculation, but the living manifestation of the way in which it were possible for man to be taken up into the fellowship of God, and his prayer to become a real factor in God's rule of this earth. And we can, as in the distance, catch glimpses of the light that from the eternal world shines out on words such as these: `THROUGH HIM we have access BY ONE SPIRIT unto THE FATHER.'

Day 31 Prayer

`LORD, TEACH US TO PRAY.'

Everlasting God! the Three-One and Thrice Holy! in deep reverence would I with veiled face worship before the holy mystery of Thy Divine Being. And if it please Thee, O most glorious God, to unveil aught of that mystery, I would bow with fear and trembling, lest I sin against Thee, as I meditate on Thy glory.

Father! I thank Thee that Thou bearest this name not only as the Father of Thy children here on earth, but as having from eternity subsisted as the Father with Thine only-begotten Son. I thank Thee that as Father Thou canst hear our prayer, because Thou hast from eternity given a place in Thy counsels to the asking of Thy Son. I thank Thee that we have seen in Him on earth, what the blessed intercourse was He had with Thee in heaven; and how from eternity in all Thy counsels and decrees there had been room left for His prayer and their answers. And I thank Thee above all that through His true human nature on Thy throne above, and through Thy Holy Spirit in our human nature here below, a way has been opened up by which every human cry of need can be taken up into and touch the Life and the Love of God, and receive in answer whatsoever it shall ask.

Blessed Jesus! in whom as the Son the path of prayer has been opened up, and who givest us assurance of the answer, we beseech Thee, teach Thy people to pray. O let this each day be the sign of our sonship, that, like Thee, we know that the Father heareth us always. Amen.

NOTE.

`"*God hears prayer.*" This simplest view of prayer is taken throughout Scripture. It dwells not on the reflex influence of prayer on our heart and life, although it abundantly shows the connection between prayer as an act, and prayer as a state. It rather fixes with great definiteness the objective or real purposes of prayer, to obtain blessing, gifts, deliverances from God. `Ask and it shall be given," Jesus says.

`However true and valuable the reflection may be, that God, foreseeing and foreordaining all things, has also foreseen and foreordained our prayers as links in the chain of events, of cause and effect, as a real power, yet we feel convinced that this is not the light in which the mind can find peace in this great subject, nor do we think that here is the attractive power to draw us in prayer. We feel rather that such a reflection *diverts* the attention from the Object whence comes the impulse, life, and strength of prayer. The living God, *cotemporary and not merely eternal,*[1] the living, merciful, holy One, God manifesting Himself to the soul, God saying, "Seek my face;" this is the magnet that draws us, this alone can open heart and lips. . .

`In Jesus Christ the Son of God we have the full solution of the difficulty. He prayed on earth, and that not merely as man, but as the Son of God incarnate. His prayer on earth is only the manifestation of His prayer from all eternity, when in the Divine counsel He was set up as the Christ. . . . The Son was appointed to be heir of all things. From all eternity the Son of God was the Way, the Mediator. He was, to use our imperfect language, from eternity speaking unto the Father on behalf of the world.'--SAPHIR, *The Hidden Life*, chapter 6. See also *The Lord's Prayer*, p. 12. Should it not rather be *cotemporary, because eternal,* in the proper meaning of this latter word?

DAY 31
REFLECTION QUESTIONS

1. Is faith in your prayers weakened because you wonder why an all-powerful, all-knowing God would allow our human requests to change his desires? _____

    _____

2. Have you spent much time contemplating why an infinite being like God can be dependent on any outside action for His doings? _____

3. What is the link that allows our prayers on earth to reach our Father in heaven?

    _____

4. In reality, the immutability of _____ counsel is ever still in perfect harmony with His liberty to do _____ He will.

5. Our power of prayer has its origin from _____

    _____.

6. Jesus through the _____ _____ takes up our human prayers and presents them to the Lord.

7. What is my main takeaway from Day 31 that will improve my prayer life? _____

    _____

    _____

Fill in the blanks- _____ *ye abide* _____ *me, and* _____ *words abide in you, ye shall* _____ *what ye* _____ *, and it shall be* _____ *unto* _____ *. - John 15:7*

Answers

1. Personal response

2. Personal response

3. Jesus Christ

4. God's, whatsoever

5. The eternal fellowship of the Father and Son and our relationship to the Son

6. Holy Spirit –Ephesians 2:18

7. Personal response

Class 5 Verse- *If ye abide in me, and my words abide in you, ye shall ask what ye will, and it shall be done unto you. - John 15:7*

Day 31 Bible Reading - Matthew 19; Mark 10

Day 31 notes

_____

_____

_____

_____

_____

_____

_____

_____

_____

_____

_____

_____

_____

_____

DAY 32

WHOSE IS THIS IMAGE? OR,
PRAYER IN HARMONY WITH THE DESTINY OF MAN

`He saith unto them, Whose is this image and superscription?--**Matthew 21:20**

`And God said, Let us make man in our image, after our likeness.'--**Genesis 1:26**

'Whose is this image?' It was by this question that Jesus foiled His enemies, when they thought to take Him, and settled the matter of duty in regard to the tribute. The question and the principle it involves are of universal application. Nowhere more truly than in man himself. The image he bears decides his destiny. Bearing God's image, he belongs to God: prayer to God is what he was created for. Prayer is part of the wondrous likeness he bears to His Divine original; of the deep mystery of the fellowship of love in which the Three-One has His blessedness, prayer is the earthly image and likeness.

The more we meditate on what prayer is, and the wonderful power with God which it has, the more we feel constrained to ask who and what man is, that such a place in God's counsels should have been allotted to him. Sin has so degraded him, that from what he is now we can form no conception of what he was meant to be. We must turn back to God's own record of man's creation to discover there what God's purpose was, and what the capacities with which man was endowed for the fulfilment of that purpose.

Man's destiny appears clearly from God's language at creation. It was to *fill*, to *subdue*, to *have dominion* over the earth and all in it. All the three expressions show us that man was meant, as God's representative, to hold rule here on earth. As God's viceroy he was to fill God's place: himself subject to God, he was to keep all else in subjection to Him. It was the will of God that all that was to be done on earth should be done through him: the history of the earth was to be entirely in his hands.

> ❧☙
>
> **It was the will of God that all that was to be done on earth should be done through him**
>
> ❧☙

In accordance with such a destiny was the position he was to occupy, and the power at his disposal. When an earthly sovereign sends a viceroy to a distant province, it is understood that he advises as to the policy to be adopted, and that that advice is acted on: that he is at liberty to apply for troops and the other means needed for carrying out the policy or maintaining the dignity of the empire. If his policy be not approved of, he is recalled to make way for someone who better understands his sovereign's desires' as long as he is trusted, his advice is carried out. As God's representative man was to have ruled; all was to have been done under his will and rule; on his advice and at his request heaven was to have bestowed its blessing on earth. His prayer was to have been the wonderful, though simple and most natural channel, in which the intercourse between the King in heaven and His faithful servant man, as lord of this world, was to have been maintained. The destinies of the world were given into the power of the wishes, the will, the prayer of man.

With sin, all this underwent a terrible change--man's fall brought all creation under the curse. With redemption the beginning was seen of a glorious restoration. No sooner had God begun in Abraham to form for Himself a people from whom kings, yea the Great King, should come forth, than we see what power the prayer of God's faithful servant has to decide the destinies of those who come into contact with him. In Abraham we see how prayer is not only, or even chiefly, the means of obtaining blessing for ourselves, but is the exercise of his royal prerogative to influence the destinies of men, and the will of God which rules them. We do not once find Abraham praying for himself. His prayer for Sodom and Lot, for Abimelech, for Ishmael, prove what power a man, who is God's friend, has to make the history of those around him.

ഇരുൻ

We do not once find Abraham praying for himself

ഇരുൻ

This had been man's destiny from the first. Scripture not only tells us this, but also teaches us how it was that God could entrust man with such a high calling. It was because He had created him *in His own image and likeness.* The external rule was not committed to him without the inner fitness: the bearing God's image in having dominion, in being lord of all, had its root in the inner likeness, in his nature. There was an inner agreement and harmony between God and man, and incipient Godlikeness, which gave man a real fitness for being the mediator between God and His world, for he was to be prophet, priest, and king, to interpret God's will, to represent nature's needs, to receive and dispense God's bounty. It was in bearing God's image that he could bear God's rule; he was indeed so like God, so capable of entering into God's purposes, and carrying out His plans, that God could trust him with the wonderful privilege of asking and obtaining what the world might need. And although sin has for a time frustrated God's plans, prayer still remains what it would have been if man had never fallen: the proof of man's Godlikeness, the vehicle of his intercourse with the Infinite Unseen One, the power that is allowed to hold the hand that holds the destinies of the universe. Prayer is not merely the cry of the suppliant for mercy; it is the highest forth-putting of his will by man, knowing himself to be of Divine origin, created for and capable of being, in king-like liberty, the executor of the counsels of the Eternal.

What sin destroyed, grace has restored. What the first Adam lost, the second has won back. In Christ man regains his original position, and the Church, abiding in Christ, inherits the promise: `Ask what ye will, and it shall be done unto you.' Such a promise does by no means, in the first place, refer to the grace or blessing we need for ourselves. It has reference to our position as the fruit-bearing branches of the Heavenly Vine, who, like Him, only live for the work and glory of the Father. It is for those who abide in Him, who have forsaken self to take up their abode in Him with His life of obedience and self-sacrifice, who have lost their life and found it in Him, who are now entirely given up to the interests of the Father and His kingdom. These are they who understand how their new creation has brought them back to their original destiny, has restored God's image and likeness, and with it the power to have dominion. Such have indeed the power, each in their own circle, to obtain and dispense the powers of heaven here on earth. With holy boldness they may make known what they will: they live as priests in God's presence; as kings the powers of the world to come begin to be at their disposal.[1] They enter upon the fulfilment of the promise: `Ask whatsoever ye will, it shall be done unto you.'

ഇരുൻ

What sin destroyed, grace has restored

ഇരുൻ

Church of the living God, thy calling is higher and holier than thou knowest. Through thy members, as kings, and priests unto God, would God rule the world; their prayers bestow and withhold the blessing of heaven. In His elect who are not just content to be themselves saved, but yield themselves wholly, that through them, even as through the Son, the Father may fulfil all His glorious counsel, in these His elect, who cry day and night unto Him, God would prove how wonderful man's original destiny was. As the image-bearer of God on earth, the earth was indeed given into his hand. When he fell, all fell with him: the whole creation groaneth and travaileth in pain together. But now he is redeemed; the restoration of the original dignity has begun. It is in very deed God's purpose that the fulfilment of His eternal purpose, and the coming of His kingdom, should depend on those of His people who, abiding in Christ, are ready to take up their position in Him their Head, the great Priest-King, and in their prayers are bold enough to say what they will that their God should do. As image-bearer and representative of God on earth, redeemed man has by his prayers to determine the history of this earth. Man was created, and has now again been redeemed, to pray, and by his prayer to have dominion.

Day 32 Prayer

`LORD, TEACH US TO PRAY.'

Lord, what is man, that Thou art mindful of him? And the son of man, that Thou visitest him? For Thou has made him a little lower than the angels, and hast crowned him with glory and honor. Thou madest him to have dominion over the work of Thy hands: Thou hast put all things under his feet. O Lord our Lord, how excellent is Thy name in all the earth!

Lord God, how low has sin made man to sink. And how terribly has it darkened his mind, that he does not even know his Divine destiny, to be Thy servant and representative. Alas! that even Thy people, when their eyes are opened, are so little ready to accept their calling and to seek to have power with God, that they may have power with men too to bless them.

Lord Jesus, it is in Thee the Father hath again crowned man with glory and honor, and opened the way for us to be what He would have us. O Lord, have mercy on Thy people, and visit Thine heritage! Work mightily in Thy Church, and teach Thy believing disciples to go forth in their royal priesthood, and in the power of prayer, to which Thou hast given such wonderful promises, to serve Thy kingdom, to have rule over the nations, and make the name of God glorious in the earth. Amen.

1'God is seeking priests among the sons of men. A human priesthood is one of the essential parts of His eternal plan. To *rule* creation by man is His design; to carry on the worship of creation by man is no less part of His design.

`Priesthood is the appointed link between heaven and earth, the channel of intercourse between the sinner and God. Such a priesthood, in so far as expiation is concerned, is in the hands of the Son of God alone; in so far as it is to be the medium of communication between Creator and creature, is also in the hands of redeemed men--of the Church of God.

`God is seeking kings. Not out of the ranks of angels. Fallen man must furnish Him with the rulers of His universe. Human hands must wield the sceptre, human heads must wear the crown.--*The Rent Veil*, by Dr. H. Bonar.

DAY 32
REFLECTION QUESTIONS

1. What does Murray say man was created for? _____

2. Man's destiny was originally to: _____, _____ and have _____ over the earth.

3. Before the fall, man was to use _____ to offer advice and make requests asking God to bestow His blessing on earth.

4. Prayers of God's faithful servants like Abraham, have the ability to _____ the destinies of men.

5. Are your prayers chiefly concerned with asking God to bless others? _____

6. Have your forsaken self and entirely given up to the interests of the Father and His kingdom?

   _____

7. Do you know anyone who fits the following description? *"His elect who are not just content to be themselves saved, but yield themselves wholly, that through them, even as through the Son, the Father may fulfill all His glorious counsel, in these His elect, who cry day and night unto Him, God would prove how wonderful man's original destiny was. As the image-bearer of God on earth, the earth was indeed given into his hand."* If so what do you remember about their Christian life? _____

   _____

   _____

8. What is my main takeaway from Day 32 that will improve my prayer life? _____

   _____

   _____

Fill in the blanks- *If _____ _____ in me, and my _____ abide in _____, ye shall _____ _____ ye will, and _____ _____ be _____ unto you. - John 15:7*

Answers

1. Prayer to God
2. Fill, subdue dominion
3. Prayer
4. Influence
5. Personal response
6. Personal response
7. Personal response
8. Personal response

Class 5 Verse- *If ye abide in me, and my words abide in you, ye shall ask what ye will, and it shall be done unto you. - John 15:7*

Day 32 Bible Reading - Matthew 20-21

Day 32 notes

_____

_____

_____

_____

_____

_____

_____

_____

_____

_____

_____

_____

_____

_____

DAY 33

I GO UNTO THE FATHER OR, POWER FOR PRAYING AND WORKING

`Verily, verily, I say unto you, He that believeth on me, the works that I do shall he do also; and greater works than these shall he do; because I go unto my Father. And whatsoever ye shall ask in my Name, that will I do.'--**John 14:12-13**

As the Savior opened His public ministry with His disciples by the Sermon on the Mount, so He closes it by the Parting Address preserved to us by John. In both He speaks more than once of prayer. But with a difference. In the Sermon on the Mount it is as to disciples who have only just entered His school, who scarcely know that God is their Father, and whose prayer chiefly has reference to their personal needs. In His closing address He speaks to disciples whose training time is now come to an end, and who are ready as His messengers to take His place and His work. In the former the chief lesson is: Be childlike, pray believingly, and trust the Father that He will give you all good gifts. Here He points to something higher: They are now His friends to whom He has made known all that He has heard of the Father; His messengers, who have entered into His plans, and into whose hands the care of His work and kingdom on earth is to be entrusted. They are now to go out and do His works, and in the power of His approaching exaltation, even greater works: prayer is now to be the channel through which that power is to be received for their work. With Christ's ascension to the Father a new epoch commences for their working and praying both.

See how clearly this connection comes out in our text. As His body here on earth, as those who are one with Him in heaven, they are now to do greater works than He had done; their success and their victories are to be greater than His. He mentions two reasons for this. The one, because He was to go to the Father, to receive all power; the other, because they might now ask and expect all in His Name. `Because I go to the Father, *and*--notice this and--*and*, whatsoever ye shall ask, I will do.' His going to the Father would thus bring the double blessing: they would ask and receive all in His Name, and as a consequence, would do the greater works. This first mention of prayer in our Savior's parting words thus teaches us two most important lessons. He that would do the works of Jesus *must pray* in His Name. He that would pray in His Name *must work* in His Name.

He who would work *must pray*: it is in prayer that the power for work is obtained. He that in faith would do the works that Jesus did, must pray in His Name. As long as Jesus was here on earth, He Himself did the greatest works: even devils the disciples could not cast out, fled at His word. When He went to the Father, He was no longer here in the body to work directly. The disciples were now His body: all His work from the throne in heaven here on earth must and could be done through them. One might have thought that now He was leaving the scene Himself, and could only work through commissioners, the works might be fewer and weaker. He assures us of the contrary: *Verily, verily,* I say unto you, He that believeth on me, the works that I do shall he do also, and he shall do greater works.' His approaching death was to be such a real breaking down and making an end of the power of sin; with the resurrection the powers of the Eternal Life were so truly to take possession of the human body and to obtain supremacy over human life; with His ascension He was to receive the power

He who would work *must pray*

189

to communicate the Holy Spirit so fully to His own; the union, the oneness between Himself on the throne and them on earth, was to be so intensely and divinely perfect, that He meant it as the literal truth: `Greater works than these shall he do, because I go to the Father.' And the issue proved how true it was. While Jesus, during three years of personal labour on earth, gathered little more than five hundred disciples, and the most of them so feeble that they were but little credit to His cause, it was given to men like Peter and Paul manifestly to do greater things than He had done. From the throne He could do through them what He Himself in His humiliation could not yet do.

But there is one condition: `He that believeth on me, he shall do greater works, because I go to the Father; *and whatsover ye shall ask in my Name, that will I do.*' His going to the Father would give Him a new power to hear prayer. For the doing of the greater works, two things were needed: His going to the Father to receive all power, our prayer in His Name to receive all power from Him again. As He asks the Father, He receives and bestows on us the power of the new dispensation for the greater works; as we believe, and ask in His Name, the power comes and takes possession of us to do the greater works.

Effectual working needs first effectual prayer

Alas, how much working there is in the work of God, in which there is little or nothing to be seen of the power to do anything like Christ's works, not to speak of greater works. There can be but one reason: the believing on Him, the believing prayer in His Name, this is so much wanting. O that every laborer and leader in church, or school, in the work of home philanthropy or foreign missions, might learn the lesson: Prayer in the Name of Jesus is the way to share in the mighty power which Jesus has received of the Father for His people, and it is in this power alone, that he that believeth can do the greater works. To every complaint as to weakness or unfitness, as to difficulties or want of success, Jesus gives this one answer: `*He that believeth* on me shall do greater works, because I go to the Father, and *whatsoever ye shall ask* in my Name, *that will I do.'* We must understand that the first and chief thing for everyone who would do the work of Jesus, is to believe, and so to get linked to Him, the Almighty One, and then to pray the prayer of faith in His Name. Without this our work is but human and carnal; it may have some use in restraining sin, or preparing the way for blessing, but the real power is wanting. Effectual working needs first effectual prayer.

And now the second lesson: He who would pray *must work.* It is for power to work that prayer has such great promises: it is in working that the power for the effectual prayer of faith will be gained. In these parting words of our blessed Lord we find that He no less than six times (John 14:13-14, 15:7 & 16, 16:23-24) repeats those unlimited prayer-promises which have so often awakened our anxious questionings as to their real meaning: `*whatsoever,*' `*anything,*' `*what ye will,*' `*ask and ye shall receive.'* How many a believer has read these over with joy and hope, and in deep earnestness of soul has sought to plead them for his own need. And he has come out disappointed. The simple reason was this: he had rent away the promise from its surrounding. The Lord gave the wonderful promise of the free use of His Name with the Father in connection with the *doing of His works.* It is the disciple who gives himself wholly to live for Jesus' work and kingdom, for His will and honor, to whom the power will come to appropriate the promise. He that would fain grasp the promise when he wants something very special for himself, will be disappointed, because he would make Jesus the servant of his own comfort. But to him who seeks to pray the effectual prayer of faith, because he needs it for the work of the Master, to him it will be given to learn it; because he has made himself the servant of his Lord's interests. Prayer not only teaches and strengthens to work: work teaches and strengthens to pray.

This is in perfect harmony with what holds good both in the natural and the spiritual world. Whosoever hath, to him shall be given; or, He that is faithful in a little, is faithful also in much. Let us with the small measure of grace already received, give ourselves to the Master for His work: work will be to us a real school of prayer. It was when Moses had to take full charge of a rebellious people that he felt the need, but also the courage, to speak boldly to God and to ask great things of Him (Ex. 33:12, 15 & 18). As you give yourself entirely to God for His work, you will feel that nothing less than these great promises are what you need, that nothing less is what you may most confidently expect.

Believer in Jesus! You are called, you are appointed, to do the works of Jesus, and even greater works, because He has gone to the Father to receive the power to do them in and through you.

Whatsoever ye shall ask in my Name, that *will I do*. Give yourself, and live, to do the works of Christ and you will learn to pray so as to obtain wonderful answers to prayer. Give yourself, and live, to pray and you will learn to do the works He did, and greater works. With disciples full of faith in Himself, and bold in prayer to ask great things, Christ can conquer the world.

Day 33 Prayer

`LORD, TEACH US TO PRAY.'

O my Lord! I have this day again heard words from Thee which pass my comprehension. And yet I cannot do aught but in simple childlike faith take and keep them as Thy gift to me too. Thou hast said that in virtue of Thy going to the Father, he that believeth on Thee will do the works which Thou hast done, and greater works. Lord! I worship Thee as the Glorified One, and look for the fulfilment of Thy promise. May my whole life just be one of continued believing in Thee. So, purify and sanctify my heart, make it so tenderly susceptible of Thyself and Thy love, that believing on Thee may be the very life it breathes.

And Thou hast said that in virtue of Thy going to the Father, whatsoever we ask, Thou wilt do. From Thy throne of power Thou wouldest make Thy people share the power given Thee, and work through them as the members of Thy body, in response to their believing prayers in Thy Name. Power in prayer with Thee, and power in work with men, is what Thou has promised Thy people and me too.

Blessed Lord! Forgive us all that we have so little believed Thee and Thy promise, and so little proved Thy faithfulness in fulfilling it. O forgive us that we have so little honored Thy all-prevailing Name in heaven or upon earth.

Lord, teach me to pray so that I may prove that Thy Name is indeed all-prevailing with God and men and devils. Yea, teach me so to work and so to pray that Thou canst glorify Thyself in me as the Omnipotent One, and do Thy great work through me too. Amen.

DAY 33
REFLECTION QUESTIONS

1. What were the differences in Jesus' teaching on prayer at the Sermon of the Mount versus His instructions before His ascension? _____

    _____

    _____

2. What is one reason Jesus gave that we can do 'greater works than these'? _____

    _____

3. What two things did Jesus teach through His parting words on prayer? _____

    _____ and _____

4. What must we do to produce greater works than Jesus? _____

5. Name the one condition this new power was dependent on. _____

6. Why do we see so few works like Christ's in today's church? _____

    _____

7. _____working for the kingdom needs first _____ prayer.

8. How much of your work is done without prayer? _____

    _____

9. What is my main takeaway from Day 33 that will improve my prayer life? _____

    _____

    _____

Fill in the blanks- *If _____ _____ in _____, and my _____ abide in _____, ye shall _____ _____ ye _____, and _____ _____ be _____ unto _____. - John 15:7*

Answers

1. At the Sermon on the Mount it was; praying for their needs and to be childlike and trust the Father to answer the prayer, at His closing address it was; praying for His work and His kingdom on earth to be established.

2. Because He would go to the Father on our behalf

3. Those who follow Jesus must pray in His Name and those who pray must work in His name

4. Pray in His name

5. Jesus going to the Father

6. Lack of believing prayer in His name

7. Effective, effectual

8. Personal response

9. Personal response

Class 5 Verse- *If ye abide in me, and my words abide in you, ye shall ask what ye will, and it shall be done unto you. - John 15:7*

Day 33 Bible Reading - Luke 18:15-19:48

Day 33 notes

_____

_____

_____

_____

_____

_____

_____

_____

_____

_____

_____

_____

DAY 34

THAT THE FATHER MAY BE GLORIFIED
OR, THE CHIEF END OF PRAYER

'I go unto the Father. And whatsoever ye shall ask in my Name, that will I do, that the Father may be glorified in the Son.'- **John 14:13**

That the Father may be glorified in the Son: it is to this end that Jesus on His throne in glory will do all we ask in His Name. Every answer to prayer He gives will have this as its object: when there is no prospect of this object being obtained, He will not answer. It follows as a matter of course that this must be with us, as with Jesus, the essential element in our petitions: the glory of the Father must be the aim and end, the very soul and life of our prayer.

The glory of the Father must be the aim and end, the very soul and life of our prayer

It was so with Jesus when He was on earth. `I seek not mine own honor: I seek the honor of Him that sent me;' in such words we have the keynote of His life. In the first words of the high-priestly prayer He gives utterance to it: Father! Glorify Thy son, *that Thy Son may glorify Thee.* `I have glorified Thee* on earth; glorify me with Thyself.' The ground on which He asks to be taken up into the glory He had with the Father, is the twofold one: He has glorified Him on earth; He will still glorify Him in heaven. What He asks is only to enable Him to glorify the Father more. It is as we enter into sympathy with Jesus on this point, and gratify Him by making the Father's glory our chief object in prayer too, that our prayer cannot fail of an answer. There is nothing of which the Beloved Son has said more distinctly that it will glorify the Father than this, His doing what we ask; He will not, therefore, let any opportunity slip of securing this object. Let us make His aim ours: let the glory of the Father be the link between our asking and His doing: such prayer must prevail.

This word of Jesus comes indeed as a sharp two-edged sword, piercing even to the dividing of soul and spirit, and quick to discern the thoughts and intents of the heart. Jesus in His prayers on earth, in His intercession in heaven, in His promise of an answer to our prayers from there, makes this His first object-the glory of His Father. Is it so with us too? Or are not, in large measure, self-interest and self-will the strongest motives urging us to pray? Or, if we cannot see that this is the case, have we not to acknowledge that the distinct, conscious longing for the glory of the Father is not what animates our prayers? And yet it must be so.

The separation between the spirit of daily life and the spirit of the hour of prayer was too wide.

Not as if the believer does not at times desire it. But he has to mourn that he has so little attained. And he knows the reason of his failure too. It was, because the separation between the spirit of daily life and the spirit of the hour of prayer was too wide. We begin to see that the desire for the glory of the Father is not something that we can awake and present to our Lord when we prepare ourselves to pray. No, it is only when the whole life, in all its parts, is given up to God's glory, that we can really pray to His glory too. `Do all to the glory of God,' and, `Ask all to the glory of God,'-these twin commands are inseparable: obedience to the former is the secret of grace for the latter. A life to the glory of God is the condition of the prayers that Jesus can answer, `that the Father may be glorified.'

This demand in connection with prevailing prayer-that it should be to the glory of God-is no more than right and natural. There is none glorious but the Lord: there is no glory but His, and what He layeth on His creatures. Creation exists to show forth His glory; all that is not for His glory is sin, and darkness, and death: it is only in the glorifying of God that the creatures can find glory. What the Son of Man did, to give Himself wholly, His whole life, to glorify the Father, is nothing but the simple duty of every redeemed one. And Christ's reward will be his too. Because He gave Himself so entirely to the glory of the Father, the Father crowned Him with glory and honor, giving the kingdom into His hands, with the power to ask what He will, and, as Intercessor, to answer our prayers. And just as we become one with Christ in this, and as our prayer is part of a life utterly surrendered to God's glory, will the Savior be able to glorify the Father to us by the fulfilment of the promise: `Whatsoever ye shall ask, *I will do it.*'

To such a life, with God's glory our only aim, we cannot attain by any effort of our own. It is only in the man Christ Jesus that such a life is to be seen: in Him it is to be found for us. Yes blessed be God! His life is our life; He gave *Himself* for us; He Himself is now our life. The discovery, and the confession, and the denial, of self, as usurping the place of God, of self-seeking and self-trusting, is essential, and yet is what we cannot accomplish in our own strength. It is the incoming and indwelling, the Presence and the Rule in the heart, of our Lord Jesus who glorified the Father on earth, and is now glorified with Him, that thence He might glorify Him in us;--it is Jesus Himself coming in, who can cast out all self-glorifying, and give us instead His own God-glorifying life and Spirit. It is Jesus, who longs to glorify the Father in hearing our prayers, who will teach us to live and to pray to the glory of God.

And what motive, what power is there that can urge our slothful hearts to yield themselves to our Lord to work this in us? Surely nothing more is needed than a sight of how glorious, how alone worthy of glory the Father is. Let our faith learn in adoring worship to bow before Him, to ascribe to Him alone the kingdom, and the power, and the glory, to yield ourselves to dwell in His light as the ever-blessed, ever-loving One. Surely we shall be stirred to say, `To Him alone be glory.' And we shall look to our Lord Jesus with new intensity of desire for a life that refuses to see or seek ought but the glory of God. When there is but little prayer that can be answered, the Father is not glorified. It is a duty, for the glory of God, to live and pray so that our prayer can be answered. For the sake of God's glory, let us learn to pray well.

What a humbling thought that so often there is earnest prayer for a child or a friend, for a work or a circle, in which the thought of our joy or our pleasure was far stronger than any yearnings for God's glory. No wonder that there are so many unanswered prayers: here we have the secret. God would not be glorified when that glory was not our object. He that would pray the prayer of faith, will have to give himself to live literally so that the Father in all things may be glorified in him. This must be his aim: without this there cannot be the prayer of faith. `How can ye believe,' said Jesus, `which receive glory of one another, and the glory that cometh from the only God ye seek not?' All seeking of our own glory with men makes faith impossible: it is the deep, intense self-sacrifice that gives up its own glory, and seeks the glory of God alone, that wakens in the soul that spiritual susceptibility of the Divine, which is faith. The surrender to God to seek His glory, and the expectation that He will show His glory in hearing us, are one at root: He that seeks God's glory will see it in the answer to his prayer, and he alone.

All seeking of our own glory with men makes faith impossible

And how, we ask again, shall we attain to it? Let us begin with confession. How little has the glory of God been an all-absorbing passion; how little our lives and our prayers have been full of it. How little have we lived in the likeness of the Son, and in sympathy with Him-for God and His glory alone. Let us take time, until the Holy Spirit discover it to us, and we see how wanting we have been in this. True knowledge and confession of sin are the sure path to deliverance.

And then let us look to Jesus. In Him we can see by what death we can glorify God. In death He glorified Him; through death He was glorified with Him. It is by dying, being dead to self and living to God, that we can glorify Him. And this-this death to self, this life to the glory of God-is what Jesus gives and lives in each one who can trust Him for it. Let nothing less than these-the desire, the decision to live only for the glory of the Father, even as Christ did; the acceptance of Him with His life and strength working it in us; the joyful assurance that we can live to the glory of God, because Christ lives in us;--let this be the spirit of our daily life. Jesus stands surety for our living thus; the Holy Spirit is given, and waiting to make it our experience, if we will only trust and let Him; O let us not hold back through unbelief, but confidently take as our watchword- All to the glory of God! The Father accepts the will, the sacrifice is well-pleasing; the Holy Spirit will seal us within with the consciousness, we are living for God and His glory.

And then what quiet peace and power there will be in our prayers, as we know ourselves through His grace, in perfect harmony with Him who says to us, when He promises to do what we ask: `That the Father may be glorified in the Son.' With our whole being consciously yielded to the inspiration of the Word and Spirit, our desires will be no longer ours but His; their chief end the glory of God. With increasing liberty we shall be able in prayer to say: Father! Thou knowest, we ask it only for Thy glory. And the condition of prayer- answers, instead of being as a mountain we cannot climb, will only give us the greater confidence that we shall be heard, because we have seen that prayer has no higher beauty or blessedness than this, that it glorifies the Father. And the precious privilege of prayer will become doubly precious because it brings us into perfect unison with the Beloved Son in the wonderful partnership He proposes: `*You ask*, and *I do*, that the Father may be glorified in the Son.'

Day 34 Prayer

`LORD, TEACH US TO PRAY.'

Blessed Lord Jesus! I come again to Thee. Every lesson Thou givest me convinces me more deeply how little I know to pray aright. But every lesson also inspires me with hope that Thou art going to teach me, that Thou art teaching me not only to know what prayer should be, but actually to pray as I ought. O my Lord! I look with courage to Thee, the Great Intercessor, who didst pray and dost hear prayer, only that the Father may be glorified, to teach me too to live and to pray to the glory of God.

Savior! To this end I yield myself to Thee again. I would be nothing. I have given self, as already crucified with Thee, to the death. Through the Spirit its workings are mortified and made dead; Thy life and Thy love of the Father are taking possession of me. A new longing begins to fill my soul, that every day, every hour, that in every prayer the glory of the Father may be everything to me. O my Lord! I am in Thy school to learn this: teach Thou it me.

And do Thou, the God of glory, the Father of glory, my God and my Father, accept the desire of a child who has seen that Thy glory is indeed alone worth living for. O Lord! Show me Thy glory. Let it overshadow me. Let it fill the temple of my heart. Let me dwell in it as revealed in Christ. And do Thou Thyself fulfil in me Thine own good pleasure, that Thy child should find his glory in seeking the glory of his Father. Amen.

1See in the note on George Muller, at the close of this volume, how he was led to make God's glory his first object.

DAY 34
REFLECTION QUESTIONS

1. The essential element or aim of all our prayers must be _____
   _____.

2. How many of your prayers are for God's glory? _____

3. What does Murray say will focus our prayers on God's glory? _____
   _____

4. For our prayers to truly seek God's glory our lives must be _____ for
   God's glory.

5. Of the following three which is the primary motivation behind most of your prayers? (circle one)
   self-interest   self-will   God's glory

6. How do we begin to attain a life focused more on bringing God glory? _____
   _____

7. What is my main takeaway from Day 34 that will improve my prayer life? _____
   _____
   _____

Fill in the blanks- *If _____ _____ in _____, and my _____ _____ in _____, ye _____ _____ _____ ye _____, and _____ _____ _____ _____ unto _____. - John 15:7*

Answers

1. The glory of God
2. Personal response
3. Daily life in all its parts, must be given up to God's glory
4. Lived
5. Personal response
6. Confession
7. Personal response

Class 5 Verse- *If ye abide in me, and my words abide in you, ye shall ask what ye will, and it shall be done unto you. - John 15:7*

Day 34 Bible Reading - Mark 11; John 12

Day 34 notes

_____

_____

_____

_____

_____

_____

_____

_____

_____

_____

_____

_____

_____

_____

DAY 35

IF YE ABIDE ME OR THE ALL-INCLUSIVE CONDITION

`If ye abide in me, and my words abide in you, ask whatsoever ye will, and it shall be done unto you.' -**John 15:7**

In all God's intercourse with us, the promise and its conditions are inseparable. If we fulfil the conditions, He fulfils the promise. What He is to be to us depends upon what we are willing to be to Him. `Draw near to God, and He will draw near to you.' And so in prayer the unlimited promise, *Ask whatsoever ye will*, has its one simple and natural condition, *if ye abide in me*. It is Christ whom the Father always hears; God is *in Christ*, and can only be reached by being in Him; to be IN HIM is the way to have our prayer heard; fully and wholly ABIDING IN HIM, we have the right to ask whatsoever we will, and the promise that it shall be done unto us.

When we compare this promise with the experiences of most believers, we are startled by a terrible discrepancy. Who can number up the countless prayers that rise and bring no answer? The cause must be either that we do not fulfil the condition, or God does not fulfil the promise. Believers are not willing to admit either, and therefore have devised a way of escape from the dilemma. They put into the promise the qualifying clause our Savior did not put there-if it be God's will; and so maintain both God's integrity and their own. O if they did but accept it and hold it fast as it stands, trusting to Christ to vindicate His truth, how God's Spirit would lead them to see the Divine propriety of such a promise to those who really abide in Christ in the sense in which He means it, and to confess that the failure in the fulfilling the condition is the one sufficient explanation of unanswered prayer. And how the Holy Spirit would then make our feebleness in prayer one of the mightiest motives to urge us on to discover the secret, and obtain the blessing, of full abiding in Christ.

The cause must be either that we do not fulfil the condition, or God does not fulfil the promise

`If ye abide in me.' As a Christian grows in grace and in the knowledge of the Lord Jesus, he is often surprised to find how the words of God grow too, in the new and deeper meaning with which they come to him. He can look back to the day when some word of God was opened up to him and he rejoiced in the blessing he had found in it. After a time some deeper experience gave it a new meaning, and it was as if he never had seen what it contained. And yet once again, as he advanced in the Christian life, the same word stood before him again as a great mystery, until anew the Holy Spirit led him still deeper into its Divine fullness. One of these ever-growing, never-exhausted words, opening up to us step by step the fullness of the Divine life, is the Master's precious `Abide in me.' As the union of the branch with the vine is one of growth, never-ceasing growth and increase, so our abiding in Christ is a life process in which the Divine life takes ever fuller and more complete possession of us. The young and feeble believer may be really abiding in Christ up to the measure of his light; it is he who reaches onward to the full abiding in the sense in which the Master understood the words, who inherits all the promises connected with it.

In the growing life of abiding in Christ, the first stage is that of faith. As the believer sees that, with all his feebleness, the command is really meant for him, his great aim is simply to believe that, as he knows he is in

199

Christ, so now, notwithstanding unfaithfulness and failure, abiding in Christ is his immediate duty, and a blessing within his reach. He is specially occupied with the love, and power, and faithfulness of the Savior: he feels his one need to be believing.

It is not long before he sees something more is needed. Obedience and faith must go together. Not as if to the faith he has the obedience must be added, but faith must be made manifest in obedience. Faith is obedience at home and looking to the Master: obedience is faith going out to do His will. He sees how he has been more occupied with the privilege and the blessings of this abiding than with its duties and its fruit. There has been much of self and of self-will that has been unnoticed or tolerated: the peace which, as a young and feeble disciple, he could enjoy in believing goes from him; it is in practical obedience that the abiding must be maintained: `If ye keep my commands, ye shall abide in my love.' As before his great aim was through the *mind*, and the truth it took hold of, to let the heart rest on Christ and His promises; so now, in this stage, the chief effort is to get his *will* united with the will of his Lord, and the heart and the life brought entirely under His rule.

And yet it is as if there is something wanting. The will and the heart are on Christ's side; he obeys and he loves his Lord. But still, why is it that the fleshly nature has yet so much power, that the spontaneous motions and emotions of the inmost being are not what they should be? The will does not approve or allow, but here is a region beyond control of the will. And why also, even when there is not so much of positive commission to condemn, why so much of omission, the deficiency of that beauty of holiness, that zeal of love, that conformity to Jesus and His death, in which the life of self is lost, and which is surely implied in the abiding, as the Master meant it? There must surely be something in our abiding in Christ and Christ in us, which he has not yet experienced.

It is so. Faith and obedience are but the pathway of blessing. Before giving us the parable of the vine and the branches, Jesus had very distinctly told what the full blessing is to which faith and obedience are to lead. Three times over He had said, `If ye love me, keep my commandments,' and spoken of the threefold blessing with which He would crown such obedient love. The Holy Spirit would come from the Father; the Son would manifest Himself; the Father and the Son would come and make their abode. It is as our faith grows into obedience, and in obedience and love our whole being goes out and clings itself to Christ, that our inner life becomes opened up, and the capacity is formed within of receiving the life, the spirit, of the glorified Jesus, as a distinct and conscious union with Christ and with the Father. The word is fulfilled in us: `In that day ye shall know that I am in my Father and ye in me, and I in you.' We understand how, just as Christ is in God, and God in Christ, one together not only in will and in love, but in identity of nature and life, because they exist in each other, so we are in Christ and Christ in us, in union not only of will and love, but of life and nature too.

Faith must be made manifest in obedience

It was after Jesus had spoken of our thus through the Holy Spirit knowing that He is in the Father, and even so we in Him and He in us, that He said, `Abide in me, and I in you. Accept, consent to receive that Divine life of union with myself, in virtue of which, as you abide in me, I also abide in you, even as I abide in the Father. So that your life is mine and mine is yours.' This is the true abiding, the occupying of the position in which Christ can come and abide; so abiding in Him that the soul has come away from self to find that He has taken the place and become our life. It is the becoming as little children who have no care, and find their happiness in trusting and obeying the love that has done all for them.

To those who thus abide, the promise comes as their rightful heritage: Ask whatsoever ye will. It cannot be otherwise. Christ has got full possession of them. Christ dwells in their love, their will, their life. Not only has their will been given up; Christ has entered it, and dwells and breathes in it by His Spirit. He whom the Father always hears, prays in them; they pray in Him: what they ask shall be done unto them.

Beloved fellow-believer, let us confess that it is because we do not abide in Christ as He would have us, that the Church is so impotent in presence of the infidelity and worldliness and heathendom, in the midst of which the Lord is able to make her more than conqueror. Let us believe that He means what He promises, and accept the condemnation the confession implies.

But let us not be discouraged. The abiding of the branch in the Vine is a life of never-ceasing growth. The abiding, as the Master meant it, is within our reach, for He lives to give it us. Let us but be ready to count all things loss, and to say, 'Not as though I had already attained; I follow after, if that I may apprehend that for which I also am apprehended of Christ Jesus.' Let us not be so much occupied with the abiding, as with *Him* to whom the abiding links us, and His fullness. Let it be *Him*, the whole Christ, in His obedience and humiliation, in His exaltation and power, in whom our soul moves and acts; He Himself will fulfil His promise in us.

And then as we abide, and grow evermore into the full abiding, let us exercise our right, the will to enter into all God's will. Obeying what that will commands, let us claim what it promises. Let us yield to the teaching of the Holy Spirit, to show each of us, according to his growth and measure, what the will of God is which we may claim in prayer. And let us rest content with nothing less than the personal experience of what Jesus gave when He said, 'If ye abide in me, ask whatsoever ye will, it shall be done unto you.'

Day 35 Prayer

'LORD, TEACH US TO PRAY!'

Beloved Lord! do teach me to take this promise anew in all its simplicity, and to be sure that the only measure of Thy holy giving is our holy willing. Lord! Let each word of this Thy promise be anew made quick and powerful in my soul.

Thou sayest: *Abide in me!* O my Master, my Life, my All, I do abide in Thee. Give Thou me to grow up into all Thy fullness. It is not the effort of faith, seeking to cling to Thee, nor even the rest of faith, trusting Thee to keep me; it is not the obedience of the will, nor the keeping the commandments; but it is Thyself living in me and in the Father, that alone can satisfy me. It is Thy self, my Lord, no longer before me and above me, but one with me, and abiding in me; it is this I need, it is this I seek. It is this I trust Thee for.

Thou sayest: *Ask whatsoever ye will!* Lord! I know that the life of full, deep abiding will so renew and sanctify and strengthen the will that I shall have the light and the liberty to ask great things. Lord! let my will, dead in Thy death, living in Thy life, be bold and large in its petitions.

Thou sayest: *It shall be done.* O Thou who art the Amen, the Faithful and True Witness, give me in Thyself the joyous confidence that Thou wilt make this word yet more wonderfully true to me than ever, because it hath not entered into the heart of man to conceive what God hath prepared for them that love Him. Amen.

NOTE

On a thoughtful comparison of what we mostly find in books or sermons on prayer, and the teaching of the Master, we shall find one great difference: the importance assigned to the answer to prayer is by no means the same. In the former we find a great deal on the blessing of prayer as a spiritual exercise even if there be no answer, and on the reasons why we should be content without it. God's fellowship ought to be more to us than the gift we ask; God's wisdom only knows what is best; God may bestow something better than what

He withholds. Though this teaching looks very high and spiritual, it is remarkable that we find nothing of it with our Lord. The more carefully we gather together all He spoke on prayer, the clearer it becomes that He wished us to think of prayer simply as the means to an end, and that the answer was to be the proof that we and our prayer are acceptable to the Father in heaven. It is not that Christ would have us count the gifts of higher value than the fellowship and favor of the Father. By no means. But the Father means the answer to be the token of His favor and of the reality of our fellowship with Him. `To-day thy servant knoweth that I have found grace in thy sight, my lord, O king, in that the king hath fulfilled the request of his servant.'

A life marked by daily answer to prayer is the proof of our spiritual maturity; that we have indeed attained to the true abiding in Christ; that our will is truly at one with God's will; that our faith has grown strong to see and take what God has prepared for us; that the Name of Christ and His nature have taken full possession of us; and that we have been found fit to take a place among those whom God admits to His counsels, and according to whose prayer He rules the world. These are they in whom something of man's original dignity hath been restored, in whom, as they abide in Christ, His power as the all-prevailing Intercessor can manifest itself, in whom the glory of His Name is shown forth. Prayer is very blessed; *the answer is more blessed still*, as the response from the Father that our prayer, our faith, our will are indeed as He would wish them to be.

> **A life marked by daily answer to prayer is the proof of our spiritual maturity**

I make these remarks with the one desire of leading my readers themselves to put together all that Christ has said on prayer, and to yield themselves to the full impression of the truth that when prayer is what it should be, or rather when we are what we should be, abiding in Christ, the answer must be expected. It will bring us out from those refuges where we have comforted ourselves with unanswered prayer. It will discover to us the place of power to which Christ has appointed His Church, and which it so little occupies. It will reveal the terrible feebleness of our spiritual life as the cause of our not knowing to pray boldly in Christ's Name. It will urge us mightily to rise to a life in the full union with Christ, and in the fulness of the Spirit, as the secret of effectual prayer. And it will so lead us on to realize our destiny: `*At that day*: Verily, verily, I say unto you, If ye shall ask anything of the Father, He will give it you in my Name: ask, and ye shall receive, that your joy may be fulfilled.' Prayer that is really, spiritually, *in union with Jesus*, is always answered.

DAY 35
REFLECTION QUESTIONS

1. What is the main condition of answered prayer? _____

2. List the two possible causes for unanswered prayers based on the promise in John 15:7.
   _____ _____

3. What qualifying clause do Christians add to the conditions for answered prayers? _____
   _____

4. Do you ever blame your unanswered prayers on God's unknown will? _____

5. The first two steps on the path to a life of abiding in Christ are _____
   _____.

6. Why does abiding in Christ result in answered prayers? _____
   _____

7. We can know we are abiding in Christ when we have _____
   _____ in our daily lives.

8. What is my main takeaway from Day 35 that will improve my prayer life? _____
   _____
   _____

Fill in the blanks- *If _____ _____ in _____, and _____ _____ _____*
_____ _____, ye _____ _____ _____ ye _____, and _____
_____ _____ _____ _____ _____. - John 15:7

203

Answers

1. Abiding in Christ
2. We do not fulfill the condition, or God does not fulfill the promise
3. If it be God's will
4. Personal response
5. Faith and obedience
6. Because Christ dwells in us and prays through us and His prayers are always heard by the Lord
7. Answered prayers
8. Personal response

Class 5 Verse- *If ye abide in me, and my words abide in you, ye shall ask what ye will, and it shall be done unto you. - John 15:7*

Day 35 Bible Reading - Matthew 22; Mark 12

Day 35 notes

_____

_____

_____

_____

_____

_____

_____

_____

_____

_____

_____

_____

_____

CLASS 5

WEEK 6

Opening Prayer –Thank God for answering our prayers.

Word- Abide, **Theme**- The chief object of prayer is God's glory

Key Questions-

1. Murray points out that the focus of our prayer meeting should be _____.

2. One of the blessings of persevering prayer is _____.

3. What is the link that allows our prayers on earth to reach our Father in heaven? _____

4. Prayers of God's faithful servants like Abraham, have the ability to _____ the destinies of men.

5. What were the differences in Jesus' teaching on prayer at the Sermon of the Mount vs. His instructions before His ascension? _____

   _____

6. What does Murray say will focus our prayers on God's glory? _____

   _____

7. How do we begin to attain a life focused more on bringing God glory? _____

8. List the two possible causes for unanswered prayers based on the promise in John 15:7.

   _____

9. We can know we are abiding in Christ when we have _____

   _____ in our daily lives.

Testimonies- What is God doing through your prayer life?

Scripture Memory-

Class 4 Verse- *If ye abide in me, and my words abide in you, ye shall ask what ye will, and it shall be done unto you. - John 15:7*

Next Class Preview-

Word- Fruit, **Theme**- Faith & obedience lead to fruit bearing.

Verse- *Ye have not chosen me, but I have chosen you, and ordained you, that ye should go and bring forth fruit, and that your fruit should remain: that whatsoever ye shall ask of the Father in my name, he may give it you. - John 15:16*

Prayer for Students-

- Time to Pray Each Day, A Desire for Prayer, A Clear Mind During Prayer, Show us God's Will

Class 5 Answers

1. Securing answers to prayer

2. Teaches us to discover, confess and give up everything that hinders the coming of the answer

3. Jesus Christ

4. Influence

5. At the Sermon on the Mount it was; praying for their needs and to be childlike and trust the Father to answer the prayer, at His closing address it was; praying for His work and His kingdom on earth to be established

6. Daily life in all its parts, must be given up to God's glory

7. Confession

8. We are not abiding in Christ, or God does not fulfill the promise

9. Answered prayers

Class 5 notes

_____

_____

_____

_____

_____

_____

_____

_____

_____

_____

_____

_____

DAY 36

MY WORDS IN YOU OR, THE WORD AND PRAYER

`If ye abide in me, and my words abide in you, ask whatsoever ye will, and it shall be done unto you.' **-John 15:7**

The vital connection between the word and prayer is one of the simplest and earliest lessons of the Christian life. As that newly-converted heathen put it: I pray-I speak to my father; I read-my Father speaks to me. Before prayer, it is God's word that prepares me for it by revealing what the Father has bid me ask. In prayer, it is God's word that strengthens me by giving my faith its warrant and its plea. And after prayer, it is God's word that brings me the answer when I have prayed, for in it the Spirit gives me to hear the Father's voice. Prayer is not monologue but dialogue; God's voice in response to mine in its most essential part. Listening to God's voice is the secret of the assurance that He will listen to mine. `Incline thine ear, and hear;' `Give ear to me;' Hearken to my voice;' are words which God speaks to man as well as man to God. His hearkening will depend on ours; the entrance His words find with me, will be the measure of the power of my words with Him. What God's words are to me, is the test of what He Himself is to me, and so of the uprightness of my desire after Him in prayer.

> **Listening to God's voice is the secret of the assurance that He will listen to mine**

It is this connection between His word and our prayer that Jesus points to when He says, `If ye abide in me, *and my words abide in you*, ask whatsoever ye will, and it shall be done unto you.' The deep importance of this truth becomes clear if we notice the other expression of which this one has taken the place. More than once Jesus had said, "Abide in me and *I in you*.' His abiding in us was the complement and the crown of our abiding in Him. But here, instead of `Ye in me *and I in you*,' He says, `Ye in me *and my words in you*.' His words abiding are the equivalent of Himself abiding.

What a view is here opened up to us of the place the words of God in Christ are to have in our spiritual life, and especially in our prayer. In a man's words *he reveals himself*. In his promises *he gives himself away*, he binds himself to the one who receives his promise. In his commands he sets forth his will, seeks *to make himself master* of him whose obedience he claims, to guide and use him as if he were part of himself. It is through our words that spirit holds fellowship with spirit, that the spirit of one man passes over and transfers itself into another. It is through the words of a man, heard and accepted, and held fast and obeyed, that he can impart himself to another. But all this in a very relative and limited sense.

> **His words abiding are the equivalent of Himself abiding**

But when God, the infinite Being, in whom everything is life and power, spirit and truth, in the very deepest meaning of the words,--when God speaks forth Himself in His words, He does indeed give HIMSELF, His Love and His Life, His Will and His Power, to those who receive these words, in a reality passing

207

comprehension. In every promise He puts *Himself* in our power to lay hold of and possess; in every command He puts *Himself* in our power for us to share with Him His Will, His Holiness, His Perfection. In God's Word God gives us HIMSELF; His Word is nothing less than the Eternal Son, Christ Jesus. And so all Christ's words are God's words, full of a Divine quickening life and power. `The words that I speak unto you, they are spirit and they are life.'

Those who have made the deaf and dumb their study, tell us how much the power of speaking depends on that of hearing, and how the loss of hearing in children is followed by that of speaking too. This is true in a wider sense: as we hear, so we speak. This is true in the highest sense of our intercourse with God. To offer a prayer-to give utterance to certain wishes and to appeal to certain promises-is an easy thing, and can be learned of man by human wisdom. But to pray in the Spirit, to speak words that reach and touch God, that affect and influence the powers of the unseen world, --such praying, such speaking, depends entirely upon our hearing God's voice. Just as far as we listen to the voice and language that God speaks, and in the words of God receive His thoughts, His mind, His life, into our heart, we shall learn to speak in the voice and the language that God hears. It is the ear of the learner, wakened morning by morning, that prepares for the tongue of the learned, to speak to God as well as men, as should be (Isa. 50:4).

It is only in the full presence of God that disobedience and unbelief become impossible

This hearing the voice of God is something more than the thoughtful study of the Word. There may be a study and knowledge of the Word, in which there is but little real fellowship with the living God. But there is also a reading of the Word, in the very presence of the Father, and under the leading of the Spirit, in which the Word comes to us in living power from God Himself; it is to us the very voice of the Father, a real personal fellowship with Himself. It is the living voice of God that enters the heart that brings blessing and strength, and awakens the response of a living faith that reaches the heart of God again.

It is on this hearing the voice that the power both to obey and believe depends. The chief thing is, not to know *what* God has said we must do, but that *God Himself* says it to us. It is not the law, and not the book, not the knowledge of what is right, that works obedience, but the personal influence of God and His living fellowship. And even so it is not the knowledge of *what* God has promised, but the presence of *God Himself* as the Promiser, that awakens faith and trust in prayer. It is only in the full presence of God that disobedience and unbelief become impossible.

`If ye abide in me, and *my words abide in you,* ask whatsoever ye will, it shall be done unto you.' We see what this means. In the words the Savior gives Himself. We must have the words *in us,* taken up into our will and life, reproduced in our disposition and conduct. We must have them *abiding* in us: our whole life one continued exposition of the words that are within, and filling us; the words revealing Christ within, and our life revealing Him without. It is as the words of Christ enter our very heart, become our life and influence it, that our words will enter His heart and influence Him. My prayer will depend on my life; what God's words are to me and in me, my words will be to God and in God. If I do what God says, God will do what I say.

How well the Old Testament saints understood this connection between God's words and ours, and how really prayer with them was the loving response to what they had heard God speak! If the word were a promise, they counted *on God to do as He had spoken.* `Do as Thou hast said;' `For Thou, Lord, hast spoken it;' `According to Thy promise;' `According to Thy word;' in such expressions they showed that what God spake in promise was the root and the life of what they spake in prayer. If the word was a command, they simply *did as the Lord had spoken:* `So Abram departed as the Lord had spoken.' Their life was fellowship with God, the interchange of word and thought. What God spoke they heard and did; what they spoke God heard and did. In each word He speaks to us, the whole Christ gives Himself to fulfil it for us. For each word He asks no less that we give the whole man to keep that word, and to receive its fulfilment.

`If my words abide in you;' the condition is simple and clear. In His words His will is revealed. As the words abide in me, His will rules me; my will becomes the empty vessel which His will fills, the willing instrument which His will wields; He fills my inner being. In the exercise of obedience and faith my will becomes ever stronger, and is brought into deeper inner harmony with Him. He can fully trust it to will nothing but what He wills; He is not afraid to give the promise, `If my words abide in you, ask whatsoever ye will, it shall be done unto you.' To all who believe it, and act upon it, He will make it literally true.

In His words, His will is revealed.

Disciples of Christ! is it not becoming more and more clear to us that while we have been excusing our unanswered prayers, our impotence in prayer, with a fancied submission to God's wisdom and will, the real reason has been that our own feeble life has been the cause of our feeble prayers. Nothing can make strong men but the word coming to us from God's mouth: by that we must live. It is the word of Christ, loved, lived in, abiding in us, becoming through obedience and action part of our being, that makes us one with Christ, that fits us spiritually for touching, for taking hold of God. All that is of the world passeth away; he that doeth the will of God abideth forever. O let us yield heart and life to the words of Christ, the words in which He ever gives HIMSELF, the personal living Savior, and His promise will be our rich experience: `If ye abide in me, and my words abide in you, ask whatsoever ye will, and it shall be done unto you.'

Day 36 Prayer

`LORD, TEACH US TO PRAY!'

Blessed Lord! Thy lesson this day has again discovered to me my folly. I see how it is that my prayer has not been more believing and prevailing. I was more occupied with my speaking to Thee than Thy speaking to me. I did not understand that the secret of faith is this: there can be only so much faith as there is of the Living Word dwelling in the soul.

 And Thy word had taught me so clearly: Let every man be swift to hear, slow to speak; let not thine heart be hasty to utter anything before God. Lord, teach me that it is only with Thy word taken up into my life that my words can be taken into Thy heart; that Thy word, if it be a living power within me, will be a living power with Thee; what Thy mouth hath spoken Thy hand will perform.

 Lord! deliver me from the uncircumcised ear. Give me the opened ear of the learner, wakened morning by morning to hear the Father's voice. Even as Thou didst only speak what Thou didst hear, may my speaking be the echo of Thy speaking to me. `When Moses went into the tabernacle to speak with Him, he heard the voice of One speaking unto him from off the mercy-seat.' Lord, may it be so with me too. Let a life and character bearing the one mark, that Thy words abide and are seen in it, be the preparation for the full blessing: `Ask whatsoever ye will, and it shall be done unto you.' Amen.

DAY 36
REFLECTION QUESTIONS

1. Reading God's word results in _____.

2. Prayer is not _____ but _____.

3. How can we have Christ abiding in us? _____

4. Murray teaches that the chief thing is not to know *what* God has said we must do, but that _____ _____ says it to us.

5. How can we know if God's words are within our life? _____
   _____

6. Do your words and actions reveal that you have Christ's words abiding in your life? _____
   _____

7. In God's words His _____ is revealed.

8. If God's words are abiding in our life then His will is controlling our will resulting in us only asking requests that will be according to his will. How confident are you that your will is His will?
   _____

9. What is my main takeaway from Day 36 that will improve my prayer life? _____
   _____
   _____

Fill in the blanks- Ye have not _____ me, but I have chosen you, and ordained you, that ye should go and _____ _____ fruit, and that your fruit should _____: that whatsoever ye _____ _____ of the Father in my name, he may give it you. - John 15:16

Answers

1. God speaking to us

2. Monologue, dialogue

3. Spending time meditating and reading God's word

4. God himself

5. Our life (words and actions) will reveal Christ

6. Personal response

7. Will

8. Personal response

9. Personal response

Class 6 Verse- *Ye have not chosen me, but I have chosen you, and ordained you, that ye should go and bring forth fruit, and that your fruit should remain: that whatsoever ye shall ask of the Father in my name, he may give it you. - John 15:16*

Day 36 Bible Reading - Matthew 23; Luke 20-21

Day 36 notes

_____

_____

_____

_____

_____

_____

_____

_____

_____

_____

_____

DAY 37

BEAR FRUIT, THAT THE FATHER MAY GIVE WHAT YE ASK
OR, OBEDIENCE THE PATH TO POWER IN PRAYER

`Ye did not choose me, but I chose you, and appointed you, that ye should go and bear fruit, and that your fruit should abide: that whatsoever ye shall ask the Father in my name, He may give it you.'-**John 15:16**

`The fervent effectual prayer of a righteous man availeth much.'-**James 5:16**

The promise of the Father's giving whatsoever we ask is here once again renewed, in such a connection as to show us to whom it is that such wonderful influence in the council chamber of the Most High is to be granted. `I chose you,' the Master says, `and appointed you that ye should go and bear fruit, and that your fruit should abide;' and then He adds, *to the end `that* whatsoever ye,' the fruit-bearing ones, `shall ask of the Father in my name, He may give it you.' This is nothing but the fuller expression of what He had spoken in the words, `If ye abide in me.' He had spoken of the object of this abiding as the bearing `fruit,' `more fruit,' `much fruit;' in this was God to be glorified, and the mark of discipleship seen. No wonder that He now adds, that where the reality of the abiding is seen in fruit abounding and abiding, this would be the qualification for praying so as to obtain what we ask. Entire consecration to the fulfilment of our calling is the condition of effectual prayer, is the key to the unlimited blessings of Christ's wonderful prayer-promises.

Entire consecration to the fulfilment of our calling is the condition of effectual prayer

There are Christians who fear that such a statement is at variance with the doctrine of free grace. But surely not of free grace rightly understood, nor with so many express statements of God's blessed word. Take the words of St. John (1 John 3:22): `Let us love in deed and truth; *hereby* shall we assure our heart before Him. And whatsoever we ask, we receive of Him, *because* we keep His commandments, and do the things that are pleasing in His sight." Or take the oft-quoted words of James: `The fervent effectual prayer of a *righteous* man availeth much;' that is, of a man of whom, according to the definition of the Holy Spirit, it can be said, `He that doeth righteousness, is righteous even as He is righteous.' Mark the spirit of so many of the Psalms, with their confident appeal to the integrity and righteousness of the supplicant. In Ps. 28, David says: `The Lord rewarded me according to my righteousness; according to the cleanness of my hands hath He recompensed me. . . . I was upright before Him, and I kept myself from mine iniquity: therefore hath the Lord recompensed me according to my righteousness.' (Ps. 28:20-26. See also Ps. 7:3-5, 25:1-2, 28:3-6, 26:1-6, 119, 121 & 153.) If we carefully consider such utterances in the light of the New Testament, we shall find them in perfect harmony with the explicit teaching of the Savior's parting words: `*If ye keep* my commandments, ye shall abide in my love;' `Ye are my friends *if ye do* what I command you.' The word is indeed meant literally: `I appointed you that ye should go and bear fruit, *that*,' then, `whatsoever ye shall ask of the Father in my name, He may give it you.'

Let us seek to enter into the spirit of what the Savior here teaches us. There is a danger in our evangelical religion of looking too much at what it offers from one side, as a certain experience to be obtained in prayer and faith. There is another side which God's word puts very strongly, that of obedience as the only path to blessing. What we need is to realize that in our relationship to the Infinite Being whom we call God who has created and redeemed us, the first sentiment that ought to animate us is that of subjection: the surrender to His supremacy, His glory, His will, His pleasure, ought to be the first and uppermost thought of our life. The question is not, how we are to obtain and enjoy His favor, for in this the main thing may still be self. But what this Being in the very nature of things rightfully claims, and is infinitely and unspeakably worthy of, is that His glory and pleasure should be my one object. Surrender to His perfect and blessed will, a life of service and obedience, is the beauty and the charm of heaven. Service and obedience, these were the thoughts that were uppermost in the mind of the Son, when He dwelt upon earth. Service and obedience, these must become with us the chief objects of desire and aim, more so than rest or light, or joy or strength: in them we shall find the path to all the higher blessedness that awaits us.

> ℰ⧉◌⧉
>
> **The question is not, how we are to obtain and enjoy His favor, for in this the main thing may still be self**
>
> ℰ⧉◌⧉

Just note what a prominent place the Master gives it, not only in the 15th chapter of John, in connection with the abiding, but in the 14th, where He speaks of the indwelling of the Three-One God. In John 14 verse 15 we have it: `If ye love me, *keep my commandments*, and the Spirit will be given you of the Father. Then verse 21: `He that hath *my commandments and keepeth them*, he it is that loveth me;' and he shall have the special love of my Father resting on him and the special manifestation of myself. And then again, verse 23, one of the highest of all the exceeding great and precious promises: `If a man love me *he will keep my words*, and the Father and I will come and take up our abode with him.' Could words put it more clearly that obedience is the way to the indwelling of the Spirit, to His revealing the Son within us, and to His again preparing us to be the abode, the home of the Father? The indwelling of the Three-One God is the heritage of them that obey. Obedience and faith are but two aspects of one act,--surrender to God and His will. As faith strengthens for obedience, it is in turn strengthened by it: faith is made perfect by works. It is to be feared that often our efforts to believe have been unavailing because we have not taken up the only position in which a large faith is legitimate or possible,--that of entire surrender to the honor and the will of God. It is the man who is entirely consecrated to God and His will who will find the power come to claim everything that His God has promised to be for him.

The application of this in the school of prayer is very simple, but very solemn. `I chose you,' the Master says, `and appointed you that ye should go and bear fruit,' much fruit (John 15 verses 5-8), `and that your fruit should abide,' that your life might be one of abiding fruit and abiding fruitfulness, `*that*' thus, as fruitful branches abiding in me, `whatsoever ye shall ask of the Father in my name, He may give it you.' O how often we have sought to be able to pray the effectual prayer for much grace to bear fruit, and have wondered that the answer came not. It was because we were reversing the Master's order. We wanted to have the comfort and the joy and the strength first, that we might do the work easily and without any feeling of difficulty or self-sacrifice. And He wanted us in faith, without asking whether we felt weak or strong, whether the work was hard or easy, in the obedience of faith to do what He said: the path of fruit-bearing would have led us to the place and the power of prevailing prayer. Obedience is the only path that leads to the glory of God. Not obedience instead of faith, nor obedience to supply the shortcomings of faith; no, but faith's obedience gives access to all the blessings our God has for us. The baptism of the Spirit (John 14:16), the manifestation of the Son (John 14:21), the indwelling of the Father (John 14:23), the abiding in Christ's love (John 15:10), the privilege of His holy friendship (John 15:14), and the power of all-prevailing prayer (John 15:16),--all wait for the obedient.

Let us take home the lessons. Now we know the great reason why we have not had power in faith to pray prevailingly. Our life was not as it should have been: simple downright obedience, abiding fruitfulness, was not its chief mark. And with our whole heart we approve of the Divine appointment: men to whom God is to give such influence in the rule of the world, as at their request to do what otherwise would not have taken place, men whose will is to guide the path in which God's will is to work, must be men who have themselves learned obedience, whose loyalty and submission to authority must be above all suspicion. Our whole soul approves the law: obedience and fruit-bearing, the path to prevailing prayer. And with shame we acknowledge how little our lives have yet borne this stamp.

Let us yield ourselves to take up the appointment the Savior gives us. Let us study His relation to us as Master. Let us seek no more with each new day to think in the first place of comfort, or joy, or blessing. Let the first thought be: I belong to the Master. Every moment and every movement I must act as His property, as a part of Himself, as one who only seeks to know and do His will. A servant, a slave of Jesus Christ,--let this be the spirit that animates me. If He says, `No longer do I call you servants, but I have called you friends,' let us accept the place of friends: `Ye are my friends if ye do the things which I command you.'

The one thing He commands us as His branches is to bear fruit

The one thing He commands us as His branches is to bear fruit. Let us live to bless others, to testify of the life and the love there is in Jesus. Let us in faith and obedience give our whole life to that which Jesus chose us for and appointed us to-fruit-bearing. As we think of His electing us to this, and take up our appointment as coming from Him who always gives all He demands, we shall grow strong in the confidence that a life of fruit-bearing, abounding and abiding, is within our reach. And we shall understand why this fruit-bearing alone can be the path to the place of all prevailing prayer. It is the man who, in obedience to the Christ of God, is proving that he is doing what his Lord wills, for whom the Father will do whatsoever he will: `Whatsoever we ask we receive, because we keep His commandments, and do the things that are pleasing in His sight.'

Day 37 Prayer

`LORD, TEACH US TO PRAY.'

Blessed Master, teach me to apprehend fully what I only partly realize, that it is only through the will of God, accepted and acted out in obedience to His commands, that we obtain the power to grasp His will in His promises and fully to appropriate them in our prayers. And teach me that it is in the path of fruit-bearing that the deeper growth of the branch into the Vine can be perfected, and we attain to the perfect oneness with Thyself in which we ask whatsoever we will.

O Lord! Reveal to us, we pray Thee, how with all the hosts of heaven, and with Thyself the Son on earth, and with all the men of faith who have glorified Thee on earth, *obedience to God is our highest privilege, because it gives access to oneness with Himself in that which is His highest glory-His all perfect will.* And reveal to us, we pray Thee, how in keeping Thy commandments and bearing fruit according to Thy will, our spiritual nature will grow up to the full stature of the perfect man, with power to ask and to receive whatsoever we will.

O Lord Jesus! Reveal Thyself to us, and the reality of Thy purpose and Thy power to make these Thy wonderful promises the daily experience of all who utterly yield themselves to Thee and Thy words. Amen.

DAY 37
REFLECTION QUESTIONS

1. Who does God offer the promise 'whatsoever ye ask' to? _____

2. _____ is the only path to God's blessing.

3. Is God's will, glory and pleasure your main aim in life? _____

4. Murray states that Jesus' focus was _____ and _____ during His ministry here on earth.

5. Do you put service and obedience to God ahead of your own comforts and desires? _____
_____

6. What is the only way to ensure the indwelling of the Father in your life? _____
_____

7. Is your first goal each morning your comfort, joy and blessings or are you focused on being God's servant and living to do only His will? _____

8. Are you a fruit bearing Christian that God can trust to do exactly what He wants when He wants it done?_____
_____

9. What is my main takeaway from Day 37 that will improve my prayer life? _____
_____
_____

Fill in the blanks- Ye have not _____ me, but I have chosen you, and ordained you, that ye should go and _____ _____ fruit, and that your fruit should _____: that whatsoever ye _____ _____ of the Father in my name, he may give it you. - John 15:16

Answers

1. Fruit bearers
2. Obedience
3. Personal response
4. Service, obedience
5. Personal response
6. Faith & obedience
7. Personal response
8. Personal response

Class 6 Verse- *Ye have not chosen me, but I have chosen you, and ordained you, that ye should go and bring forth fruit, and that your fruit should remain: that whatsoever ye shall ask of the Father in my name, he may give it you. - John 15:16*

Day 37 Bible Reading - Mark 13

Day 37 notes

_____

_____

_____

_____

_____

_____

_____

_____

_____

_____

_____

_____

DAY 38

IN MY NAME OR, THE ALL-PREVAILING PLEA

`Whatsoever ye shall ask in my Name, that will I do. If ye shall ask me anything in my Name, that will I do. That whatsoever ye shall ask the Father in my Name, He may give it you. Verily, verily, I say unto you, If ye shall ask anything of the Father, He will give it you in my Name. Hitherto ye have asked nothing in my Name: ask, and ye shall receive. In that day ye shall ask in my Name.'-**John 14:13-14, 15:16, 16:23-24 & 26**

Hitherto the disciples had not asked in the Name of Christ, nor had He Himself ever used the expression. The nearest approach is, `met together in my Name.' Here in His parting words, He repeats the word unceasingly in connection with those promises of unlimited meaning, `*Whatsoever,*' `*Anything,*' `*What ye will,*' to teach them and us that His Name is our only, but also our all-sufficient plea. The power of prayer and the answer depend on the right use of the Name.

The Name of Christ is the expression of all He has done and all He is and lives to do as our Mediator

What is a person's name? That word or expression in which the person is called up or represented to us. When I mention or hear a name, it calls up before me the whole man, what I know of him, and also the impression he has made on me. The name of a king includes his honor, his power, and his kingdom. His name is the symbol of his power. And so each name of God embodies and represents some part of the glory of the Unseen One. And the Name of Christ is the expression of all He has done and all He is and lives to do as our Mediator.

And what is it to do a thing in the name of another? It is to come with the power and authority of that other, as his representative and substitute. We know how such a use of another's name always supposes a community of interest. No one would give another the free use of his name without first being assured that his honor and interest were as safe with that other as with himself.

And what is it when Jesus gives us power over His Name, the free use of it, with the assurance that whatever we ask in it will be given to us? The ordinary comparison of one person giving another, on some special occasion, the liberty to ask something in his name, comes altogether short here,--Jesus solemnly gives to *all* His disciples a general and unlimited power of the free use of His Name at *all* times for *all* they desire. He could not do this if He did not know that He could trust us with His interests, that His honor would be safe in our hands. The free use of the name of another is always the token of great confidence, of close union. He who gives his name to another stands aside, to let that other act for him; he who takes the name of another, gives up his own as of no value. When I go in the name of another, I deny myself, I take not only his name, but himself and what he is, instead of myself and what I am.

Such a use of the name of a person may be in virtue of *a legal union.* A merchant leaving his home and business, gives his chief clerk a general power, by which he can draw thousands of pounds in the merchant's name. The clerk does this, not for himself, but only in the interests of the business. It is because the merchant knows and trusts him as wholly devoted to his interests and business, that he dares put his name and property at his command. When the Lord Jesus went to heaven, He left His work, the management of His kingdom on earth, in the hands of His servants. He could not do otherwise than also give them His Name to draw all the supplies they needed for the due conduct of His business. And they have the spiritual power to avail themselves of the Name of Jesus just to the extent to which they yield themselves to live only for the interests and the work of the Master. The use of the Name always supposes the surrender of our interests to Him whom we represent.

Or such a use of the name may be in virtue of a *life union*. In the case of the merchant and his clerk, the union is temporary. But we know how oneness of life on earth gives oneness of name: a child has the father's name because he has his life. And often the child of a good father has been honored or helped by others for the sake of the name he bore. But this would not last long if it were found that it was only a name, and that the father's character was wanting. The name and the character or spirit must be in harmony. When such is the case, the child will have a double claim on the father's friends: the character secures and increases the love and esteem rendered first for the name's sake. So it is with Jesus and the believer: we are one, we have one life, one Spirit with Him; for this reason we may come in His Name. Our power in using that Name, whether with God, or men, or devils *depends on the measure of our spiritual life-union*. The use of the name rests on the unity of life; the Name and the Spirit of Jesus are one.1

Or the union that empowers to the use of the Name may be *the union of love*. When a bride whose life has been one of poverty, becomes united to the bridegroom, she gives up her own name, to be called by his, and has now the full right to use it. She purchases in his name, and that name is not refused. And this is done because the bridegroom has chosen her for himself, counting on her to care for his interests: they are now one. And so the Heavenly Bridegroom could do nothing less; having loved us and made us one with Himself, what could He do but give those who bear His Name the right to present it before the Father, or to come with it to Himself for all they need. And there is no one who gives himself really to live in the Name of Jesus, who does not receive in ever-increasing measure the spiritual capacity to ask and receive in that Name what he will. The bearing of the name of another supposes my having given up my own, and with it my own independent life; but then, as surely, my possession of all there is in the name I have taken instead of my own.

Such illustrations show us how defective the common view is of a messenger sent to ask in the name of another, or a guilty one appealing to the name of a surety. No Jesus Himself is with the Father; it is not an absent one in whose name we come. Even when we pray to Jesus Himself, it must be in His Name. The name represents the person; to ask in the Name is to ask in full union of interest and life and love with Himself, as one who lives in and for Him. Let the Name of Jesus only have undivided supremacy in my heart and life, my faith will grow to the assurance that what I ask in that Name cannot be refused. The name and the power of asking go together: when the Name of Jesus has become the power that rules my life, its power in prayer with God will be seen too.

We see thus that everything depends on our own relation to the Name: the power it has on my life is the power it will have in my prayers. There is more than one expression in Scripture which can make this clear to us. When it says, `Do all in the Name of the Lord Jesus,' we see how this is the counterpart of the other, `Ask all.' To do all and to ask all in His Name, these go together. When we read, `We shall walk in the Name of our God,' we see how the power of the Name must rule in the whole life; only then will it have power in prayer. It is not to the lips but to the life God looks to see what the Name is to us. When Scripture speaks of `men who have given their lives for the Name of the Lord Jesus,' or of one `ready to die for the Name of the Lord Jesus,' we see what our relation to the Name must be: when it is everything to me, it will obtain everything for me. If I let it have all I have, it will let me have all it has.

> ❧☙
>
> **It is not to the lips but to the life God looks to see what the Name is to us**
>
> ❧☙

218

`WHATSOEVER ye shall ask in my Name, that will I do.' Jesus means the promise literally. Christians have sought to limit it: it looked too free; it was hardly safe to trust man so unconditionally. We did not understand that the word `in my Name' is its own safeguard. It is a spiritual power which no one can use further than he obtains the capacity for, by his living and acting in that Name. As we bear that Name before men, we have power to use it before God. O let us plead for God's Holy Spirit to show us what the Name means, and what the right use of it is. It is through the Spirit that the Name, which is above every name in heaven, will take the place of supremacy in our heart and life too.

Disciples of Jesus! Let the lessons of this day enter deep into your hearts. The Master says: Only pray in my Name; whatsoever ye ask will be given. Heaven is set open to you; the treasures and powers of the world of spirit are placed at your disposal on behalf of men around you. O come, and let us learn to pray in the Name of Jesus. As to the disciples, He says to us, `Hitherto ye have not asked in my Name: ask, and ye shall receive.' Let each disciple of Jesus seek to avail himself of the rights of his royal priesthood, and use the power placed at his disposal for his circle and his work. Let Christians awake and hear the message: your prayer can obtain what otherwise will be withheld, can accomplish what otherwise remains undone. O awake, and use the name of Jesus to open the treasures of heaven for this perishing world. Learn as the servants of the King to use His Name: `WHATSOEVER ye shall ask in my Name, THAT WILL I DO.'

Day 38 Prayer

`LORD, TEACH US TO PRAY.'

Blessed Lord! It is as if each lesson Thou givest me has such fullness and depths of meaning, that if I can only learn that one, I shall know how to pray aright. This day I feel again as if I needed but one prayer every day: Lord! Teach me what it is to pray in Thy Name. Teach me so to live and act, to walk and speak, so to do all in the Name of Jesus, that my prayer cannot be anything else but in that blessed Name too.

And teach me, Lord! to hold fast the precious promise that WHATSOEVER we ask in Thy Name, Thou wilt do, the Father will give. Though I do not yet fully understand, and still less have fully attained, the wondrous union Thou meanest when Thou sayest, IN MY NAME, I would yet hold fast the promise until it fills my heart with the undoubting assurance: Anything in the Name of Jesus.

O my Lord, let Thy Holy Spirit teach me this. Thou didst say of Him, `The Comforter, whom the Father shall send IN MY NAME.' He knows what it is to be sent from heaven in Thy Name, to reveal and to honor the power of that Name in Thy servants, to use that Name alone, and so to glorify Thee. Lord Jesus! let Thy Spirit dwell in me, and fill me. I would, I do yield my whole being to His rule and leading. Thy Name and Thy Spirit are one; through Him Thy Name will be the strength of my life and my prayer. Then I shall be able for Thy Name's sake to forsake all, in Thy Name to speak to men and to God, and to prove that this is indeed the Name above every name.

Lord Jesus! O teach me by Thy Holy Spirit to pray in Thy Name. Amen.

NOTE.

What is meant by praying in Christ's name? It cannot mean simply appearing before God with faith in the mediation of the Savior. When the disciples asked Jesus to teach them to pray, He supplied them with petitions. And afterwards Jesus said to them, "Hitherto have ye asked nothing in my Name." Until the Spirit came, the seven petitions of the Lord's prayer lay as it were dormant within them. When by the Holy Ghost

Christ descended into their hearts, they desired the very blessings which Christ as our High Priest obtains for us by His prayer from the Father. And such petitions are always answered. The Father is always willing to give what Christ asks. The Spirit of Christ always teaches and influences us to offer the petitions which Christ ratifies and presents to the Father. To pray in Christ's name is therefore to be identified with Christ as to our righteousness, and *to be identified with Christ in our desires by the indwelling of the Holy Ghost.* To pray *in the Spirit*, to pray *according to the will of the Father*, to pray *in Christ's name, are identical expressions.* The Father Himself loveth us, and is willing to hear us: two intercessors, Christ the Advocate above, and the Holy Ghost, the Advocate within, are the gifts of His love.

`This view may appear at first less consoling than a more prevalent one, which refers prayer in Christ's name chiefly to our trust in Christ's merit. The defect of this opinion is, that it does not combine the intercession of the Saviour with the will of the Father, and the indwelling Spirit's aid in prayer. Nor does it fully realize the mediation of Christ; for the mediation consists not merely in that for Christ's sake the Holy Father is able to regard me and my prayer; but also, in that Christ Himself presents my petitions as His petitions, desired by Him for me, even as all blessings are purchased for me by His precious blood.

Praying in Christ's name is impossible without self-examination, without reflection, without self-denial

`In all prayer, the one essential condition is that we are able to offer it in the name of Jesus, as according to His desire for us, according to the Father's will, according to the Spirit's teaching. And thus praying in Christ's name is impossible without self-examination, without reflection, without self-denial; in short, without the aid of the Spirit.'-*Saphiv, The Lord's Prayer,* pp. 411, 142.

1 'Whatsoever ye shall ask in my Name,' that is, in my nature; for things with God are called according to their nature. We ask in Christ's Name, not when at the end of some request we say, `This I ask in the Name of Jesus Christ,' but when we pray *according to His nature,* which is love, which seeketh not its own but only the will of God and the good of all creatures. Such asking is the cry of His own Spirit in our hearts.-*Jukes. The New Man.*

DAY 38
REFLECTION QUESTIONS

1. The answer to prayer depends on the right use of _____.

2. Is God's honor and interest safe when He gives you use of His name? _____
_____

3. The use of Jesus' name always supposes the _____ of our interests to Him whom we represent.

4. In the illustrations (merchant, son and wife) of today's lesson, whose interest were they representing?
_____

5. As you pray in Jesus' name do your prayer requests focus on your interests or His? _____
_____

6. The power Jesus' name has on my _____ is the power His name will have in my prayers.

7. Praying in Christ's name is impossible without _____,
_____, _____.

8. What is my main takeaway from Day 38 that will improve my prayer life? _____
_____
_____

Fill in the blanks- Ye have not chosen me, but I have _____ you, and _____ you, that ye should go and bring forth fruit, and that your _____ should remain: that _____ ye shall ask of the _____ in my name, he may _____it you. - John 15:16

Answers

1. Jesus' name
2. Personal response
3. Surrender
4. The person who's name they represented -merchant, father, husband
5. Personal response
6. Life
7. Self-examination, reflection, self-denial
8. Personal response

Class 6 Verse- *Ye have not chosen me, but I have chosen you, and ordained you, that ye should go and bring forth fruit, and that your fruit should remain: that whatsoever ye shall ask of the Father in my name, he may give it you. - John 15:16*

Day 38 Bible Reading - Matthew 24

Day 38 notes

_____

_____

_____

_____

_____

_____

_____

_____

_____

_____

_____

_____

_____

DAY 39

AT THAT DAY OR, THE HOLY SPIRIT AND PRAYER

*`In that day ye shall ask me nothing. Verily, verily, I say unto you, Whatsoever ye shall ask the Father in my Name, He will give it you. Hitherto have ye asked nothing in my Name: ask, and ye shall receive, that your joy may be full. At that day ye shall ask in my Name: and I say not, that I will pray the Father for you, for the Father Himself loveth you.'-*John 16:23-26

*'Praying in the Holy Spirit, keep yourselves in the love of God.'-*Jude 20:21

The words of John (I John 2:12-14) to little children, to young men, and to fathers suggest the thought that there often are in the Christian life three great stages of experience. The first, that of the new-born child, with the assurance and the joy of forgiveness. The second, the transition stage of struggle and growth in knowledge and strength: young men growing strong, God's word doing its work in them and giving them victory over the Evil One. And then the final stage of maturity and ripeness: the Fathers, who have entered deeply into the knowledge and fellowship of the Eternal One.

In Christ's teaching on prayer there appear to be three stages in the prayer-life, somewhat analogous. In the Sermon on the Mount we have the initial stage: His teaching is all comprised in one word, Father. Pray to your Father, your Father sees, hears, knows, and will reward: *how much more* than any earthly father! Only be childlike and trustful. Then comes later on something like the transition stage of conflict and conquest, in words like these: `This sort goeth not out but by fasting and prayer;' `Shall not God avenge His own elect who cry day and night unto Him?' And then we have in the parting words, a higher stage. The children have become men: they are now the Master's friends, from whom He has no secrets, to whom He says, `All things that I heard from my Father I made known unto you;' and to whom, in the oft-repeated `whatsoever ye will,' He hands over the keys of the kingdom. Now the time has come for the power of prayer in His Name to be proved.

The contrast between this final stage and the previous preparatory ones our Savior marks most distinctly in the words we are to meditate on: `*Hitherto* ye have asked nothing in my Name;' `*At that day* ye shall ask in my Name. `We know what `*at that day*' means. It is the day of the outpouring of the Holy Spirit. The great work Christ was to do on the cross, the mighty power and the complete victory to be manifested in His resurrection and ascension, were to issue in the coming down from heaven, as never before, of the glory of God to dwell in men. The Spirit of the glorified Jesus was to come and be the life of His disciples. And one of the marks of that wonderful spirit-dispensation was to be a power in prayer hitherto unknown-prayer in the Name of Jesus, asking and obtaining whatsoever they would, is to be the manifestation of the reality of the Spirit's indwelling.

To understand how the coming of the Holy Spirit was indeed to commence a new epoch in the prayer-world, we must remember who He is, what His work, and what the significance of His not being given until Jesus was glorified. It is in the Spirit that God exists, for He is Spirit. It is in the Spirit that the Son was begotten of the Father: it is in the fellowship of the Spirit that the Father and the Son are one. The eternal never-ceasing giving to the Son which is the Father's prerogative and the eternal asking and receiving which is the

Son's right and blessedness-it is through the Spirit that this communion of life and love is maintained. It has been so from all eternity. It is so specially now, when the Son as Mediator ever liveth to pray. The great work which Jesus began on earth of reconciling in His own body God and man, He carries on in heaven. To accomplish this He took up into His own person the conflict between God's righteousness and our sin. On the cross He once for all ended the struggle in His own body. And then He ascended to heaven, that thence He might in each member of His body carry out the deliverance and manifest the victory He had obtained. It is to do this that He ever liveth to pray; in His unceasing intercession He places Himself in living fellowship with the unceasing prayer of His redeemed ones. Or rather, it is His unceasing intercession which shows itself in their prayers, and gives them a power they never had before.

And He does this through the Holy Spirit. The Holy Spirit, the Spirit of the glorified Jesus, was not (John 7:39), could not be, until He had been glorified. This gift of the Father was something distinctively new, entirely different from what Old Testament saints had known. The work that the blood effected in heaven when Christ entered within the veil, was something so true and new, the redemption of our human nature into fellowship with His resurrection-power and His exaltation-glory was so intensely real, the taking up of our humanity in Christ into the life of the Three-One God was an event of such inconceivable significance, that the Holy Spirit, who had to come from Christ's exalted humanity to testify in our hearts of what Christ had accomplished, was indeed no longer only what He had been in the Old Testament. It was literally true `the Holy Spirit was not yet, for Christ was not yet glorified.' He came now first as the Spirit of the glorified Jesus. Even as the Son, who was from eternity God, had entered upon a new existence as man, and returned to heaven with what He had not before, so the Blessed Spirit, whom the Son, on His ascension, received from the Father (Acts 2:33) into His glorified humanity, came to us with a new life, which He had not previously to communicate. Under the Old Testament He was invoked as the Spirit of God: at Pentecost He descended as the Spirit of the glorified Jesus, bringing down and communicating to us the full fruit and power of the accomplished redemption.

෨෬

It is in the intercession of Christ that the continued efficacy and application of His redemption is maintained

෨෬

It is in the intercession of Christ that the continued efficacy and application of His redemption is maintained. And it is through the Holy Spirit descending from Christ to us that we are drawn up into the great stream of His ever-ascending prayers. The Spirit prays for us without words: in the depths of a heart where even thoughts are at times formless, the Spirit takes us up into the wonderful flow of the life of the Three-One God. Through the Spirit, Christ's prayers become ours, and ours are made His: we ask what we will, and it is given to us. We then understand from experience, `Hitherto ye have not asked in my Name. *At that day* ye shall ask in my Name.'

Brother, what we need to pray in the Name of Christ, to ask that we may receive that our joy may be full, is the baptism of this Holy Ghost. This is more than the Spirit of God under the Old Testament. This is more than the Spirit of conversion and regeneration the disciples had before Pentecost. This is more than the Spirit with a measure of His influence and working. This is the Holy Spirit, the Spirit of the glorified Jesus in His exaltation-power, coming on us as the Spirit of the indwelling Jesus, revealing the Son and the Father within. (John xiv. 16-23.) It is when this Spirit is the Spirit not of our hours of prayer, but of our whole life and walk, when this Spirit glorifies Jesus in us by revealing the completeness of His work, and making us wholly one with Him and like Him, that we can pray in His Name, because we are in very deed one with Him. Then it is that we have that immediateness of access to the Father of which Jesus says, `I say not that I will pray the Father for you.' Oh! we need to understand and believe that to be filled with this, the Spirit of the glorified One, is the one need of God's believing people. Then shall we realize what it is, `with all prayer and supplication to be praying at all seasons in the Spirit,' and what it is, `praying in the Holy Ghost, to keep ourselves in the love of God.' `*At that day* ye shall ask in my Name.'

And so once again the lesson comes: What our prayer avails, depends upon what we are and what our life is. It is living in the Name of Christ that is the secret of praying in the Name of Christ; living in the Spirit that fits for praying in the Spirit. It is abiding in Christ that gives the right and power to ask what we will: the extent of the abiding is the exact measure of the power in prayer. It is the Spirit dwelling within us that prays, not in words and thoughts always, but in a breathing and a being deeper than utterance. Just so much as there is of Christ's Spirit in us, is there real prayer. Our lives, our lives, O let our lives be full of Christ, and full of His Spirit, and the wonderfully unlimited promises to our prayer will no longer appear strange. `Hitherto ye have asked nothing in my Name. Ask, and ye shall receive, that your joy may be full. At that day ye shall ask in my Name. Verily, verily, I say unto you, Whatsoever ye shall ask the father in my Name, He will give it you.'

ဆာ‌ဟာ

What our prayer avails, depends upon what we are and what our life is

ဆာ‌ဟာ

Day 39 Prayer

`LORD, TEACH US TO PRAY.'

O my God, in holy awe I bow before Thee, the Three in One. Again I have seen how the mystery of prayer is the mystery of the Holy Trinity. I adore the Father who ever hears, and the Son who ever lives to pray, and the Holy Spirit, proceeding from the Father and the Son, to lift us up into the fellowship of that ever-blessed, never-ceasing asking and receiving. I bow, my God, in adoring worship, before the infinite condescension that thus, through the Holy Spirit, takes us and our prayers into the Divine Life, and its fellowship of love.

O my Blessed Lord Jesus! Teach me to understand Thy lesson, that it is the indwelling Spirit, streaming from Thee, uniting to Thee, who is the Spirit of prayer. Teach me what it is as an empty, wholly consecrated vessel, to yield myself to His being my life. Teach me to honor and trust Him, as a living Person, to lead my life and my prayer. Teach me especially in prayer to wait in holy silence, and give Him place to breathe within me His unutterable intercession. And teach me that through Him it is possible to pray without ceasing, and to pray without failing, because He makes me partaker of the never-ceasing and never-failing intercession in which Thou, the Son, dost appear before the Father. Yea, Lord, fulfil in me Thy promise, at that day ye shall ask in my Name. Verily, verily, I say unto you, whatsoever ye shall ask the Father in my Name, that will He give.' Amen.

NOTE.

Prayer has often been compared to breathing: we have only to carry out the comparison fully to see how wonderful the place is which the Holy Spirit occupies. With every breath we expel the impure air which would soon cause our death, and inhale again the fresh air to which we owe our life. So we give out from us, in confession the sins, in prayer the needs and the desires of our heart. And in drawing in our breath again, we inhale the fresh air of the promises, and the love, and the life of God in Christ. We do this through the Holy Spirit, who is the breath of our life.

And this He is because He is the breath of God. The Father breathes Him into us, to unite Himself with our life. And then just as on every expiration there follows again the inhaling or drawing in of the breath, so God draws in again His breath, and the Spirit returns to Him laden with the desires and needs of our hearts. And thus the Holy Spirit is the breath of the life of God, and the breath of the new life in us. As God breathes Him out, we receive Him in answer to prayer; as we breathe Him back again, He rises to God laden with our supplications. As the Spirit of God, in whom the Father and the Son are one, and the intercession of the Son reaches the Father, He is to us the Spirit of prayer. True prayer is the living experience of the truth of the Holy Trinity. The Spirit's breathing, the Son's intercession, the Father's will, these three become one in us.

DAY 39
REFLECTION QUESTIONS

1. Explain the three stages of the Christian life? 1._____

   _____

   2._____

   _____

   3._____

   _____

2. Explain the three stages of the Christian prayer life? 1._____

   _____

   2._____

   _____

   3._____

   _____

3. Does Jesus's unceasing intersession show itself in your prayers? _____

4. What does Murray say 'at that day' means? _____

5. Per Murray what our prayer avails, depends on? _____

6. What is my main takeaway from Day 39 that will improve my prayer life? _____

   _____

   _____

Fill in the blanks- Ye have not _____ me, but I have _____ you, and ordained _____, that ye should go and _____ forth fruit, and that _____ fruit should _____: that _____ ye shall _____ of the _____ in my name, he _____ give it you. - John 15:16

Answers

1. New born child- forgiveness; Young man –fighting temptation and growing closer to God; Mature- in close communion with the Lord

2. Childlike stage- asking the Father for needs; Conflict stage- battling Satan and persevering in prayer; Friend stage- working for the advancement of the kingdom

3. Personal response

4. The outpouring of the Holy Spirit at Pentecost

5. What our life is

6. Personal response

Class 6 Verse- *Ye have not chosen me, but I have chosen you, and ordained you, that ye should go and bring forth fruit, and that your fruit should remain: that whatsoever ye shall ask of the Father in my name, he may give it you. - John 15:16*

Day 39 Bible Reading - Matthew 25

Day 39 notes

_____

_____

_____

_____

_____

_____

_____

_____

_____

_____

_____

_____

_____

DAY 40

I HAVE PRAYED FOR THEE OR, CHRIST THE INTERCESSOR

`But I have prayed for thee, that thy faith fail not.'-**Luke 22:32**

`I say not unto you, that I will pray the Father for you.'-**John 16:26**

`He ever liveth to make intercession.'-**Hebrews 7:25**

All growth in the spiritual life is connected with the clearer insight into what Jesus is to us. The more I realize that Christ must be all to me and in me, that all in Christ is indeed for me, the more I learn to live the real life of faith, which, dying to self, lives wholly in Christ. The Christian life is no longer the vain struggle to live right, but the resting in Christ and finding strength in Him as our life, to fight the fight and gain the victory of faith. This is especially true of the life of prayer. As it too comes under the law of faith alone, and is seen in the light of the fullness and completeness there is in Jesus, the believer understands that it need no longer be a matter of strain or anxious care, but an experience of what Christ will do for him and in him-a participation in that life of Christ which, as on earth, so in heaven, ever ascends to the Father as prayer. And he begins to pray, not only trusting in the merits of Jesus, or in the intercession by which our unworthy prayers are made acceptable, but in that near and close union in virtue of which He prays in us and we in Him. The whole of salvation is Christ Himself: He has given HIMSELF to us; He Himself lives in us. Because He prays, we pray too. As the disciples, when they saw Jesus pray, asked Him to make them partakers of what He knew of prayer, so we, now we see Him as intercessor on the throne, know that He makes us participate with Himself in the life of prayer.

How clearly this comes out in the last night of His life. In His high-priestly prayer (John 17,) He shows us how and what He has to pray to the Father, and will pray when once ascended to heaven. And yet He had in His parting address so repeatedly also connected His going to the Father with *their* new life of prayer. The two would be ultimately connected: His entrance on the work of His eternal intercession *would be the commencement and the power of their new prayer-life in His Name.* It is the sight of Jesus in His intercession that gives us power to pray in His Name: all right and power of prayer is Christ's; He makes us share in His intercession.

All right and power of prayer is Christ's; He makes us share in His intercession

To understand this, think first of *His intercession:* He ever liveth to make intercession. The work of Christ on earth as Priest was but a beginning. It was as Aaron He shed His blood; it is as Melchizedek that He now lives within the veil to continue His work, after the power of the eternal life. As Melchizedek is more glorious than Aaron, so it is in the work of intercession that the atonement has its true power and glory. `It is Christ that died: *yea more*, who is even at the right hand of God, who maketh intercession for us.' That intercession is an intense reality, a work that is absolutely necessary, and without which the continued application of redemption cannot take place. In the incarnation and resurrection of Jesus the wondrous reconciliation took place, by which man became partaker of the Divine life and blessedness. But the real personal appropriation of this reconciliation in each of His members here below cannot take place without the unceasing exercise of His Divine power by the head in heaven. In all conversion and sanctification, in every victory over sin and the world, there is a real forth-putting of the power of Him who is mighty to save. And this exercise of His power only takes place through His prayer: He asks of the Father, and receives from the Father. `He is able to save to the uttermost, *because* He ever liveth to make intercession.' There is not a need of His people but He receives in intercession what the Godhead has to give: His mediation on the throne is as real and indispensable as on the cross. Nothing takes place without His intercession: it engages all His time and powers, is His unceasing occupation at the right hand of the Father.

And we participate not only in the benefits of this His work, but in the work itself. This because we are His body. Body and members are one: `The head cannot say to the feet, I have no need of thee.' We share with Jesus in all He is and has: `The glory which Thou gavest me, I have given them.' We are partakers of His life, His righteousness, His work: we share with Him in His intercession too; it is not a work He does without us.

We do this because we are partakers of His life: `Christ is our life;' `No longer I, but Christ liveth in me.' The life in Him and in us is identical, one and the same. His life in us is an *ever-praying* life. When it descends and takes possession of us, it does not lose its character; in us too it is the *every-praying* life-a life that without ceasing asks and receives from God. And this not as if there were two separate currents of prayer rising upwards, one from Him, and one from His people. No, but the substantial life-union is also prayer-union: what He prays passes through us, what we pray passes through Him. He is the angel with the golden censer: `UNTO HIM there was given much incense,' the secret

We share with Him in His intercession too; it is not a work He does without us

of acceptable prayer, `that He should add it unto the prayers of all the saints upon the golden altar.' We live, we abide in Him, the Interceding One.

The Only-begotten is the only one who has the right to pray: to Him alone it was said, `Ask, and it shall be given Thee.' As in all other things the fullness dwells in Him, so the true prayer-fullness too; He alone has the power of prayer. And just as the growth of the spiritual life consists in the clearer insight that all the treasures are *in Him,* and that we too are *in Him,* to receive each moment what we possess in Him, grace for grace, so with the prayer-life too. Our faith in the intercession of Jesus must not only be that He prays in our stead, when we do not or cannot pray, but that, as the Author of our life and our faith, He draws us on to pray in unison with Himself. Our prayer must be a work of faith in this sense too, that as we know that Jesus communicates His whole life in us, He also out of that prayerfulness which is His alone breathes into us our praying.

To many a believer it was a new epoch in his spiritual life when it was revealed to him how truly and entirely Christ was his life, standing good as surety for his remaining faithful and obedient. It was then first that he really began to live a *faith-life.* No less blessed will be the discovery that Christ is surety for our prayer-life too, the center and embodiment of all prayer, to be communicated by Him through the Holy Spirit to His people. `He ever liveth to make intercession' as the Head of the body, as the Leader in that new and living way which He hath opened up, as the Author and the Perfecter of our faith. He provides in everything for the life of His redeemed ones by giving His own life in them: He cares for their life of prayer, by taking them up into His heavenly prayer-life, by giving and maintaining His prayer-life within them. `I have prayed for thee,' not to render thy faith needless, but `that *thy faith* fail not:' our faith and prayer of faith is rooted in His. It is, `if ye abide in me,' the ever-living Intercessor, and pray with me and in me: `ask whatsoever ye will, and it shall be done unto you.'

The thought of our fellowship in the intercession of Jesus reminds us of what He has taught us more than once before, how all these wonderful prayer-promises have as their aim and their justification, the glory of God in the manifestation of His kingdom and the salvation of sinners. As long as we only or chiefly pray for ourselves, the promises of the last night must remain a sealed book to us. It is to the fruit-bearing branches of the Vine; it is to disciples sent into the world as the Father sent Him, to live for perishing men; it is to His faithful servants and intimate friends who take up the work He leaves behind, who have like their Lord become as the seed-corn, losing its life to multiply it manifold;--it is to such that the promises are given. Let us each find out what the work is, and who the souls are entrusted to our special prayers; let us make our intercession for them our life of fellowship with God, and we shall not only find the promises of power in prayer made true to us, but we shall then first begin to realize how our abiding in Christ and His abiding in us makes us share in His own joy of blessing and saving men.

O most wonderful intercession of our Blessed Lord Jesus, to which we not only owe everything, but in which we are taken up as active partners and fellow-workers! Now we understand what it is to pray in the Name of Jesus, and why it has such power. In His Name, in His Spirit, in Himself, in perfect union with Him. O wondrous, ever active, and most efficacious intercession of the man Christ Jesus! When shall we be wholly taken up into it and always pray in it?

Day 40 Prayer

'LORD, TEACH US TO PRAY.'

Blessed Lord! In lowly adoration I would again bow before Thee. Thy whole redemption work has now passed into prayer; all that now occupies Thee in maintaining and dispensing what Thou didst purchase with Thy blood is only prayer. Thou ever livest to pray. And because we are and abide in Thee, the direct access to the Father is always open, our life can be one of unceasing prayer, and the answer to our prayer is sure.

Blessed Lord! Thou hast invited Thy people to be Thy fellow-workers in a life of prayer. Thou hast united Thyself with Thy people and makest them as Thy body share with Thee in that ministry of intercession through which alone the world can be filled with the fruit of Thy redemption and the glory of the Father. With more liberty than ever I come to Thee, my Lord, and beseech Thee: Teach me to pray. Thy life is prayer, Thy life is mine. Lord, teach me to pray, in Thee, like Thee.

And, O my Lord! Give me specially to know, as Thou didst promise Thy disciples, that Thou art in the Father, and I in Thee, and Thou in me. Let the uniting power of the Holy Spirit make my whole life an abiding in Thee and Thy intercession, so that my prayer may be its echo, and the Father hear me in Thee and Thee in me. Lord Jesus, let Thy mind in everything be in me, and my life in everything by in Thee. So shall I be prepared to be the channel through which Thy intercession pours its blessing on the world. Amen.

NOTE.

'The new epoch of prayer in the Name of Jesus is pointed out by Christ as the time of the outpouring of the Spirit, in which the disciples enter upon a more enlightened apprehension of the economy of redemption, and become as clearly conscious of their oneness with Jesus as of His oneness with the Father. Their prayer in the Name of Jesus is now directly to the Father Himself. "*I say not that I will pray* for you, for the Father Himself loveth you," Jesus says; while He had previously spoken of the time before the Spirit's coming: "*I will pray* the Father, and He will give you the Comforter." This prayer thus has as its central thought the insight into our being united to God in Christ as on both sides the living bond of union between God and us (John 17:23 "I in them and Thou in me"), so that in Jesus we behold the Father as united to us, and ourselves as united to the Father. Jesus Christ must have been revealed to us, not only through the truth in the mind, but in our inmost personal consciousness as the living personal reconciliation, as He in whom God's Fatherhood and Father-love have been perfectly united with human nature and it with God. Not that with the immediate prayer to the Father, the mediatorship of Christ is set aside; but it is no longer looked at as something external, existing outside of us, but as a real living spiritual existence within us, so that the Christ *for us*, the Mediator, has really become Christ *in us*.

`When the consciousness of this oneness between God in Christ and us in Christ still is wanting, or has been darkened by the sense of guilt, then the prayer of faith looks to our Lord as the Advocate, who pays the Father *for us*. (Compare John 16:26 with 14:16-17, 9:20; Luke 21:32; I John 2:1.) To take Christ thus in prayer as Advocate, is according to John 16:26 not perfectly the same as the prayer in His Name. Christ's advocacy is meant to lead us on to that inner self-standing life-union with Him, and with the Father in Him, in virtue of which Christ is He in whom God enters into immediate relation and unites Himself with us, and in whom we in all circumstances enter into immediate relation with God. Even so the prayer in the Name of Jesus does not consist in our prayer at His command: the disciples had prayed thus ever since the Lord had given them His "Our Father," and yet He says, "Hitherto ye have not prayed in my Name." Only when the mediation of Christ has become, through the indwelling of the Holy Spirit, life and power within us, and so *His mind, as it found expression in His word and work, has taken possession of and filled our personal consciousness and will,* so that in faith and love we have Jesus in us as the Reconciler who has actually made us one with God: only then His Name, which included His nature and His work, is become truth and power in us (not only for us), and we have in the Name of Jesus the free, direct access to the Father which is sure of being heard. Prayer in the Name of Jesus is the liberty of a son with the Father, just as Jesus had this as the First-begotten. We pray in the place of Jesus, not as if we could put ourselves in His place, but in as far as we are in Him and He in us. We go direct to the Father, but only as the Father is in Christ, not as if He were separate from Christ. Wherever thus the inner man does not live in Christ and has Him not present as the Living One, where His word is not ruling in the heart in its Spirit-power, where His truth and life have not become the life of our soul, it is vain to think that a formula like "for the sake of Thy dear Son" will avail.'-*Christliche Ethik, von Dr. I. T. Beck, Tubingen, 3:39.*

1 See on the difference between having Christ as an Advocate or Intercessor who stands outside of us, and the having Him within us, we abiding in Him and He in us through the Holy Spirit perfecting our union with Him, so that we ourselves can come directly to the Father in His Name,--the note above from Beck of Tubingen.

DAY 40
REFLECTION QUESTIONS

1. Knowing Christ is on the right hand of God making intersession for us should _____ _____.

2. The exercise of _____ power only takes place through _____ prayers.

3. Does Jesus involve us in His interceding work? _____

4. How involved are you in the intercession work of Christ? _____ _____

5. What is the aim of all the prayer promises? _____ _____

6. How much of your prayer time is spent joined with Christ in interceding for God's glory or lost sinners? _____ _____

7. How much fruit are you bearing? _____

8. What is my main takeaway from Day 40 that will improve my prayer life? _____ _____ _____

Fill in the blanks- _____ have not _____ me, but _____ have _____ you, and _____ _____, that ye should go and _____ forth _____, and that _____ fruit should _____: that _____ ye shall _____ of the _____ in my name, he _____ give it _____. - John 15:16

233

Answers

1. Strengthen faith in our prayers
2. Christ's, Christ's
3. Yes, we are part of the body participating in His work
4. Personal response
5. The glory of God and the salvation of sinners
6. Personal response
7. Personal response
8. Personal response

Class 6 Verse- *Ye have not chosen me, but I have chosen you, and ordained you, that ye should go and bring forth fruit, and that your fruit should remain: that whatsoever ye shall ask of the Father in my name, he may give it you. - John 15:16*

Day 40 Bible Reading - Matthew 26; Mark 14

Day 40 notes

_____

_____

_____

_____

_____

_____

_____

_____

_____

_____

_____

_____

_____

_____

DAY 41

FATHER, I WILL OR, CHRIST THE HIGH PRIEST

'Father, I will that they also whom Thou hast given me may be with me where I am.'-**John 17:24**

In His parting address, Jesus gives His disciples the full revelation of what the New Life was to be, when once the kingdom of God had come in power. In the indwelling of the Holy Spirit, in union with Him the heavenly Vine, in their going forth to witness and to suffer for Him, they were to find their calling and their blessedness. In between His setting forth of their future new life, the Lord had repeatedly given the most unlimited promises as to the power their prayers might have. And now in closing, He Himself proceeds to pray. To let His disciples have the joy of knowing what His intercession for them in heaven as their High Priest will be, He gives this precious legacy of His prayer to the Father. He does this at the same time because they as priests are to share in His work of intercession, that they and we might know how to perform this holy work. In the teaching of our Lord on this last night, we have learned to understand that: these astonishing prayer-promises have not been given in our own behalf, but in the interest of the Lord and His kingdom it is from the Lord Himself alone that we can learn what the prayer in His Name is to be and to obtain. We have understood that to pray in His Name is to pray in perfect unity with Himself: the high-priestly prayer will teach all that the prayer in the Name of Jesus may ask and expect.

> **These astonishing prayer-promises have not been given in our own behalf, but in the interest of the Lord and His kingdom**

This prayer is ordinarily divided into three parts. Our Lord first prays for Himself (John 17:1-5), then for His disciples (6-19), and last for all the believing people through all ages (20-26). The follower of Jesus, who gives himself to the work of intercession, and would fain try how much of blessing he can pray down upon his circle in the Name of Jesus, will in all humility let himself be led of the Spirit to study this wonderful prayer as one of the most important lessons of the school of prayer.

First of all, Jesus prays for Himself, for His being glorified, that so He may glorify the Father. `Father! Glorify Thy Son. And now, Father, glorify me.' And He brings forward the grounds on which He thus prays. A holy covenant had been concluded between the Father and the Son in heaven. The Father had promised Him power over all flesh as the reward of His work: He had done the work, He had glorified the Father, and His one purpose is now still further to glorify Him. With the utmost boldness He asks that the Father may glorify Him that He may now be and do for His people all He has undertaken.

Disciple of Jesus, here you have the first lesson in your work of priestly intercession, to be learned from the example of your great High Priest. To pray in the Name of Jesus is to pray in unity, in sympathy with Him. As the Son began His prayer by making clear His relation to the Father, pleading His work and obedience and His desire to see the Father glorified, do so too. Draw near and appear before the Father in Christ. Plead His finished work. Say that you are one with it, that you trust on it, live in it. Say that you too have given yourself to finish the work the Father has given you to do, and to live alone for His glory. And ask then confidently that the Son may be glorified in you. This is praying in the Name, in the very words, in the Spirit of Jesus, in union with Jesus Himself. Such prayer has power. If with Jesus you glorify the Father, the Father will glorify Jesus by doing what you ask in His Name. It is only when your own personal relation on this point, like Christ's, is clear with God, when you are glorifying Him, and seeking all for His glory, that like Christ, you will have power to intercede for those around you.

Our Lord next prays for the circle of His disciples. He speaks of them as those whom the Father has given Him. Their chief mark is that they have received Christ's word. He says of them that He now sends them into the world in His place, just as the Father had sent Himself. And He asks two things for them: that the Father keep them from the evil one, and sanctify them through His Word, because He sanctifies Himself for them.

When you are glorifying Him, and seeking all for His glory, that like Christ, you will have power to intercede for those around you

Just like the Lord, each believing intercessor has his own immediate circle for whom he first prays. Parents have their children, teachers their pupils, pastors their flocks, all workers their special charge, all believers those whose care lies upon their hearts. It is of great consequence that intercession should be personal, pointed, and definite. And then our first prayer must always be that they may receive the word. But this prayer will not avail unless with our Lord we say, `I have given them Thy word:' it is this gives us liberty and power in intercession for souls. Not only pray for them, but speak to them. And when they have received the word, let us pray much for their being kept from the evil one, for their being sanctified through that word. Instead of being hopeless or judging or giving up those who fall, let us pray for our circle, `Father! Keep them in Thy Name;' `Sanctify them through Thy truth.' Prayer in the Name of Jesus availeth much: `What ye will shall be done unto you.'

And then follows our Lord's prayer for a still wider circle. `I pray not only for these, but for them who through their word shall believe.' His priestly heart enlarges itself to embrace all places and all time, and He prays that all who belong to Him may everywhere be one, as God's proof to the world of the divinity of His mission, and then that they may ever be with Him in His glory. Until then `that the love wherewith Thou hast loved me may be in them, and I in them.'

The disciple of Jesus, who has first in his own circle proved the power of prayer, cannot confine himself within its limits: he prays for the Church universal and its different branches. He prays specially for the unity of the Spirit and of love. He prays for its being one in Christ, as a witness to the world that Christ, who hath wrought such a wonder as to make love triumph over selfishness and separation, is indeed the Son of God sent from heaven. Every believer ought to pray much that the unity of the Church, not in external organizations, but in spirit and in truth, may be made manifest.

So much for the matter of the prayer. Now for its mode. Jesus says, `FATHER! I WILL.' On the ground of His right as Son, and the Father's promise to Him, and His finished work, He might do so. The Father had said to Him, `Ask of me, and I will give Thee.' He simply availed Himself of the Father's promise. Jesus has given us a like promise: `*Whatsoever ye will* shall be done unto you.' He asks me in His Name to say what

Not only pray for lost souls, but speak to them

I will. Abiding in Him, in a living union with Him in which man is nothing and Christ all, the believer has the liberty to take up that word of His High Priest and, in answer to the question `*What wilt thou?*' to say, `FATHER! I WILL all that Thou hast promised.' This is nothing but true faith; this is honoring God: to be assured that such confidence in saying what I will is indeed acceptable to Him. At first sight, our heart shrinks from the expression; we feel neither the liberty nor the power to speak thus. It is a word for which alone in the most entire abnegation of our will grace will be given, but for which grace will most assuredly be given to each one who loses his will in his Lord's. He that loseth his will shall find it; he that gives up his will entirely shall find it again renewed and strengthened with a Divine Strength. `FATHER! I WILL:' this is the keynote of the everlasting, ever-active, all-prevailing intercession of our Lord in heaven. It is only in union with Him that our prayer avails; in union with Him it avails much. If we but abide in Him, living, and walking, and doing all things in His Name; if we but come and bring each separate petition, tested and touched by His Word and Spirit, and cast it into the mighty stream of intercession that goes up from Him, to be borne upward and presented before the Father;--we shall have the full confidence that we receive the petitions we ask: the `Father! *I will*' will be breathed into us by the Spirit Himself. We shall lose ourselves in Him, and become nothing, to find that in our impotence we have power and prevail.

Disciples of Jesus! Called to be like your Lord in His priestly intercession, when, O when! Shall we awaken to the glory, passing all conception, of this our destiny to plead and prevail with God for perishing men? O when shall we shake off the sloth that clothes itself with the pretense of humility, and yield ourselves wholly to God's Spirit, that He may fill our wills with light and with power, to know, and to take, and to possess all that our God is waiting to give to a will that lays hold on Him.

Day 41 Prayer

`LORD, TEACH US TO PRAY.'

O my Blessed High Priest, who am I that Thou shouldest thus invite me to share with Thee in Thy power of prevailing intercession! And why, O my Lord, am I so slow of heart to understand and believe and exercise this wonderful privilege to which Thou hast redeemed Thy people. O Lord, give Thy grace that this may increasingly be my unceasing life-work-in praying without ceasing to draw down the blessing of heaven on all my surroundings on earth.

Blessed Lord! I come now to accept this my calling. For this I would forsake all and follow Thee. Into Thy hands I would believingly yield my whole being: form, train, inspire me to be one of Thy prayer-legion, wrestlers who watch and strive in prayer, Israel's, God's princes, who have power and prevail. Take possession of my heart, and fill it with the one desire for the glory of God in the ingathering, and sanctification, and union of those whom the Father hath given Thee. Take my mind and let this be my study and my wisdom, to know when prayer can bring a blessing. Take me wholly and fit me as a priest ever to stand before God and to bless in His Name.

Blessed Lord! Be it here, as through all the spiritual life: Thou all, I nothing. And be it here my experience too that he that has and seeks nothing for himself, receives all, even to the wonderful grace of sharing with Thee in Thine everlasting ministry of intercession. Amen.

DAY 41
REFLECTION QUESTIONS

1. What ministry did Jesus' last prayer show that His disciples were to share in? _____
   _____

2. Who were the prayer-promises the Lord gave on his last night for? (Circle one)   our personal interests
   or   the Lord's kingdom interests

3. What are the three parts to Jesus's last prayer in John 17? 1._____
   2._____   3._____
   _____

4. Is your life following Christ's example of advancing God's kingdom and seeking to glorify the Lord?
   _____
   _____

5. What two things did Christ ask God to grant His disciples? 1._____
   _____ 2. _____

6. Who are some of the people in your circle of influence that you pray for? _____
   _____

7. Have you shared God's Word with them? _____

8. How often do you pray for unity between all believers? _____

9. What is my main takeaway from Day 41 that will improve my prayer life? _____
   _____
   _____

Fill in the blanks- _____ have not _____ me, but _____ have _____ you,
and _____ _____, that ye should go and _____ forth _____,
and that _____ fruit should _____: that _____ ye shall _____ of
the _____ in my name, he _____ give it _____. - John 15:16

Answers

1. His work of intercession

2. The Lord's kingdom interests

3. For Himself (John 17:1-5), for His disciples (v. 6-19), for all the believing people through all ages (v. 20-26)

4. Personal response

5. Keep them from the evil one, sanctify them through His Word

6. Personal response

7. Personal response

8. Personal response

9. Personal response

Class 6 Verse- *Ye have not chosen me, but I have chosen you, and ordained you, that ye should go and bring forth fruit, and that your fruit should remain: that whatsoever ye shall ask of the Father in my name, he may give it you. - John 15:16*

Day 41 Bible Reading - Luke 22; John 13

Day 41 notes

_____

_____

_____

_____

_____

_____

_____

_____

_____

_____

_____

_____

_____

DAY 42

FATHER, NOT WHAT I WILL OR, CHRIST THE SACRIFICE

'And He said, Abba, Father, all things are possible unto Thee; remove this cup from me: howbeit not what I will, but what Thou wilt.'-**Mark 14:36**

What a contrast within the space of a few hours! What a transition from the quiet elevation of that, He lifted up His eyes to heaven, and said, FATHER I WILL,' to that falling on the ground and crying in agony. `My Father! Not what I will.' In the one we see the High Priest within the veil in His all-prevailing intercession; in the other, the sacrifice on the altar opening the way through the rent veil. The high-priestly `Father! I will,' in order of time precedes the sacrificial `Father! Not what I will;' but this was only by anticipation, to show what the intercession would be when once the sacrifice was brought. In reality it was that prayer at the altar, `Father! Not what I will,' in which the prayer before the throne, `Father! I will,' had its origin and its power. It is from the entire surrender of His will in Gethsemane that the High Priest on the throne has the power to ask what He will, has the right to make His people share in that power too, and ask what they will.

For all who would learn to pray in the school of Jesus, this Gethsemane lesson is one of the most sacred and precious. To a superficial scholar it may appear to take away the courage to pray in faith. If even the earnest supplication of the Son was not heard, if even the Beloved had to say, `NOT WHAT I WILL!' how much more do we need to speak so. And thus it appears impossible that the promises which the Lord had given only a few hours previously, `WHATSOEVER YE SHALL ASK,' `WHATSOEVER YE WILL,' could have been meant literally. A deeper insight into the meaning of Gethsemane would teach us that we have just here the sure ground and the open way to the assurance of an answer to our prayer. Let us draw nigh in reverent and adoring wonder, to gaze on this great sight-God's Son thus offering up prayer and supplications with strong crying and tears, and not obtaining what He asks. He Himself is our Teacher, and will open up to us the mystery of His holy sacrifice, as revealed in this wondrous prayer.

To understand the prayer, let us note the infinite difference between what our Lord prayed a little ago as a Royal High Priest, and what He here supplicates in His weakness. *There* it was for the glorifying of the Father He prayed, and the glorifying of Himself and His people as the fulfilment of distinct promises that had been given Him. He asked what He knew to be according to the word and the will of the Father; He might boldly say, `FATHER! I WILL.' *Here* He prays for something in regard to which the Father's will is not yet clear to Him. As far as He knows, it is the Father's will that He should drink the cup. He had told His disciples of the cup He must drink: a little later He would again say, `The cup which my Father hath given me, shall I not drink it?' It was for this He had come to this earth. But when, in the unutterable agony of soul that burst upon him as the power of darkness came upon Him, and He began to taste the first drops of death as the wrath of God against sin, His human nature, as it shuddered in presence of the awful reality of being made a curse, gave utterance in this cry of anguish, to its desire that, if God's purpose could be accomplished without it, He might be spared the awful cup: `Let this cup pass from me.' That desire was the evidence of the intense reality of His humanity. The `Not as I will' kept that desire from being sinful: as He pleadingly cries, `All things are possible with Thee,' and returns again to still more earnest prayer that the cup may be removed, it

240

is His thrice-repeated `NOT WHAT I WILL' that constitutes the very essence and worth of His sacrifice. He had asked for something of which He could not say: I know it is Thy will. He had pleaded God's power and love, and had then withdrawn it in His final, `THY WILL BE DONE.' The prayer that the cup should pass away could not be answered; the prayer of submission that God's will be done was heard, and gloriously answered in His victory first over the fear, and then over the power of death.

It is in this denial of His will, this complete surrender of His will to the will of the Father, that Christ's obedience reached its highest perfection. It is from the sacrifice of the will in Gethsemane that the sacrifice of the life on Calvary derives its value. It is here, as Scripture saith, that He learned obedience, and became the author of everlasting salvation to all that obey Him. It was because He there, in that prayer, became obedient unto death, even the death of the cross, that God hath highly exalted Him, and given Him the power to ask what He will. It was in that `Father! Not what I will,' that He obtained the power for that other `FATHER! I will.' It was by Christ's submittal in Gethsemane to have not His will done, that He secured for His people the right to say to them, `Ask whatsoever ye will.'

Let me look at them again, the deep mysteries that Gethsemane offers to my view. There is the first: the Father offers His Well-beloved the cup, the cup of wrath. The second: the Son, always so obedient, shrinks back, and implores that He may not have to drink it. The third: the Father does not grant the Son His request, but still gives the cup. And then the last: the Son yields His will, is content that His will be not done, and goes out to Calvary to drink the cup. O Gethsemane! in thee I see how my Lord could give me such unlimited assurance of an answer to my prayers. As my surety He won it for me, by His consent to have His petition unanswered.

This is in harmony with the whole scheme of redemption. Our Lord always wins for us the opposite of what He suffered. He was bound that we might go free. He was made sin that we might become the righteousness of God. He died that we might live. He bore God's curse that God's blessing might be ours. He endured the not answering of His prayer, that our prayers might find an answer. Yea, He spake, `*Not as I will,'* that He might say to us, `If ye abide in me, *ask what ye will;* it shall be done unto you.'

Yes, `If ye abide in me;' here in Gethsemane the word acquires new force and depth. Christ is our Head, who as surety stands in our place, and bears what we must for ever have borne. We had deserved that God should turn a deaf ear to us, and never listen to our cry. Christ comes, and suffers this too for us: He suffers what we had merited; for our sins He suffers beneath the burden of that unanswered prayer. But now His suffering this avails for me: what He has borne is taken away for me; His merit has won for me the answer to every prayer, if I abide in Him.

Yes, in Him, as He bows there in Gethsemane, I must abide. As my Head, He not only once suffered for me, but ever lives in me, breathing and working His own disposition in me too. The Eternal Spirit, through which He offered Himself unto God, is the Spirit that dwells in me too, and makes me partaker of the very same obedience, and the sacrifice of the will unto God. That Spirit teaches me to yield my will entirely to the will of the Father, to give it up even unto the death, in Christ to be dead to it. Whatever is my own mind and thought and will, even though it be not directly sinful, He teaches me to fear and flee. He opens my ear to wait in great gentleness and teachableness of soul for what the Father has day by day to speak and to teach. He discovers to me how union with God's will in the love of it is union with God Himself; how entire surrender to God's will is the Father's claim, the Son's example, and the true blessedness of the soul. He leads my will into the fellowship of Christ's death and resurrection, my will dies in Him, in Him to be made alive again. He breathes into it, as a renewed and quickened will, a holy insight into God's perfect will, a holy joy in yielding itself to be an instrument of that will, a holy liberty and power to lay hold of God's will to answer prayer. With my whole will I learn to live for the interests of God and His kingdom, to exercise the power of that will-crucified but risen again-in nature and in prayer, on earth and in heaven, with men and with God. The more deeply I enter into the `FATHER! NOT WHAT I WILL' of Gethsemane, and into Him who spake it, to abide in Him, the fuller is my spiritual access into the power of His `FATHER! I WILL. And the soul experiences that it is the will, which has become nothing that God's will may be all, which now becomes inspired with a Divine strength to really will what God wills, and to claim what has been promised it in the name of Christ.

O let us listen to Christ in Gethsemane, as He calls, `If ye abide in me, ask whatsoever ye will, and it shall be done unto you.' Being of one mind and spirit with Him in His giving up everything to God's will, living like Him in obedience and surrender to the Father; this is abiding in Him; this is the secret of power in prayer.

Day 42 Prayer

`LORD, TEACH US TO PRAY.'

Blessed Lord Jesus! Gethsemane was Thy school, where Thou didst learn to pray and to obey. It is still Thy school, where Thou leadest all Thy disciples who would fain learn to obey and to pray even as Thou. Lord! teach me there to pray, in the faith that Thou has atoned for and conquered our self-will, and canst indeed give us grace to pray like Thee.

O Lamb of God! I would follow Thee to Gethsemane, there to become one with Thee, and to abide in Thee as Thou dost unto the very death yield Thy will unto the Father. With Thee, through Thee, in Thee, I do yield my will in absolute and entire surrender to the will of the Father. Conscious of my own weakness, and the secret power with which self-will would assert itself and again take its place on the throne, I claim in faith the power of Thy victory. Thou didst triumph over it and deliver me from it. In Thy death I would daily live; in Thy life I would daily die. Abiding in Thee, let my will, through the power of Thine eternal Spirit, only be the tuned instrument which yields to every touch of the will of my God. With my whole soul do I say with Thee and in Thee, `Father! Not as I will, but as Thou wilt.'

And then, Blessed Lord! Open my heart and that of all Thy people, to take in fully the glory of the truth, that a will given up to God is a will accepted of God to be used in his service, to desire, and purpose, and determine, and will what is according to God's will. A will which, in the power of the Holy Spirit the indwelling God, is to exercise its royal prerogative in prayer, to loose and to bind in heaven and upon earth, to ask whatsoever it will, and to say it shall be done.

O Lord Jesus, teach me to pray. Amen.

DAY 42
REFLECTION QUESTIONS

1. How did Christ's obedience reach its highest perfection? _____

2. What are the four steps Murray identified in the Gethsemane prayer?

    1. _____

    2. _____

    3. _____

    4. _____

3. Have you given up your will to God's Will? _____

4. Murray defines abiding in Christ as: _____
_____

5. What is my main takeaway from Day 42 that will improve my prayer life? _____
_____
_____

Fill in the blanks- _____ _____ not _____ me, but ___ _____
_____ you, and _____ _____, that ye should _____ and
_____ forth _____, and that _____ _____ should _____:
that _____ ye _____ _____ of _____ _____ in _____
name, he _____ give it _____. - John 15:16

Answers

1. He surrendered His will to the Fathers will

2. **First**: the Father offers His well-beloved the cup, the cup of wrath.

   Second: the Son, always so obedient, shrinks back, and implores that He may not have to drink.

   Third: the Father does not grant the Son His request, but still gives the cup.

   Fourth: the Son yields His will, is content that His will be not done, and goes out to Calvary to drink the cup.

3. Personal response

4. Being of one mind and spirit with God, giving up everything to God's will, living like Jesus in obedience and surrender to the Father

5. Personal response

Class 6 Verse- *Ye have not chosen me, but I have chosen you, and ordained you, that ye should go and bring forth fruit, and that your fruit should remain: that whatsoever ye shall ask of the Father in my name, he may give it you. - John 15:16*

Day 42 Bible Reading - John 14-17

Day 42 notes

_____

_____

_____

_____

_____

_____

_____

_____

_____

_____

_____

_____

CLASS 6

WEEK 7

Opening Prayer –Thank God for answering our prayers.

Word- Fruit, **Theme**- Faith & obedience lead to fruit bearing.

Key Questions-

1. How can we know if God's words are within our life? _____

2. Who does God offer the promise 'whatsoever ye ask' to? _____

3. The use of Jesus' name always supposes the _____ of our interests to Him whom we represent.

4. Explain the three stages of the Christian life. 1._____
    2._____ 3._____

5. Explain the three stages of the Christian prayer life. 1._____
    2._____ 3._____

6. What is the aim of all the prayer promises? _____

7. What are the three parts to Jesus' last prayer in John 17?   1._____
    2._____ 3._____

8. What are the four steps Murray identified in the Gethsemane prayer?

    1. _____

    2. _____

    3. _____

    4. _____

Testimonies- What is God doing through your prayer life?

Scripture Memory- Class 6 Verse- Verse- *Ye have not chosen me, but I have chosen you, and ordained you, that ye should go and bring forth fruit, and that your fruit should remain: that whatsoever ye shall ask of the Father in my name, he may give it you. - John 15:16*

Next Class Preview-

Word- Intersession, **Theme**- Believing and persistent prayer for His kingdom.

Prayer for Students- Time to Pray Each Day, A Desire for Prayer, A Clear Mind During Prayer, Show us God's Will

Class 6 Answers

1. Our life (words and actions) will reveal Christ

2. Fruit bearers

3. Surrender

4. New born child- forgiveness, Young man –fighting temptation and growing closer to God, Mature- in close communion with the Lord

5. Childlike stage- asking the Father for needs; Conflict stage- battling Satan and preserving in prayer; Friend stage- working for the advancement of the kingdom

6. Glory of God and salvation of sinners

7. For Himself (v. 1-5), for His disciples (v. 6-19), for all the believing people through all ages (v. 20-26)

8. **First**: the Father offers His well-beloved the cup, the cup of wrath. **Second**: the Son, always so obedient, shrinks back, and implores that He may not have to drink it. **Third**: the Father does not grant the Son His request, but still gives the cup. **Fourth:** the Son yields His will, is content that His will be not done, and goes out to Calvary to drink the cup

Class 6 notes

_____

_____

_____

_____

_____

_____

_____

_____

_____

_____

_____

_____

DAY 43

IF WE ASK ACCORDING TO HIS WILL OR, OUR BOLDNESS IN PRAYER

`And this is the boldness which we have toward Him, that, if we ask anything according to His will, He heareth us. And if we know that He hear us, whatsoever we ask, we know that we have the petitions which we have asked of Him.'-1 John 5:14-15*

One of the greatest hindrances to believing prayer is with many undoubtedly this: they know not if what they ask is according to the will of God. As long as they are in doubt on this point, they cannot have the boldness to ask in the assurance that they certainly shall receive. And they soon begin to think that, if once they have made known their requests, and receive no answer, it is best to leave it to God to do according to His good pleasure. The words of John, `If we ask anything *according to His will*, He heareth us,' as they understand them, make certainty as to answer to prayer impossible, because they cannot be sure of what really may be the will of God. They think of God's will as His hidden counsel-how should man be able to fathom what really may be the purpose of the all-wise God.

This is the very opposite of what John aimed at in writing thus. He wished to rouse us to boldness, to confidence, to full assurance of faith in prayer. He says, `*This is the boldness which we have toward Him,'* that we can say: Father! Thou knowest and I know that I ask according to Thy will: I know Thou hearest me. `This is the boldness, that if we ask anything according to His will, He heareth us.' On this account He adds at once: `If we know that He heareth us whatsoever we ask, we *know*,' through this faith, that we have,' that we now while we pray receive `the petition,' the special things, `we have asked of Him.' John supposes that when we pray, we first find out if our prayers are according to the will of God. They may be according to God's will, and yet not come at once, or without the persevering prayer of faith. It is to give us courage thus to persevere and to be strong in faith, that He tells us: This gives us boldness or confidence in prayer, if we ask anything according to His will, He heareth us. It is evident that if it be a matter of uncertainty to us whether our petitions be according to His will, we cannot have the comfort of what he says, `We know that we have the petitions which we have asked of Him.'

But just this is the difficulty. More than one believer says: `I do not know if what I desire be according to the will of God. God's will is the purpose of His infinite wisdom: it is impossible for me to know whether He may not count something else better for me than what I desire, or may not have some reasons for withholding what I ask.' Everyone feels how with such thoughts the prayer of faith, of which Jesus said, `Whosoever shall believe that *these things which he saith* shall come to pass, he shall have *whatsoever* he saith,' becomes an impossibility. There may be the prayer of submission, and of trust in God's wisdom; there cannot be the prayer of faith. The great mistake here is that God's children do not really believe that it is possible to know God's will. Or if they believe this, they do not take the time and trouble to find it out. What we need is to see clearly in what way it is that the Father leads His waiting, teachable child to know that his petition is according to His will. It is

247

through God's holy word, taken up and kept in the heart, the life, the will; and through God's Holy Spirit, accepted in His indwelling and leading, that we shall learn to know that our petitions are according to His will.

Through the word. There is a secret will of God, with which we often fear that our prayers may be at variance. It is not with this will of God, but His will as revealed in His word, that we have to do in prayer. Our notions of what the secret will may have decreed, and of how it might render the answers to our prayers impossible, are mostly very erroneous. Childlike faith as to what He is willing to do for His children, simply keeps to the Father's assurance, that it is His will to hear prayer and to do what faith in His word desires and accepts. In the word the Father has revealed, in general promises, the great principles of His will with His people. The child has to take the promise and apply it to the special circumstances in His life to which it has reference. Whatever he asks within the limits of that revealed will, he can know to be according to the will of God, and he may confidently expect. In His word, God has given us the revelation of His will and plans with us, with His people, and with the world, with the most precious promises of the grace and power with which through His people He will carry out His plans and do His work. As faith becomes strong and bold enough to claim the fulfilment of the general promise in the special case, we may have the assurance that our prayers are heard: they are according to God's will. Take the words of John in the verse following our text as an illustration: `If any man see his brother sinning a sin not unto death, he shall ask and *God will give him life*.' Such is the general promise; and the believer who pleads on the ground of this promise, prays according to the will of God, and John would give him boldness to know that he has the petition which he asks.

But this apprehension of God's will is something spiritual, and must be spiritually discerned. It is not as a matter of logic that we can argue it out: God has said it; I must have it. Nor has every Christian the same gift or calling. While the general will revealed in the promise is the same for all, there is for each one a special different will according to God's purpose. And herein is the wisdom of the saints, to know this special will of God for each of us, according to the measure of grace given us, and so to ask in prayer just what God has prepared and made possible for each. It is to communicate this wisdom *that the Holy Ghost dwells in us*. The personal application of the general promises of the word to our special personal needs-*it is for this that the leading of the Holy Spirit is given us.*

It is this union of the teaching of the word and Spirit that many do not understand, and so there is a twofold difficulty in knowing what God's will may be. Some seek the will of God in an inner feeling or conviction, and would have the Spirit lead them without the word. Others seek it in the word, without the living leading of the Holy Spirit. The two must be united: only in the word, only in the Spirit, but in these most surely, can we know the will of God, and learn to pray according to it. In the heart the word and the Spirit must meet: it is only by indwelling that we can experience their teaching. The word must dwell, must abide in us: heart and life must day by day be under its influence. Not from without, but from within, comes the quickening of the word by the Spirit. It is only he who yields himself entirely in his whole life to the supremacy of the word and the will of God, who can expect in special cases to discern what that word and will permit him boldly to ask. And even as with the word, just so with the Spirit: if I would have the leading of the Spirit in prayer to assure me what God's will is, my whole life must be yielded to that leading; so only can mind and heart become spiritual and capable of knowing God's holy will. It is he who, through word and Spirit, *lives in the will* of God by doing it, who will know to pray according to that will in the confidence that He hears us.

Would that Christians might see what incalculable harm they do themselves by the thought that because possibly their prayer is not according to God's will, they must be content without an answer. God's word tells us that the great reason of unanswered prayer is that we do not pray aright: `Ye ask and receive not, because ye ask amiss.' In not granting an answer, the Father tells us that there is something wrong in our praying. He wants to teach us to find it out and confess it, and so to educate us to true believing and prevailing prayer. He can only attain His object when He brings us to see that we are to blame for the withholding of the answer; our aim, or our faith, or our life is not what it should be. But this purpose of God is frustrated as long as we are content to say: It is perhaps because my prayer is not according to His will that He does not hear me. O let us no longer throw the blame of our unanswered prayers on the secret will of God, but on our praying amiss. Let that word, `Ye receive not because ye ask amiss,' be as the lantern of the Lord, searching heart and life to prove that we are indeed such as those to whom Christ gave His promises of certain answers. Let us believe that we *can know* if our prayer be according to God's will. Let us yield our heart to have the word of the Father dwell richly there, to have Christ's word abiding in us. Let us live day by day with the anointing which teacheth us all things. Let us yield ourselves unreservedly to the Holy Spirit as He teaches us to abide in Christ, to dwell in the Father's presence, and we shall soon understand how the Father's love longs that the child should know His will, and should, in the confidence that that will includes all that His power and love have promised to do, know too that He hears the petitions which we ask of Him. `*This is* the boldness which we have, that if we ask anything according to His will, He heareth us.'

୫୬୦୯୫ O let us no longer throw the blame of our unanswered prayers on the secret will of God, but on our praying amiss ୫୬୦୯୫

Day 43 Prayer

`LORD, TEACH US TO PRAY.'

Blessed Master! With my whole heart I thank Thee for this blessed lesson, that the path to a life full of answers to prayer is through the will of God. Lord! Teach me to know this blessed will by living it, loving it, and always doing it. So shall I learn to offer prayers according to that will, and to find in their harmony with God's blessed will, my boldness in prayer and my confidence in accepting the answer.

Father, *it is Thy will* that Thy child should enjoy Thy presence and blessing. *It is Thy will* that everything in the life of Thy child should be in accordance with Thy will, and that the Holy Spirit should work this in Him. *It is Thy will* that Thy child should live in the daily experience of distinct answers to prayer, so as to enjoy living and direct fellowship with Thyself. *It is Thy will* that Thy Name should be glorified in and through Thy children, and that it will be in those who trust Thee. O my Father! let this Thy will be my confidence in all I ask.

Blessed Savior! Teach me to believe in the glory of this will. That will is the eternal love, which with Divine power works out its purpose in each human will that yields itself to it. Lord! Teach me this. Thou canst make me see how every promise and every command of the word is indeed the will of God, and that its fulfilment is secured to me by God Himself. Let thus the will of God become to me the sure rock on which my prayer and my assurance of an answer ever rest. Amen.

NOTE.

There is often great confusion as to the will of God. People think that what God wills must inevitably take place. This is by no means the case. God wills a great deal of blessing to His people, which never comes to them. He wills it most earnestly, but they do not will it, and it cannot come to them. This is the great mystery of man's creation with a free will, and also of the renewal of his will in redemption, that God has made the execution of His will, in many things, dependent on the will of man. Of God's will revealed in His promises, so much will be fulfilled as our faith accepts. Prayer is the power by which that comes to pass which otherwise would not take place. And faith, the power by which it is decided how much of God's will shall be done in us. When once God reveals to a soul what He is willing to do for it, the responsibility for the execution of that will rests with us.

Some are afraid that this is putting too much power into the hands of man. But all power is put into the hands of man in Christ Jesus. The key of all prayer and all power is His, and when we learn to understand that He is just as much with us as with the Father, and that we are also just as much one with Him as He with the Father, we shall see how natural and right and safe it is that to those who abide in Him as He in the Father, such power should be given. It is Christ the Son who has the right to ask what He will: it is through the abiding in Him and His abiding in us (in a Divine reality of which we have too little apprehension) that His Spirit breathes in us what He wants to ask and obtain through us. We pray in His Name: the prayers are really ours and as really His.

Others again fear that to believe that prayer has such power is limiting the liberty and the love of God. O if we only knew how we are limiting His liberty and His love by not allowing Him to act in the only way in which He chooses to act, now that He has taken us up into fellowship with himself-through our prayers and our faith. A brother in the ministry once asked, as we were speaking on this subject, whether there was not a danger of our thinking that our love to souls and our willingness to see them blessed were to move God's love and God's willingness to bless them. We were just passing some large water-pipes, by which water was being carried over hill and dale from a large mountain stream to a town at some distance. Just look at these pipes, was the answer; they did not make the water willing to flow downwards from the hills, nor did they give it its power of blessing and refreshment: this is its very nature. All that they could do is to decide its direction: by it the inhabitants of the town said they want the blessing there. And just so, it is the very nature of God to love and to bless. Downward and ever downward His love longs to come with its quickening and refreshing streams. But He has left it to prayer to say where the blessing is to come. He has committed it to His believing people to bring the living water to the desert places: the will of God to bless is dependent upon the will of man to say where the blessing must descend. `Such honor have His saints.' `And this is *the boldness* which we have toward him that if we ask anything according to His will, He heareth us. And if *we know* that He hear us, whatsoever we ask, *we know that we have* the petitions which we have asked of Him.'

1See this illustrated in the extracts from George Muller at the end of this volume.

DAY 43
REFLECTION QUESTIONS

1. What is one of the great hindrances to believing prayer? _____
    _____

2. The promise in 1 John 5:14 should give us _____ in our prayers.

3. Is it possible for you to know God's Will? +_____

4. Have you taken to time and trouble to learn God's Will? _____

5. How can we know God's Will? _____
    _____

6. God's Word and the indwelling Holy Spirit must be _____ to fully
    understand God's Will for your life.

7. One reason the leading of the Holy Spirit was given to us is _____
    _____.

8. How often do you blame God's secret will on your unanswered prayers? _____
    _____

9. What is my main takeaway from Day 43 that will improve my prayer life? _____
    _____
    _____

Fill in the blanks- *And this is the _____ that we have in him, that, if we ask _____ thing according to his will, he heareth us: And if we know that he _____ us, whatsoever we ask, we know that we have the _____ that we desired of him. - 1 John 5:14-15*

Answers

1. We do not know if our request is according to God's Will

2. Boldness

3. Yes

4. Personal response

5. Through reading the Word, listening to the Holy Spirit

6. United

7. To communicate the personal application of the general promises of God's Word to our special personal needs

8. Personal response

9. Personal response

Class 7 Verse- *And this is the confidence that we have in him, that, if we ask any thing according to his will, he heareth us: And if we know that he hear us, whatsoever we ask, we know that we have the petitions that we desired of him. - 1 John 5:14-15*

Day 43 Bible Reading - Matthew 27; Mark 15

Day 43 notes

_____

_____

_____

_____

_____

_____

_____

_____

_____

_____

_____

_____

DAY 44

AN HOLY PRIESTHOOD OR, THE MINISTRY OF INTERCESSION

`An holy priesthood, to offer up spiritual sacrifices acceptable to God by Jesus Christ.'-**1st Peter 2:5**

`Ye shall be named the Priests of the Lord.'-**Isaiah 61:6**

The Spirit of the Lord God is upon me: because the Lord hath anointed me.' These are the words of Jesus in Isaiah. As the fruit of His work all redeemed ones are priests, fellow-partakers with Him of His anointing with the Spirit as High Priest. `Like the precious ointment upon the beard of Aaron, that went down to the skirts of his garments.' As every son of Aaron, so every member of Jesus' body has a right to the priesthood. But not everyone exercises it: many are still entirely ignorant of it. And yet it is the highest privilege of a child of God, the mark of greatest nearness and likeness to Him, `whoever liveth to pray.' Do you doubt if this really be so? Think of what constitutes priesthood. There is, first, the *work of the priesthood*. This has two sides, one Godward, the other manward. `Every priest is *ordained for men* in things *pertaining to God'* (Heb. 5:1); or, as it is said by Moses (Deut. 10:8, see also 11:5, 33:10; Mal. 2:6): `The Lord separated the tribe of Levi, *to stand before the Lord* to minister unto Him, and *to bless His Name.'* On the one hand, the priest had the power to draw nigh to God, to dwell with Him in His house, and to present before Him the blood of the sacrifice or the burning incense. This work he did not do, however, on his own behalf, but for the sake of the people whose representative he was. This is the other side of his work. He received from the people their sacrifices, presented them before God, and then came out to bless in His Name, to give the assurance of His favor and to teach them His law.

> **God's priests, who in conformity to Jesus, the Great High Priest, are to be the ministers and stewards of the grace of God to all around them.**

A priest is thus a man who does not at all live for himself. *He lives with God and for God.* His work is as God's servant to care for His house, His honor, and His worship, to make known to men His love and His will. *He lives with men and for men* (Heb. 5:2). His work is to find out their sin and need, and to bring it before God, to offer sacrifice and incense in their name, to obtain forgiveness and blessing for them, and then to come out and bless them in His Name. This is the high calling of every believer. `Such honor have all His saints.' They have been redeemed with the one purpose to be in the midst of the perishing millions around them, God's priests, who in conformity to Jesus, the Great High Priest, are to be the ministers and stewards of the grace of God to all around them.

And then there is *the walk of the priesthood*, in harmony with its work. As God is holy, so the priest was to be especially holy. This means not only separated from everything unclean, but *holy unto God*, being set apart and given up to God for His disposal. The separation from the world and setting apart unto God was indicated in many ways.

It was seen in the clothing: the holy garments, made after God's own order, marked them as His (Ex. 28). It was seen in the command as to their special purity and freedom from all contact from death and defilement (Lev. 11:22). Much that was allowed to an ordinary Israelite was forbidden to them. It was seen in the injunction that the priest must have no bodily defect or blemish; bodily perfection was to be the type of wholeness and holiness in God's service. And it was seen in the arrangement by which the priestly tribes were to have no inheritance with the other tribes; God was to be their inheritance. Their life was to be one of faith: set apart unto God, they were to live on Him as well as for Him.

All this is the emblem of what the character of the New Testament priest is to be. Our priestly power with God depends on our personal life and walk. We must be of them of whose walk on earth Jesus says, `They have not defiled their garments.'

The world needs, greatly needs, priests who will bear the burden of the perishing ones, and intercede on their behalf

In the surrender of what may appear lawful to others in our separation from the world, we must prove that our consecration to be holy to the Lord is whole-hearted and entire. The bodily perfection of the priest must have its counterpart in our too being `without spot or blemish;' `the man of God perfect, thoroughly furnished unto all good works,' `perfect and entire, wanting nothing' (Lev. 21:17-21; Eph. 5:27; 2 Tim. 2:7; Jas. 1:4). And above all, we consent to give up all inheritance on earth; to forsake all, and like Christ to have only God as our portion: to possess as not possessing, and hold all for God alone: this marks the true priest, the man who only lives for God and his fellow-men.

And now *the way to the priesthood*. In Aaron God had chosen all his sons to be priests: each of them was a priest by birth. And yet he could not enter upon his work without a special act of ordinance-his consecration. Every child of God is priest in light of his birth, his blood relationship to the Great High Priest; but this is not enough: he will exercise his power only as he accepts and realizes his consecration.

With Aaron and his sons it took place thus (Ex. 29): After being washed and clothed, they were anointed with the holy oil. Sacrifices were then offered, and with the blood the right ear, the right hand, and the right foot were touched. And then they and their garments were once again sprinkled with the blood and the oil together. And so it is as the child of God enters more fully into what THE BLOOD and THE SPIRIT of which he already is partaker, are to him, that the power of the Holy Priesthood will work in him. The blood will take away all sense of unworthiness; the Spirit, all sense of unfitness.

Let us notice what there was new in the application of the blood to the priest. If ever he had as a penitent brought a sacrifice for his sin, seeking forgiveness, the blood was sprinkled on the altar, but not on his person. But now, for priestly consecration, there was to be closer contact with the blood; ear and hand and foot were by a special act brought under its power, and the whole being taken possession of and sanctified for God. And so, when the believer, who had been content to think chiefly of the blood sprinkled on the mercy-seat as what he needs for pardon, is led to seek full priestly access to God, he feels the need of a fuller and more abiding experience of the power of the blood, as really sprinkling and cleansing the heart from an evil conscience, so that he has `no more conscience of sin' (Heb. 10:2) as cleansing from all sin. And it is as he gets to enjoy this, that the consciousness is awakened of his wonderful right of most intimate access to God, and of the full assurance that his intercessions are acceptable.

And as the blood gives the right, the Spirit gives the power, and fits for believing intercession. He breathes into us the priestly spirit-burning love for God's honor and the saving of souls. He makes us so one with Jesus that prayer in His Name is a reality. He strengthens us to believing, importunate prayer. The more the Christian is truly filled with the Spirit of Christ, the more spontaneous will be his giving himself up to the life of priestly intercession. Beloved fellow-Christians! God needs, greatly needs, priests who can draw near to Him, who live in His presence, and by their intercession draw down the blessings of His grace on others. And the world needs, greatly needs, priests who will bear the burden of the perishing ones, and intercede on their behalf.

Are you willing to offer yourself for this holy work? You know the surrender it demands-nothing less than the Christ-like giving up of all, that the saving purposes of God's love may be accomplished among men. Oh, be no longer of those who are content if they have salvation, and just do work enough to keep themselves warm and lively. O let nothing keep you back from giving yourselves to be wholly and only priests-nothing else, nothing less than the priests of the Most High God. The thought of unworthiness, of unfitness, need not keep you back. In *the Blood*, the objective power of the perfect redemption works in you: in *the Spirit* its full subjective personal experience as a divine life is secured. *The Blood* provides an infinite worthiness to make your prayers most acceptable: *The Spirit* provides a Divine fitness, teaching you to pray just according to the will of God. *Every priest knew that when he presented a sacrifice according to the law of the sanctuary, it was accepted:* under the covering of the Blood and Spirit you have the assurance that all the wonderful promises to prayer in the Name of Jesus will be fulfilled in you. Abiding in union with the Great High Priest, `you shall ask what you will, and it shall be done unto you.' You will have power to pray the effectual prayer of the righteous man that availeth much. You will not only join in the general prayer of the Church for the world, but be able in your own sphere to take up your special work in prayer-as priests, to transact it with God, to receive and know the answer, and so to bless in His Name. Come, brother, come, and be a priest, *only* priest, *all* priest. Seek now to walk before the Lord in the full consciousness that you have been set apart for the holy Ministry of Intercession. This is the true blessedness of conformity to the image of God's Son.

Day 44 Prayer

`LORD TEACH US TO PRAY.'

O Thou my blessed High Priest, accept the consecration in which my soul now would respond to Thy message.

I believe in the HOLY PRIESTHOOD OF THY SAINTS, and that I too am a priest, with power to appear before the Father, and in the prayer that avails much bring down blessing on the perishing around me.

I believe in the POWER OF THY PRECIOUS BLOOD to cleanse from all sin, to give me perfect confidence toward God, and bring me near in the full assurance of faith that my intercession will be heard.

I believe in the ANOINTING OF THE SPIRIT, coming down daily from Thee, my Great High Priest, to sanctify me, to fill me with the consciousness of my priestly calling, and with love to souls, to teach me what is according to God's will, and how to pray the prayer of faith.

I believe that, as Thou my Lord Jesus art Thyself in all things my life, so Thou, too, art THE SURETY FOR MY PRAYER-LIFE, and wilt Thyself draw me up into the fellowship of Thy wondrous work of intercession. In this faith I yield myself this day to my God, as one of His anointed priests, to stand before His face to intercede in behalf of sinners, and to come out and bless in His Name.

Holy Lord Jesus! accept and seal my consecration. Yea, Lord, do Thou lay Thy hands on me, and Thyself consecrate me to this Thy holy work. And let me walk among men with the consciousness and the character of a priest of the Most High God. Unto Him that loved us, and washed us from our sins IN HIS OWN BLOOD, AND HATH MADE US kings and priests unto God and His Father; TO HIM be glory and dominion forever and ever. Amen

DAY 44
REFLECTION QUESTIONS

1. What were the things included in a priest's work? _____
   _____
   _____

2. Our priestly power with God depends on our personal _____ and _____.

3. Can Jesus say of your walk on earth, `He has not defiled his garments?' _____
   _____

4. In our work as a Holy priest of God the _____ will take away all sense of
   unworthiness; the _____, all sense of unfitness.

5. Do you know anyone who lives as God's priest drawing near to Him, living in His presence, and by
   his or her intercession draws down the blessings of His grace on others?_____
   _____

6. Are you willing to offer yourself for this holy work? _____

7. What is my main takeaway from Day 44 that will improve my prayer life? _____
   _____
   _____

Fill in the blanks- *And this is the _____ that we have in _____, that, if we ask
_____ thing according to his _____, he heareth us: And if we know that he _____ us,
whatsoever we ask, we know that we _____ the _____ that we desired of him. - 1 John 5:14-15*

Answers

1. Care for God's house, God's honor, and God's worship, to make known to men God's love and God's will

2. Life, Walk

3. Personal response

4. Blood, spirit

5. Personal response

6. Personal response

Class 7 Verse - *And this is the confidence that we have in him that, if we ask any thing according to his will, he heareth us: And if we know that he hear us, whatsoever we ask, we know that we have the petitions that we desired of him. - 1 John 5:14-15*

Day 44 Bible Reading - Luke 23; John 18-19

Day 44 notes

_____

_____

_____

_____

_____

_____

_____

_____

_____

_____

_____

_____

_____

_____

_____

DAY 45

PRAY WITHOUT CEASING OR, A LIFE OF PRAYER

`Rejoice evermore. Pray without ceasing. In everything give thanks.'-1 Thessalonians 5:16-18*

Our Lord spake the parable of the widow and the unjust judge to teach us that men ought to pray always and not faint. As the widow persevered in seeking one definite thing, the parable appears to have reference to persevering prayer for someone blessing, when God delays or appears to refuse. The words in the Epistles, which speak of continuing instant in prayer, continuing in prayer and watching in the same, of praying always in the Spirit, appear more to refer to the whole life being one of prayer. As the soul is filling with the longing for the manifestation of God's glory to us and in us, through us and around us, and with the confidence that He hears the prayers of His children; the inmost life of the soul is continually rising upward in dependence and faith, in longing desire and trustful expectation.

At the close of our meditations it will not be difficult to say what is needed to live such a life of prayer. The first thing is undoubtedly the entire sacrifice of the life to God's kingdom and glory. He who seeks to pray without ceasing because he wants to be very pious and good, will never attain to it. It is the forgetting of self and yielding ourselves to live for God and His honor that enlarges the heart, that teaches us to regard everything in the light of God and His will, and that instinctively recognizes in everything around us the need of God's help and blessing, an opportunity for His being glorified. Because everything is weighed and tested by the one thing that fills the heart-the glory of God, and because the soul has learnt that only what is of God can really be to Him and His glory, the whole life becomes a looking up, a crying from the inmost heart, for God to prove His power and love and so show forth His glory. The believer awakes to the consciousness that he is one of the watchmen on Zion's walls, one of the Lord's remembrances, whose call does really touch and move the King in heaven to do what would otherwise not be done. He understands how real Paul's exhortation was, `praying always with all prayer and supplication in the Spirit for all the saints and for me,' and `continue in prayer, withal praying also for us.' To forget oneself, to live for God and His kingdom among men, is the way to learn to pray without ceasing.

> ℬℭ
>
> **He who seeks to pray without ceasing because he wants to be very pious and good, will never attain to it**
>
> ℬℭ

This life devoted to God must be accompanied by the deep confidence that our prayer is effectual. We have seen how our Blessed Lord insisted upon nothing so much in His prayer-lessons as faith in the Father as a God who most certainly does what we ask. `Ask and ye shall receive;' count confidently on an answer, is with Him the beginning and the end of His teaching (compare Matt. 7:8 and John 16:24). In proportion as this assurance masters us, and it becomes a settled thing that our prayers do tell and that God does what we ask, we dare not neglect the use of this wonderful power: the soul turns wholly to God, and our life becomes prayer. We see that the Lord needs and takes time, because we and all around us are the creatures of time, under the law of growth; but knowing that not one single prayer of faith can possibly be lost that there is sometimes a needs-be for the storing up and accumulating of prayer, that persevering prayer is irresistible, prayer becomes the quiet, persistent living of our life of desire and faith in the presence of our God. O do not let us any longer by our reasoning's limit and enfeeble such free and sure promises of the living God, robbing them of their power, and ourselves of the wonderful confidence they are meant to inspire. Not in God, not in His secret will, not in the limitations of His promises, but in us, in ourselves is the hindrance; we are not what we should be to obtain the promise. Let us open our whole heart to God's words of promise in all their simplicity and truth: they will search us and humble us; they will lift us up and make us glad and strong. And to the faith that knows it gets what it asks, prayer is not a work or a burden, but a joy and a triumph; it becomes a necessity and a second nature.

This union of strong desire and firm confidence again is nothing but the life of the Holy Spirit within us. The Holy Spirit dwells in us, hides Himself in the depths of our being, and stirs the desire after the Unseen and the Divine, after God Himself. Now in groaning's that cannot be uttered, then in clear and conscious assurance; now in special distinct petitions for the deeper revelation of Christ to ourselves, then in pleadings for a soul, a work, the Church or the world, it is always and alone the Holy Spirit who draws out the heart to thirst for God, to long for His being made known and glorified. Where the child of God really lives and walks in the Spirit, where he is not content to remain carnal, but seeks to be spiritual, in everything a fit organ for the Divine Spirit to reveal the life of Christ and Christ Himself, there the never-ceasing intercession-life of the Blessed Son cannot but reveal and repeat itself in our experience. Because it is the Spirit of Christ who prays in us, our prayer must be heard; because it is we who pray in the Spirit, there is need of time, and patience, and continual renewing of the prayer, until every obstacle be conquered, and the harmony between God's Spirit and ours is perfect.

But the chief thing we need for such a life of unceasing prayer is, to know that Jesus teaches us to pray. We have begun to understand a little what *His* teaching is. Not the communication of new thoughts or views, not the discovery of failure or error, not the stirring up of desire and faith, of however much importance all this be, but the taking us up into the fellowship of His own prayer-life before the Father-this it is by which Jesus really teaches. It was the sight of the praying Jesus that made the disciples long and ask to be taught to pray. It is the faith of the ever-praying Jesus, whose alone is the power to pray, that teaches us truly to pray. We know why: He who prays is our Head and our Life. All He has is ours and is given to us when we give ourselves all to Him. By His blood He leads us into the immediate presence of God. The inner sanctuary is our home, we dwell there. And He that lives so near God, and knows that He has been brought near to bless those who are far, cannot but pray. Christ makes us partakers with Himself of His prayer-power and prayer-life. We understand then that our true aim must not be to work much and have prayer enough to keep the work right, but to pray much and then to work enough for the power and blessing obtained in prayer to find its way through us to men. It is Christ who ever lives to pray, who saves and reigns. He communicates His prayer-life to us: He maintains it in us if we trust Him. He is surety for our praying without ceasing. Yes, Christ teaches to pray by showing how He does it, by doing it in us, by leading us to do it in Him and like Him. Christ is all, the life and the strength too for a never-ceasing prayer-life.

ॐ

The highest conformity to Christ, is that we take part in His work of intercession

ॐ

It is the sight of this, the sight of the ever-praying Christ as our life that enables us to pray without ceasing. Because His priesthood is the power of an endless life, that resurrection-life that never fades and never fails, and because His life is our life, praying without ceasing can become to us nothing less than the life-joy of heaven. So the Apostle says: `Rejoice *evermore;* pray *without ceasing;* in everything give thanks.' Borne up between the never-ceasing joy and the never-ceasing praise, never-ceasing prayer is the manifestation of the power of the eternal life, where Jesus always prays. The union between the Vine and the branch is in very deed a prayer-union. The highest conformity to Christ, the most blessed participation in the glory of His heavenly life, is that we take part in His work of intercession: He and we live ever to pray. In the experience of our union with Him, praying without ceasing becomes a possibility, a reality, and the holiest and most blessed part of our holy and blessed fellowship with God. We have our abode within the veil, in the presence of the Father. What the Father says, we do; what the Son says, the Father does. Praying without ceasing is the earthly manifestation of heaven come down to us, the foretaste of the life where they rest not day or night in the song of worship and adoration.

NOTE.

GEORGE MULLER, AND THE SECRET OF HIS POWER IN PRAYER

WHEN God wishes anew to teach His Church a truth that is not being understood or practiced, He mostly does so by raising some man to be in word and deed a living witness to its blessedness. And so God has raised up in this nineteenth century, among others, George Muller to be His witness that He is indeed the Hearer of prayer. I know of no way in which the principal truths of God's word in regard to prayer can be more effectually illustrated and established than a short review of his life and of what he tells of his prayer-experiences.

He was born in Prussia on 25th September 1805, and is thus now eighty years of age. His early life, even after having entered the University of Halle as a theological student, was wicked in the extreme. Led by a friend one evening, when just twenty years of age, to a prayer meeting, he was deeply impressed, and soon after brought to know the Savior. Not long after he began reading missionary papers, and in course of time offered himself to the London Society for promoting Christianity to the Jews. He was accepted as a student, but soon found that he could not in all things submit to the rules of the Society, as leaving too little liberty for the leading of the Holy Spirit. The connection was dissolved in 1830 by mutual consent, and he became the pastor of a small congregation at Teignmouth. In 1832 he was led to Bristol, and it was as pastor of Bethesda Chapel that he was led to the Orphan Home and other work, in connection with which God has so remarkably led him to trust His word and to experience how God fulfils that word.

A few extracts in regard to his spiritual life will prepare the way for what we specially wish to quote of his experiences in reference to prayer.

"In connection with this I would mention, that the Lord very graciously gave me, from the very commencement of my divine life, a measure of simplicity and of childlike disposition in spiritual things, so that whilst I was exceedingly ignorant of the Scriptures, and was still from time to time overcome even by outward sins, yet I was enabled to carry most minute matters to the *Lord in prayer*. And I have found "godliness profitable unto all things, having promise of the life that now is, and of that which is to come." Though very weak and ignorant, yet I had now, by the grace of God, some desire to benefit others, and he who so faithfully had once served Satan, sought now to win souls for Christ." [1]

It was at Teignmouth that he was led to know how to use God's Word, and to trust the Holy Spirit as the Teacher given by God to make that word clear. He writes:--

"God then began to show me that the word of God alone is our standard of judgment in spiritual things; that it can be explained only by the Holy Spirit; and that in our day, as well as in former times. He is the Teacher of His people. The office of the Holy Spirit I had not experimentally understood before that time.

It was my beginning to understand this latter point in particular, which had a great effect on me; for the Lord enabled me to put it to the test of experience, by laying aside commentaries, and almost every other book and

260

simply reading the word of God and studying it.

The result of this was, that the first evening that I shut myself into my room, to give myself to prayer and meditation over the Scriptures, I learned more in a few hours than I had done during a period of several months previously.

But the particular difference was that I received real strength for my soul in so doing. I now began to try by the test of the Scriptures the things which I had learned and seen, and found that only those principles which stood the test were of real value" 1

Of obedience to the word of God, he writes as follows, in connection with his being baptized: --

"It had pleased God, in His abundant mercy, to bring my mind into such a state, that I was willing to carry out into my life whatever I should find in the Scriptures. I could say, 'I will do His will,' and it was on that account, I believe, that I saw which *'doctrine is of God.'*-And I would observe here, by the way, that the passage to which I have just alluded (John 7:17) has been a most remarkable comment to me on many doctrines and precepts of our most holy faith. For instance: 'Resist not evil; but whosoever shall smite thee on thy right cheek, turn to him the other also. And if any man will sue thee at the law, and take away thy coat, let him have thy cloak also. And whosoever shall compel thee to go a mile, go with him twain. Give to him that asketh thee, and from him that would borrow of thee, turn not thou away. Love your enemies, bless them that curse you, do good to them that hate you, and pray for them which despitefully use you, and persecute you' (Matt. 5:39-44). 'Sell that ye have, and give alms'(Luke 12:33). "Owe no man anything, but to love one another"(Rom. 12:8). It may be said, 'Surely these passages cannot be taken literally, for how then would the people of God be able to pass through the world?' The state of mind enjoined in John 7:17 will cause such objections to vanish. WHOSOEVER IS WILLING TO ACT OUT these commandments of the Lord LITERALLY, will, I believe, be led with me to see that to take them LITERALLY is the will of God.-Those who do *so* take them will doubtless often be brought into difficulties, hard to the flesh to bear, but these will have a tendency to make them constantly feel that they are strangers and pilgrims here, that this world is not their home, and thus to throw them more upon God, who will assuredly help us through any difficulty into which we may be brought by seeking to act in obedience to His word." 1

This implicit surrender to God's word led him to certain views and conduct in regard to money, which mightily influenced his future life. They had their root in the conviction that money was a Divine stewardship, and that all money had therefore to be received and dispensed in direct fellowship with God Himself. This led him to the adoption of the following four great rules: 1. Not *to receive any fixed salary*, both because in the collecting of it there was often much that was at variance with the freewill offering with which God's service is to be maintained, and in the receiving of it a danger of placing more dependence on human sources of income than in the living God Himself. 2. *Never to ask any human being for help*, however great the need might be, but to make his wants known to the God who has promised to care for His servants and to hear their prayer. 3. To take this command (Luke 12:33) literally, `*Sell that thou hast and give alms,*' and never to save up money, but to spend all God entrusted to him on God's poor, on the work of His kingdom. 4. Also to take Rom. 13:8, `Owe no man anything,' literally, and never to buy on credit, or be in debt for anything, but to trust God to provide.

This mode of living was not easy at first. But Muller testifies it was most blessed in bringing the soul to rest in God, and drawing it into closer union with Himself when inclined to backslide. *"For it will not do, it is not possible, to live in sin, and at the same time, by communion with God, to draw down from heaven everything one needs for the life that now is."*

Not long after his settlement at Bristol, `THE SCRIPTURAL KNOWLEDGE INSTITUTION FOR HOME AND ABROAD' was established for aiding in Day, Sunday School, Mission and Bible work. Of this Institution the Orphan Homework, by which Mr. Muller is best known, became a branch. It was in 1834 that his heart was touched by the case of an orphan brought to Christ in one of the schools, but who had to go to a poorhouse where its spiritual wants would not be cared for. Meeting shortly after with a life of Franke, he writes (Nov, 20, 1835): "Today I have had it very much laid on my heart no longer merely to *think* about the establishment of an Orphan Home, but actually to set about it, and I have been very much in prayer respecting it, in order to ascertain the Lord's mind. May God make it plain." And again, Nov. 25: "I have been again much in prayer yesterday and today about the Orphan Home, and am more and more convinced that it is of God. May He in mercy guide me. The three chief reasons are-1. That God may be glorified, should He be pleased to furnish me with the means, in its being seen that it is not a vain thing to trust Him; and that thus the faith of His children may be strengthened. 2. The spiritual welfare of fatherless and motherless children. 3. Their temporal welfare." 1

After some months of prayer and waiting on God, a house was rented, with room for thirty children, and in course of time three more, containing in all 120 children. The work was carried on it this way for ten years, the supplies for the needs of the orphans being asked and received of God alone. It was often a time of sore need and much prayer, but a trial of faith more precious than of gold was found unto praise and honor and glory of God. The Lord was preparing His servant for greater things. By His providence and His Holy Spirit, Mr. Muller was led to desire, and to wait upon God till he received from Him, the sure promise of £15,000 for a Home to contain 300 children. This first Home was opened in 1849. In 1858, a second and third Home, for 950 more orphans, was opened, costing £35,000. And in 1869 and 1870, a fourth and a fifth Home, for 850 more, at an expense of £50,000, making the total number of the orphans 2100.

In addition to this work, God has given him almost as much as for the building of the Orphan Homes, and the maintenance of the orphans, for other work, the support of schools and missions, Bible and tract circulation. In all he has received from God, to be spent in His work, during these fifty years, more than one million pounds sterling. How little he knew, let us carefully notice, that when he gave up his little salary of £35 a year in obedience to the leading of God's word and the Holy Spirit, what God was preparing to give him as the reward of obedience and faith; and how wonderfully the word was to be fulfilled to him: `Thou hast been faithful over few things; I will set thee over many things.'

And these things have happened for an ensample to us. God calls us to be followers of George Muller, even as he is of Christ. His God is our God; the same promises are for us; the same service of love and faith in which he labored is calling for us on every side. Let us in connection with our lessons in the school of prayer study the way in which God gave George Muller such power as a man of prayer: we shall find in it the most remarkable illustration of some of the lessons which we have been studying with the blessed Master in the word. We shall specially have impressed upon us His first great lesson, that if we will come to Him in the way He has pointed out, with definite petitions, made known to us by the Spirit through the word as being according to the will of God, we may most confidently believe that whatsoever we ask it shall be done.

1 The extracts are from a work in four volumes, *The Lord's Dealings with George Muller.* J. Nisbet & Co., London

Day 45 Prayer

`LORD, TEACH US TO PRAY.'

O my Father, with my whole heart do I praise Thee for this wondrous life of never-ceasing prayer, never-ceasing fellowship, never-ceasing answers, and never-ceasing experience of my oneness with Him who ever lives to pray. O my God, keep me ever so dwelling and walking in the presence of Thy glory, that prayer may be the spontaneous expression of my life with Thee.

Blessed Savior, with my whole heart I praise Thee that Thou didst come from heaven to share with me in my needs and cries, that I might share with Thee in Thy all-prevailing intercession. And I thank Thee that Thou hast taken me into the school of prayer, to teach the blessedness and the power of a life that is all prayer. And most of all, that Thou hast taken me up into the fellowship of Thy life of intercession, that through me too Thy blessings may be dispensed to those around me.

Holy Spirit, with deep reverence I thank Thee for Thy work in me. It is through Thee I am lifted up into a share in the intercourse between the Son and the Father, and enter so into the fellowship of the life and love of the Holy Trinity Spirit of God, perfect Thy work in me; bring me into perfect union with Christ my Intercessor. Let Thine unceasing indwelling make my life one of unceasing intercession. And let so my life become one that is unceasingly to the glory of the Father and to the blessing of those around me. Amen.

DAY 45
REFLECTION QUESTIONS

1. Murray says the first thing needed to pray without ceasing is. _____
    _____.

2. To forget _____, to live for _____ and His kingdom among men, is the
    way to learn to pray without ceasing.

3. As our _____ that our prayers are _____ grows, so will our
    _____ to pray without ceasing.

4. And to those who believe God will grant what they ask, prayer is not a _____ or a
    _____, but a _____ and a _____; it becomes a necessity and a
    second nature.

5. Murray said the chief things we must understand for a life of unceasing prayer is. _____
    _____

6. What are your thoughts on George Muller's prayer life? _____
    _____

7. What is my main takeaway from Day 45 that will improve my prayer life? _____
    _____
    _____

Fill in the blanks- *And this is the _____ that we have in _____, that, if we ask
_____ thing _____ to his _____, he heareth us: And if we know that he
_____ us, whatsoever we ask, we know that we _____ the _____ that we
_____ of him. - 1 John 5:14-15*

Answers

1. The entire sacrifice of our life to God's kingdom and glory

2. Oneself, God

3. Faith, answered, ability

4. Work, burden, joy, triumph

5. That Jesus teaches us to pray and is an example of unceasing intercession

6. Personal response

7. Personal response

Class 7 Verse- *And this is the confidence that we have in him, that, if we ask any thing according to his will, he heareth us: And if we know that he hear us, whatsoever we ask, we know that we have the petitions that we desired of him. - 1 John 5:14-15*

Day 45 Bible Reading - Matthew 28; Mark 16

Day 45 notes

_____

_____

_____

_____

_____

_____

_____

_____

_____

_____

_____

_____

_____

_____

_____

_____

DAY 46

GEORGE MULLER ON PRAYER AND THE WILL OF GOD

One of the greatest difficulties with young believers is to know how they can find out whether what they desire is according to God's will. I count it one of the most precious lessons God wants to teach through the experience of George Muller, that He is willing to make known, of things of which His word says nothing directly, that they are His will for us, and that we may ask them. The teaching of the Spirit, not without or against the word, but as something above and beyond it, in addition to it, without which we cannot see God's will, is the heritage of every believer. It is through THE WORD, AND THE WORD ALONE, that the Spirit teaches, applying the general principles or promises to our special need. And it is THE SPIRIT, AND THE SPIRIT ALONE, who can really make the word a light on our path, whether the path of duty in our daily walk, or the path of faith in our approach to God. Let us try and notice in what childlike simplicity and teachableness it was that the discovery of God's will was so surely and so clearly made known to His servant.

With regard to the building of the first Home and the assurance he had of its being God's will, he writes in May 1850, just after it had been opened, speaking of the great difficulties there were, and how little likely it appeared to nature that they would be removed: "But while the prospect before me would have been overwhelming had I looked at it naturally, I was never even for once permitted to question how it would end. For as from the beginning I was sure *it was the will of God* that I should go to the work of building for Him this large Orphan Home, so also from the beginning I was as certain that the whole would be finished as if the Home had been already filled." [1]

It is through the WORD, and the WORD alone, that the Spirit teaches

The way in which he found out what was God's will, comes out with special clearness in his account of the building of the second Home; and I ask the reader to study with care the lesson the narrative conveys: --

Dec. 5, 1850.- "Under these circumstances I can only pray that the Lord in His tender mercy would not allow Satan to gain an advantage over me. By the grace of God my heart says: Lord, if I could be sure that it is Thy will that I should go forward in this matter, I would do so cheerfully; and, on the other hand, if I could be sure that these are vain, foolish, proud thoughts, that they are not from Thee, I would, by Thy grace, hate them, and entirely put them aside.

My hope is in God: He will help and teach me. Judging, however, from His former dealings with me, it would not be a strange thing to me, nor surprising, if He called me to labor yet still more largely in this way.

The thoughts about enlarging the Orphan work have not yet arisen on account of an abundance of money having lately come in; for I have had of late to wait for about seven weeks upon God, whilst little, very little comparatively, came in, *i.e.* about four times as much was going out as came in; and, had not the Lord previously sent me large sums, we should have been distressed indeed.

Lord! how can Thy servant know Thy will in this matter? Wilt Thou be pleased to teach him!"

December 11.- "During the last six days, since writing the above, I have been, day after day, waiting upon God concerning this matter. It has generally been more or less all the day on my heart. When I have been awake at night, it has not been far from my thoughts. Yet all this without the least excitement. I am perfectly calm and quiet respecting it. My soul would be rejoiced to go forward in this service, could I be sure that the Lord would have me to do so; for then, notwithstanding the numberless difficulties, all would be well; and His Name would be magnified.

On the other hand, were I assured that the Lord would have me to be satisfied with my present sphere of service, and that I should not pray about enlarging the work, by His grace I could, *without an effort*, cheerfully yield to it; for He has brought me into such a state of heart, that I only desire to please Him in this matter. Moreover, hitherto I have not spoken about this thing even to my beloved wife, the sharer of my joys, sorrows, and labors for more than twenty years; nor is it likely that I shall do so for some time to come: for I prefer quietly to wait on the Lord, without conversing on this subject, in order that thus I may be kept the more easily, by His blessing, from being influenced by things from without. The burden of my prayer concerning this matter is, that the Lord would not allow me to make a mistake, and that He would teach me to do His will."

December 26.- "Fifteen days have elapsed since I wrote the preceding paragraph. Every day since then I have continued to pray about this matter, and that with a goodly measure of earnestness, by the help of God. There has passed scarcely an hour during these days, in which, whilst awake, this matter has not been more or less before me. But all without even a shadow of excitement. I converse with no one about it. Hitherto have I not even done so with my dear wife. For this I refrain still, and deal with God alone about the matter, in order that no outward influence and no outward excitement may keep me from attaining unto *a clear discovery of His will. I have the fullest and most peaceful assurance that He will clearly show me His will.* This evening I have had again an especial solemn season for prayer, to seek to know the will of God. But whilst I continue to entreat and beseech the Lord, that He would not allow me to be deluded in this business, I may say I have scarcely any doubt remaining on my mind as to what will be the issue, even that I should go forward in this matter. As this, however, is one of the most momentous steps that I have ever taken, I judge that I cannot go about this matter with too much caution, prayerfulness, and deliberation. I am in no hurry about it. I could wait for years, by God's grace, were this His will, before even taking one single step toward this thing, or even speaking to anyone about it; and, on the other hand, I would set to work tomorrow, were the Lord to bid me do so. This calmness of mind, this having no will of my own in the matter, this only wishing to please my Heavenly Father in it, this only seeking His and not my honor in it; this state of heart, I say, is the fullest assurance to me that my heart is not under a fleshly excitement, and that, if I am helped thus to go on, *I shall know the will of God to the full.* But, while I write this, I cannot but add at the same time, that I do crave the honor and the glorious privilege to be more and more used by the Lord.

I desire to be allowed to provide scriptural instruction for a thousand orphans, instead of doing so for 300. I desire to expound the Holy Scriptures regularly to a thousand orphans, instead of doing so to 300. I desire that it may be yet more abundantly manifest that God is still the Hearer and Answerer of prayer, and that He is the living God now as He ever was and ever will be, when He shall simply, in answer to prayer, have condescended to provide me with a house for 700 orphans and with means to support them. This last consideration is the most important point in my mind. The Lord's honor is the principal point with me in this whole matter; and just because this is the case, if He would be more glorified by not going forward in this business, I should by His grace be perfectly content to give up all thoughts about another Orphan House. Surely in such a state of mind, obtained by the Holy Spirit, Thou, O my Heavenly Father, *wilt not suffer Thy child to be mistaken, much less deluded.* By the help of God I shall continue further day by day to wait upon Him in prayer, concerning this thing, till He shall bid me act."

Jan. 2, 1851.- "A week ago I wrote the preceding paragraph. During this week I have still been helped day by day, and more than once every day, to seek the guidance of the Lord about another Orphan House. The burden of my prayer has still been, that He in His great mercy would keep me from making a mistake. During the last week the book of Proverbs has come in the course of my Scripture reading, and my heart has been refreshed in reference to this subject by the following passages: "Trust in the Lord with all thine heart; and lean not unto thine own understanding. In all thy ways acknowledge Him, and He shall direct thy paths" (Prov. 3:5-6). By the grace of God I do acknowledge the Lord in all my ways, and in this thing in particular; I have therefore the comfortable assurance that He will direct my paths concerning this part of my service, as to whether I shall be occupied in it or not. Further: "The integrity of the upright shall preserve them" (Prov. 11:3). By the grace of God I am upright in this business. My honest purpose is to get glory to God. Therefore I expect to be guided aright. Further: "Commit thy works unto the Lord, and thy thoughts shall be established" (Prov. 16:3). I do commit my works unto the Lord, and therefore expect that my thoughts will be established. My heart is more and more coming to a calm, quiet, and settled assurance that the Lord will condescend to use me still further in the orphan work. Here Lord is Thy servant." [1]

When later he decided to build two additional houses, Nos. 4 and 5, he writes thus again: --

"Twelve days have passed away since I wrote the last paragraph. I have still day by day been enabled to wait upon the Lord with reference to enlarging the Orphan work, and have been during the whole of this period also in perfect peace, which is the result of seeking in this thing only the Lord's honor and the temporal and spiritual benefit of my fellow-men. Without an effort could I by His grace put aside all thoughts about this whole affair, if only assured that it is the will of God that I should do so; and, on the other hand, would at once go forward, if He would have it be so. I have still kept this matter entirely to myself. Though it be now about seven weeks, since day by day, more or less, my mind has been exercised about it, and since I have been daily praying about it, yet not one human being knows of it. As yet I have not even mentioned it to my dear wife in order that thus, by quietly waiting upon God, I might not be influenced by what might be said to me on the subject. This evening has been particularly set apart for prayer, beseeching the Lord once more not to allow me to be mistaken in this thing, and much less to be deluded by the devil. I have also sought to let all the reasons *against* building another Orphan House, and all the reasons *for* doing so pass before my mind: and now for the clearness and definiteness, write them down. . . .

Much, however, as the nine previous reasons weigh with me, yet they would not decide me were there not one more. It is this. After having for months pondered the matter, and having looked at it in all its bearings and with all its difficulties, and then having been finally led, after much prayer, to decide on this enlargement, my mind is at peace. The child who has again and again besought His Heavenly Father not to allow him to be deluded, nor even to make a mistake, is at peace, perfectly at peace concerning this decision; and has thus the assurance that the decision come to, after much prayer during weeks and months, is the leading of the Holy Spirit; and therefore purposes to go forward, assuredly believing that he will not be confounded, for he trusts in God. Many and great may be his difficulties; thousands and ten thousands of prayers may have ascended to God, before the full answer may be obtained; much exercise of faith and patience may be required; but in the end it will again be seen, that His servant, who trusts in Him, has not been confounded." [1]

[1] The extracts are from a work in four volumes, *The Lord's Dealings with George Muller*. J. Nisbet & Co., London.

DAY 46
REFLECTION QUESTIONS

1. What is the only way we can know God's will for our lives? _____

   _____

2. Why did George Muller not ask his wife about expanding the orphanage? _____

   _____

3. What did Muller say was the principle point for him in the matter of expanding the orphanage house?

   _____

4. How did Muller incorporate the scripture into his prayers? _____

   _____

5. Have you ever set aside a whole evening for prayer about God's will for a need or direction in your

   life? _____

6. When you are seeking God's will about major decisions in your life how long do you pray to God?

   _____

7. What is my main takeaway from Day 46 that will improve my prayer life? _____

   _____

   _____

Fill in the blanks- *And this is the _____ that we have in _____, that, ____ we ask _____ thing _____ to his _____, he heareth us: And _____ we know that he _____ us, whatsoever we _____, we know that we _____ the _____ that we _____ of him. - 1 John 5:14-15*

Answers

1. Reading the Word of God, as the Spirit teaches, applying the general principles or promises of the Bible to our special need

2. He wanted no outward influence on his decision

3. God's glory

4. He claimed God's promises and examined his life to ensure he was fulfilling the conditions

5. Personal response

6. Personal response

7. Personal response

Class 7 Verse- *And this is the confidence that we have in him, that, if we ask any thing according to his will, he heareth us: And if we know that he hear us, whatsoever we ask, we know that we have the petitions that we desired of him. - 1 John 5:14-15*

Day 46 Bible Reading - Luke 24; John 20-21

Day 46 notes

_____

_____

_____

_____

_____

_____

_____

_____

_____

_____

_____

_____

DAY 47

GEORGE MULLER ON PRAYER AND THE GLORY OF GOD

We have sought more than once to enforce the truth, that while we ordinarily seek the reasons of our prayers not being heard in the thing we ask not being according to the will of God, Scripture warns us to find the cause in ourselves, in our not being in the right state or not asking in the right spirit. The thing may be in full accordance with His will, but the asking, the spirit of the supplicant, not; then we are not heard. As the great root of all sin is self and self-seeking, so there is nothing that even in our more spiritual desires so effectually hinders God in answering as this: we pray for our own pleasure or glory. Prayer to have power and prevail must ask for the glory of God; and he can only do this as he is living for God's glory.

In George Muller we have one of the most remarkable instances on record of God's Holy Spirit leading a man deliberately and systematically, at the outset of a course of prayer, to make the glorifying of God his first and only object. Let us ponder well what he says, and learn the lesson God would teach us through him:--

"I had constantly cases brought before me, which proved that one of the especial things which the children of God needed in our day, was *to have their faith strengthened.*

I longed, therefore, to have something to point my brethren to, as a visible proof that our God and Father is the same faithful God as ever He was; as willing as ever to PROVE Himself to be the LIVING GOD in our day as formerly, *to all who put their trust in Him.*

My spirit longed to be instrumental in strengthening their faith, by giving them not only instances from the word of God, of His willingness and ability to help all who rely upon Him, but to *show* them *by proofs* that He is the same in our day. I knew that the word of God ought to be enough, and it was by grace enough for me; but still I considered I ought to lend a helping hand to my brethren.

I therefore judged myself bound to be the servant of the Church of Christ, in the particular point in which I had obtained mercy; namely, in being able to take God at His word and rely upon it. The first object of the work was, and is still: *that God might be magnified* by the fact that the orphans under my care are provided with all they need, *only by prayer and faith,* without any one being asked; thereby it may be seen that God is FAITHFUL STILL, AND HEARS PRAYER STILL.

ॐ)ⱌ

The great root of all sin is self and self-seeking,

ॐ)ⱌ

I have again these last days prayed much about the Orphan House, and have frequently examined my heart; that if it were at all my desire to establish it for the sake of gratifying myself, I might find it out. For as I desire only the Lord's glory, I shall be glad to be instructed by the instrumentality of my brother, if the matter be not of Him.

When I began the Orphan work in 1835, my chief object was the glory of God, by giving a practical demonstration as to what could be accomplished simply through the instrumentality of prayer and faith, in order thus to benefit the Church at large, and to lead a careless world to see the reality of the things of God, by showing them in this work, that the living God is still, as 4000 years ago, the living God. This my aim has been abundantly honored. Multitudes of sinners have been thus converted, multitudes of the children of God in all parts of the world have been benefited by this work, even as I had anticipated. But the larger the work as grown, the greater has been the blessing, bestowed in the very way in which I looked for blessing: for the attention of hundreds of thousands has been drawn to the work; and many tens of thousands have come to see it. All this leads me to desire further and further to labor on in this way, in order to bring yet greater glory to the Name of the Lord. *That He may be looked at, magnified, admired, trusted in,* relied on at all times, is my aim in this service; and so particularly in this intended enlargement. That it may be seen how much one poor man, simply by trusting in God, can bring about by prayer; and that thus other children of God may be led to carry on the work of God in dependence upon Him; and that children of God may be led increasingly to trust in Him in their individual positions and circumstances, therefore I am led to this further enlargement."[1]

[1] The extracts are from a work in four volumes, *The Lord's Dealings with George Muller.* J. Nisbet & Co., London.

DAY 47
REFLECTION QUESTIONS

1. We tend to blame unanswered prayers on not being God's will, but Murray says scripture warns us to find the cause _____.

2. What is the main thing that hinders God in answering our prayers? _____
_____

3. Muller believed one of the key things Christians needed was. _____
_____

4. How often do you examine your heart and ask God to show you if your prayers are seeking your own glory? _____

5. What is my main takeaway from Day 47 that will improve my prayer life? _____
_____

_____

Fill in the blanks- *And this is the _____ that we have in _____, that, _____ we ask _____ thing _____ to his _____, he heareth us: And _____ we _____ that he _____ us, whatsoever we _____, we _____ that we _____ the _____ that we _____ of him. - 1 John 5:14-15*

Answers

1. In ourselves, in our not being in the right state or not asking in the right spirit

2. We pray for our own pleasure or glory

3. To have their faith strengthened

4. Personal response

5. Personal response

Class 7 Verse- *And this is the confidence that we have in him, that, if we ask any thing according to his will, he heareth us: And if we know that he hear us, whatsoever we ask, we know that we have the petitions that we desired of him. - 1 John 5:14-15*

Day 47 Bible Reading - Acts 1-3

Day 47 notes

_____

_____

_____

_____

_____

_____

_____

_____

_____

_____

_____

_____

_____

_____

_____

_____

DAY 48

GEORGE MULLER ON PRAYER AND TRUST IN GOD

There are other points on which I would be glad to point out what is to be found in Mr. Muller's narrative, but one more must suffice. It is the lesson of firm and unwavering trust in God's promise as the secret of persevering prayer. If once we have, in submission to the teaching of the Spirit in the word, taken hold of God's promise, and believed that the Father has heard us, we must not allow ourselves by any delay or unfavorable appearances be shaken in our faith.

"The full answer to my daily prayers was far from being realized; yet there was abundant encouragement granted by the Lord, to continue in prayer. But suppose, even, that far less had come in than was received, still, after having come to the conclusion, upon scriptural grounds, after much prayer and self-examination, I ought to have gone on without wavering, in the exercise of faith and patience concerning this object; and thus all the children of God, when once satisfied that anything which they bring before God in prayer, is according to His will, ought to continue in believing, expecting, persevering prayer until the blessing is granted. Thus am I myself now waiting upon God for certain blessings, for which I have daily besought Him for ten years and six months without one day's intermission. Still the full answer is not yet given concerning the conversion of certain individuals, though in the meantime I have received many thousands of answers to prayer. I have also prayed daily without intermission for the conversion of other individuals about ten years, for others six or seven years, for others from three or two years; and still the answer is not yet granted concerning those persons, while in the meantime many thousands of my prayers have been answered, and also souls converted, for whom I had been praying. I lay particular stress on this for the benefit of those who may suppose that I need only to ask of God, and receive at once; or that I might pray concerning anything, and the answer would surely come. One can only expect to obtain answers to prayers which are according to the mind of God; and even then, patience and faith may be exercised for many years, even as mine are exercised, in the matter to which I have referred; and yet am I daily continuing in prayer, and expecting the answer, and so surely expecting the answer, that I have often thanked God that He will surely give it, though now for nineteen years faith and patience have thus been exercised. Be encouraged, dear Christians, with fresh earnestness to give yourselves to prayer, if you can only be sure that you ask things which are for the glory of God.

Be slow to take new steps in the Lord's service, or in your business, or in your family's decisions

But the most remarkable point is this, that 6 pounds, 6 shillings and 6 pence from Scotland supplied me, as far as can be known now, with all the means necessary for fitting up and promoting the New Orphan Houses. Six years and eight months I have been day by day, and generally several times daily, asking the Lord to give me the needed means for this enlargement of the Orphan work, which, according to calculations made in the spring of 1861, appeared to be about fifty thousand pounds: the total of this amount I had now received. I praise and magnify the Lord for putting this enlargement of the work into my heart, and for giving me courage and faith for it; and above all, for sustaining my faith day by day without wavering. When the last portion of the money was received, I was no more assured concerning the whole, that I was at the time I had not received one single donation towards this large sum. I was at the beginning, after once having ascertained His mind, through most patient and heart-searching waiting upon God, as fully assured that He would bring it about, as if the two houses, with their hundreds of orphans occupying them, had been already before me. I make a few remarks here for the sake of young believers in connection with this subject: 1. Be slow to take new steps in the Lord's service, or in your business, or in your families: weigh everything well; weigh all in the light of the Holy Scriptures and in the fear of God. 2. Seek to have no will of your own, in order to ascertain the mind of God, regarding any steps you propose taking, so that you can honestly say you are willing to do the will of God, if He will only please to instruct you. 3. But when you have found out what the will of God is, seek for His help, and seek it earnestly, perseveringly, patiently, believingly, expectantly; and you will surely in His own time and way obtain it.

To suppose that we have difficulty about money only would be a mistake: there occur hundreds of other wants and of other difficulties. It is a rare thing that a day occurs without some difficulty or some want; but often there are many difficulties and many wants to be met and overcome the same day. All these are met by prayer and faith, our universal remedy; and we have never been confounded. Patient, persevering, believing prayer, offered up to God, in the Name of the Lord Jesus, has always, sooner or later, brought the blessing. I do not despair, by God's grace, of obtaining any blessing, provided I can be sure it would be for any real good, and for the glory of God."[1]

[1] The extracts are from a work in four volumes, *The Lord's Dealings with George Muller.* J. Nisbet & Co., London.

DAY 48
REFLECTION QUESTIONS

1. What did George Muller do to ensure his prayer was God's will? _____
    _____

2. Once you are confident you are praying according to God's will, when should you stop?
    _____

3. Muller gave three suggestions to praying Christians 1._____
    2._____3._____

4. Which of these three do you believe prevents your prayers from being answered? _____
    _____

5. The answer to our daily difficulties and wants is _____.

6. What is my main takeaway from Day 48 that will improve my prayer life? _____
    _____
    _____

Fill in the blanks- *And this is the _____ that we _____ in _____, that, _____
we ask _____ thing _____ to his _____, he _____ us: And _____ we
_____ that he _____ us, whatsoever we _____, we _____ that we _____
the _____ that we _____ of _____. - 1 John 5:14-15*

Answers

1. Searched scripture, prayed, self-examination
2. Not until He answers
3. 1. Move slow in making plans, 2. Have no will of your own, 3. Earnestly and expectantly seek God's help
4. Personal response
5. Prayer and faith
6. Personal response

Class 7 Verse- *And this is the confidence that we have in him, that, if we ask any thing according to his will, he heareth us: And if we know that he hear us, whatsoever we ask, we know that we have the petitions that we desired of him. - 1 John 5:14-15*

Day 48 Bible Reading - Acts 4-6

Day 48 notes

_____

_____

_____

_____

_____

_____

_____

_____

_____

_____

_____

_____

_____

_____

DAY 49

GEORGE MULLER ON PRAYER AND THE WORD OF GOD

𝖂e have more than once seen that God's listening to our voice depends upon our listening to His voice. (See Days 36 and 37.) We must not only have a special promise to plead, when we make a special request, but our whole life must be under the supremacy of the word: the word must be dwelling in us. The testimony of George Muller on this point is most instructive. He tells us how the discovery of the true place of the word of God, and the teaching of the Spirit with it, was the commencement of a new era in his spiritual life. Of it he writes:--

"Now the scriptural way of reasoning would have been: God Himself has condescended to become an author, and I am ignorant about that precious book which His Holy Spirit has caused to be written through the instrumentality of His servants, and it contains that which I ought to know, and the knowledge of which will lead me to true happiness; therefore I ought to read again and again this most precious book, this book of books, most earnestly, most prayerfully, and with much meditation; and in this practice I ought to continue all the days of my life. For I was aware, though I read it but little, that I knew scarcely anything of it. But instead of acting thus and being led by my ignorance of the word of God to study it more, my difficulty in understanding it, and the little enjoyment I had in it, made me careless of reading it (for much prayerful reading of the word gives not merely more knowledge, but increases the delight we have in reading it); and thus, like many believers, I practically preferred, for the first four years of my divine life, the works of uninspired men to the oracles of the living God. The consequence was that I remained a babe, both in knowledge and grace. In knowledge, I say; for all *true* knowledge must be derived, by the Spirit, from the word. And as I neglected the word, I was for nearly four years so ignorant, that I did not *clearly* know even the *fundamental* points of our holy faith. And this lack of knowledge most sadly kept me back from walking steadily in the ways of God. For when it pleased the Lord in August 1829 to bring me really to the Scriptures, my life and walk became very different. And though ever since that I have very much fallen short of what I might and ought to be, yet by the grace of God I have been enabled to live much nearer to Him than before. If any believers read this who practically prefer other books to the Holy Scriptures, and who enjoy the writings of men much more than the word of God, may they be warned by my loss. I shall consider this book to have been the means of doing much good, should it please the Lord, through its instrumentality, to lead some of His people no longer to neglect the Holy Scriptures, but to give them that preference which they have hitherto bestowed on the writings of men.

Before I leave this subject, I would only add: If the reader understands very little of the word of God, he ought to read it very much; for the Spirit explains the word by the word. And if he enjoys the reading of the word little, that is just the reason why he should read it much; for the frequent reading of the Scriptures creates a delight in them, so that the more we read them, the more we desire to do so.

ॐ ॐ

Therefore I ought to read again and again this most precious book, this book of books, most earnestly, most prayerfully, and with much meditation

ॐ ॐ

Above all, he should seek to have it settled in his own mind that God alone by His Spirit can teach him, and that therefore, as God will be inquired of for blessings, it becomes him to seek God's blessing previous to reading, and also whilst reading.

He should have it, moreover, settled in his mind that although the Holy Spirit is the *best* and *sufficient* Teacher, yet that this Teacher does not always teach immediately *when* we desire it, and that therefore we may have to entreat Him again and again for the explanation of certain passages; but that He will surely teach us at last, if indeed we are seeking for light prayerfully, patiently, and with a view to the glory of God."[1]

We find in his journal frequent mention made of his spending two and three hours in prayer over the word for the feeding of his spiritual life. As the fruit of this, when he had need of strength and encouragement in prayer, the individual promises were not to him so many arguments from a book to be used with God, but living words which he had heard the Father's living voice speak to him, and which he could now bring to the Father in living faith.

[1] The extracts are from a work in four volumes, *The Lord's Dealings with George Muller.* J. Nisbet & Co., London.

DAY 49
REFLECTION QUESTIONS

1. God listens to our voice when we _____.

2. How often do you read God's Word? _____

3. Do you pray and meditate on the scripture when you read it? _____

4. Do you spend more time reading Christian books than the Bible? _____

5. Who is our teacher as we read God's Word? _____

6. What is my main takeaway from Day 49 that will improve my prayer life? _____

_____

_____

Fill in the blanks- Fill in the blanks- *And _____ is the _____ that we _____ in _____, that, _____ we ask _____ thing _____ to his _____, he _____ us: And _____ we _____ that he _____ us, _____ we _____, we _____ that we _____ the _____ that we _____ of _____. - 1 John 5:14-15*

Answers

1. We listen to God's voice
2. Personal response
3. Personal response
4. Personal response
5. Holy Spirit
6. Personal response

Class 7 Verse- *And this is the confidence that we have in him, that, if we ask any thing according to his will, he heareth us: And if we know that he hear us, whatsoever we ask, we know that we have the petitions that we desired of him.* - *1 John 5:14-15*

Day 49 Bible Reading - Acts 7-8

Day 49 notes

_____

_____

_____

_____

_____

_____

_____

_____

_____

_____

_____

_____

_____

_____

CLASS 7

WEEK 8

Opening Prayer –Thank God for answering our prayers.

Word- Intercession, **Theme**- Believing and persistent prayer for His kingdom

Key Questions-

1. How can we know God's Will? _____

2. In our work as a holy priest of God the _____ will take away all sense of unworthiness; the _____, all sense of unfitness.

3. As our _____ that our prayers are _____ grows, so will our _____ to pray without ceasing.

4. How did Muller incorporate the scripture into his prayers? _____ _____

5. We tend to blame unanswered prayers on not being God's will, but Murray says scripture warns us to find the cause _____

6. What is the main thing that hinders God in answering our prayers? _____ _____

7. What did George Muller do to ensure his prayer was God's will? _____ _____, _____

8. Muller gave three suggestions to praying Christians 1. _____ 2._____ 3._____

9. Who is our teacher as we read God's Word? _____

Testimonies- What is God doing through your prayer life?

Class 7 Verse- *And this is the confidence that we have in him, that, if we ask any thing according to his will, he heareth us: And if we know that he hear us, whatsoever we ask, we know that we have the petitions that we desired of him. - 1 John 5:14-15*

Next Class Preview-

Students should review their takeaways from all 49 days and prepare their testimony of their answered prayers and how this study helped them.

Class 7 Answers

1. Through reading the Word, listening to the Holy Spirit

2. Blood, spirit

3. Faith, answered, ability

4. Reminded God of His promises

5. In ourselves, in our not being in the right state or not asking in the right spirit

6. We pray for our own personal glory

7. Searched scripture, prayed, self-examination

8. 1. Move slow in making plans, 2. Have no will of your own, 3. Earnestly and expectantly seek God's help

9. Holy Spirit

Class 7 notes

_____

_____

_____

_____

_____

_____

_____

_____

_____

_____

_____

_____

_____

_____

_____

_____

FURTHER STUDY

Below is a list of resources to help any believer learn more about prayer. Of course, reading the gospels as you ask the Holy Spirit to teach you is always the best way to join Christ in His work of intercessory prayer.

1. *"The Complete Works of E. M. Bounds On Prayer"* by E.M. Bounds
2. *"The Power of Prayer in a Believer's Life"* by Charles Spurgeon
3. *"Developing a Healthy Prayer Life"* by James & Joel Beeke
4. *"How to Pray"* by Dr. Ronnie Floyd
5. *"The Power of Prayer and Fasting"* by Dr. Ronnie Floyd
6. *"Answers to Prayer From George Muller's Narratives"* by George Muller
7. *"The Autobiography of George Muller"* by George Muller
8. *"Release the Power to Prayer"* by George Muller
9. *"The Practice of the Presence of God"* by Brother Lawrence
10. *"The Ministry of Intercession"* by Andrew Murray
11. *"The Battle Plan for Prayer-Bible Study"* by Stephen Kindrick, Alex Kindrick & Travis Agnew

NEXT STEPS

We hope this study has created a stronger desire for you to spend more time in prayer each day. But now that you are done with the study and the classes have ended, life with all its cares and responsibilities will work to keep you from praying. What can you do to keep these lessons on your mind and in your heart? Here is a short list of just a few things to help you stay in the presence of God each day.

1. Continue to have a quiet time of prayer and Bible reading each day.

2. Attend your church's weekly prayer meeting and if they don't have one…start one.

3. Make a monthly prayer calendar for the needs of your church (see sample on page 287).

4. Start a list of prayer needs for your church and its members (see sample on page 289).

5. Make a monthly prayer calendar for missionaries, Bible translators, persecuted Christians and other laborers around the world. Operation World has a good prayer plan for missions around the world. www.operationworld.org

6. Lead a *Prayer Warrior Bootcamp* for your Christian friends at church, work, neighborhood or school.

We know from these lessons that God is depending on YOU to pray to advance His kingdom. We know, *"The fervent prayer of a righteous man availeth much."* Commit yourself to being that type of Christian. Your fervent prayers will cause God to move mightily in your church, community and all around the world!

No longer can we claim ignorance of what moves God in the lives of men. It takes Christians living obedient lives and exercising their faith through prayer. We must not blame lazy preachers, or backsliding Christians, or a failing educational system, or a corrupt government, or a godless entertainment industry or anything else. The responsibility is on us, success depends on our obedience, on our faith, and on our perseverance in fervent prayer.

Christ has promised to answer YOUR prayers, if you obey His commands, have faith, and pray according to His will and for His glory. Dear prayer warrior, we have learned that it is God's will to save souls and advance His kingdom here on earth. Remember in one of the few instances when Jesus told us WHAT to pray for, He said, *"The harvest is plenteous, but the laborers are few. Pray ye therefore the Lord of the harvest, that He will send forth laborers into His harvest."* We know what we are called to do and now is the time to do it by living an obedient life and spending more time in prayer. Truly, the only person we can blame for a lack of God's glory on the earth and His power in our life, in our churches life and in the life of our family and friends is… US. But praise God our faithful prayers and obedient lives can change things! Thank God He hears us when we intercede. Have faith because God is eagerly waiting to use your prayers to change everything around you and advance His kingdom here on earth. *"For the eyes of the LORD run to and fro throughout the whole earth, to shew himself strong in the behalf of them whose heart is perfect toward him."* 2 Chronicles 16:9.

SAMPLE CHURCH PRAYER CALANDER
Monthly Prayer Calendar

You also must help us by prayer, so that many will give thanks on our behalf
for the blessing granted us through the prayers of many. -2 Corinthians 1:11

Day 1 –Pray for Pastor Ray. Ask God to give him good health and the direction of the Holy Spirit as he leads our church. **1 Th 3:1**

Day 2 -Pray for the children who attend our church. Ask God to protect them from temptation and give them wisdom. **Job 28:28**

Day 3 –Pray for the Children's teachers. Tila and Mary. Ask God to give them patience with our kids. **Matt 18:6**

Day 4 –Pray for our church building. Ask God to protect our facility and provide the funds to keep it clean and in good repair **Psa 27:4**

Day 5 –Pray for a spirit of unity and love between all the members of our church, as well as all Christians worldwide. **John 17: 23**

Day 6 –Pray for the lost in the areas where our members live. Ask God to make us a light that leads to Christ. **Luke 8:16**

> *"Ask and it will be given to you; seek and you will find;*
>
> *knock and the door will be opened to you.*
>
> *For everyone who asks receives; and he who seeks finds;*
>
> *and to him who knocks, the door will be opened." - Matthew 7:7-8*

Day 7 –Pray for Bryan as he leads the youth and that they would turn to God when making important life decisions. **Pro 1:7**

Day 8 -Pray for our Sunday morning worship services. Ask for God's glory to come down and draw us closer to Him. **Num 20:6**

Day 9 –Pray for the Cotton Belt neighborhood and ask God to help our church reach these people for Christ. **Acts 1:8**

Day 10–Pray for our missionaries all over the world. Ask God to keep them fruitful, encouraged and healthy. **Matt 28:19**

Day 11 –Pray for our Wednesday night bible study. Ask God to teach us how to apply His statues to our daily lives. **Psa 119:125**

Day 12 –Pray our church will be protected from Satan's attacks. Ask God to deliver our families from the evil one. **Matt 6:13**

Day 13 –Pray for those who have secret sins in their lives. Ask God to give them the grace to seek forgiveness. **1 John 1:9**

Day 14 -Pray for a spirit of forgiveness to fill each of our member's hearts. Let us be forgiving of each other's faults. **Mark 11:25**

Day 15 –Pray for our church finances. Ask God to help us be cheerful givers of our tithes and offerings. **2 Cor 9:7**

Day 16 –Pray for the poor in our community. Ask God that our church would be willing to help the hungry and needy. **2 Cor 9:9**

Day 17 -Pray for our Sunday school teachers. Ask God to bless their efforts and for each class to grow closer to God. **Ezra 7:10**

Day 18 –Pray that our members will honor the Sabbath and faithfully attend church services. **Luke 13:10**

Day 19–Pray that we all will spend time praying for our church's ministry. Ask the Holy Spirit to guide our prayer lives. **Matt 26:41**

Day 20 -Pray that our members will have a burden for lost souls. Ask God to lay a lost person on each of our hearts. **John 21:15-17**

Day 21 –Pray for laborers for Gods harvest. Ask God to make us His laborers and allow us to help our fellow laborers. **Luke 10:2**

Day 22 –Pray for the sick in our church. Ask God to heal their bodies, relieve any pain and draw them closer to His will. **Jas 5:14**

Day 23 –Pray for our pastor's wife. Ask God to bless Sister Liz and let her be a source of strength to Pastor Ray. **Ecc 4:9-11**

Day 24 –Pray for lost family members of those in our church. Ask God to send laborers to direct them to Christ. **Acts 16:31**

Day 25 –Pray for those fighting addictions from drugs and alcohol. Ask God to rebuke Satan's attack on their lives. **Mark 9:29**

Day 26 -Pray that someone who needs to hear about Jesus would meet you this week. Ask God to give you boldness **Ezk 3:18-21**

Day 27 –Pray that our Wednesday night meals will be a time of Christian fellowship and draw others to Christ. **Matt 25:35**

Day 28–Pray for those dealing with troubles, or thinking of suicide. Ask God to use our church to give them hope. **Rom 15:13**

Day 29 –Pray that God would prosper church members in our business and jobs. Ask for His blessings on our efforts. **Due 28:2**

Day 30 –Ask God to rebuke any attack on marriages in our church. Pray that love, honor and respect would grow. **1 Cor 13:4-13**

Our Father which art in heaven, Hallowed be thy name.

Thy kingdom come. Thy will be done in earth, as it is in heaven.

Give us this day our daily bread.

And forgive us our debts, as we forgive our debtors.

And lead us not into temptation, but deliver us from evil:

For thine is the kingdom, and the power, and the glory, forever. Amen.

Matthew 6:9-13

Lost

1. _____
2. _____
3. _____
4. _____
5. _____
6. _____
7. _____
8. _____
9. _____
10. _____
11. _____
12. _____
13. _____
14. _____
15. _____
16. _____
17. _____
18. _____
19. _____

Spiritual Needs

1. _____
2. _____
3. _____
4. _____
5. _____
6. _____
7. _____
8. _____
9. _____

This Weeks Church Prayer

Pray that we all will spend time praying for our church's ministry. Ask the Holy Spirit to guide our prayer lives. **Matt 26:41**

Date

Sample Church
PRAYER REQUESTS

Church Needs

1. _____
2. _____
3. _____
4. _____
5. _____
6. _____
7. _____
8. _____

Community Needs

1. _____
2. _____
3. _____
4. _____
5. _____
6. _____
7. _____
8. _____
9. _____

Unspoken

1. _____
2. _____
3. _____
4. _____
5. _____
6. _____
7. _____
8. _____
9. _____
10. _____

Sick

1. _____
2. _____
3. _____
4. _____
5. _____
6. _____
7. _____
8. _____
9. _____
10. _____
11. _____
12. _____
13. _____
14. _____
15. _____
16. _____
17. _____
18. _____
19. _____

Missions

1. _____
2. _____
3. _____
4. _____
5. _____
6. _____
7. _____
8. _____
9. _____

This Weeks Missions Prayer

Albania -Population: 3.1 million, Pray for Albania's least reached minorities & that God would reach them and protect them from human trafficking.

Again I say unto you, That if two of you shall agree on earth as touching anything that they

shall ask, it shall be done for them of my Father which is in heaven. **Mat 18:19**

Lost

1. _____
2. _____
3. _____
4. _____
5. _____
6. _____
7. _____
8. _____
9. _____
10. _____

Spiritual Needs

1. _____
2. _____
3. _____
4. _____
5. _____

Church Needs

1. _____
2. _____
3. _____
4. _____
5. _____

Community Needs

1. _____
2. _____
3. _____
4. _____
5. _____

Temporal Needs

1. _____
2. _____
3. _____
4. _____
5. _____

Sick

1. _____
2. _____
3. _____
4. _____
5. _____
6. _____
7. _____
8. _____
9. _____
10. _____

Temporal Needs

1. _____
2. _____
3. _____
4. _____
5. _____

ANWSERED PRAYERS & PRAISES TO GOD

1. _____
2. _____
3. _____
4. _____
5. _____
6. _____
7. _____
8. _____
9. _____
10. _____

11. _____
12. _____
13. _____
14. _____
15. _____
16. _____
17. _____
18. _____
19. _____
20. _____

"Ask and it will be given to you; seek and you will find; knock and the door will be opened to you
For everyone who asks receives; and he who seeks finds; and to him who knocks, the door will be
opened."

AUTHOR'S NOTE

I first stumbled onto E.M. Bounds while in the Marine Corps in 1994. His teaching on prayer inspired me to a much stronger prayer life. But somewhere along life's highway the cares of this world combined with my pursuit of popularity, power and prominence took me away from the prayer closet. Soon after that I experienced a devastating fall and lost all those temporal things I had been working so hard to obtain. In my sad state of affairs I finally gave in to God and dropped to my knees as I repented from my wicked lifestyle and pleaded for God's forgiveness of my many sins.

In His grace and mercy He forgave me my trespasses and revealed the power of prayer as I read the gospels. In my new desire to draw closer to the Lord, I dusted off E.M. Bounds teachings on prayer and immediately saw my faith in God answering my prayers increase. Through divine direction I was lead to Andrew Murray's *"With Christ in the School of Prayer"* which only increased my faith and desire to pray. My faith increased because I saw my specific prayers answered. It was absolutely amazing, and I never want to forget what God has graciously revealed to me about the power of prayer.

As I've read and reread these books since 2010 I felt an increasing burden to share with others the wonderful way these great men of faith explained our Lord's teaching on the power of prayer. In 2013 I began to search for a study guide or small group discussion guide that would allow a group of believers to make an in-depth study of their writings about what Jesus taught concerning prayer. Unfortunately, I came up empty handed.

This nine week prayer bootcamp was my simple way of making prayer a habit in my daily life while meditating on the promises about prayer in the scriptures. Developing questions for each day's reading was a bit harder than I expected, but it did cause me to reflect much deeper on what Christ taught about prayer. It's my hope that these readings and reflection questions will help others learn how a habit of daily prayer opens up a powerful channel to God, which will advance His kingdom here on earth.

Prayerful readers should have no problem understanding these simple lessons despite their 19th century grammar. The authors also referenced the King James Bible and I saw no need to change that. I was impressed to leave their writings unedited because of the danger that my revisions might alter their intent, so only basic spelling changes have been made. We have included a chronological Bible reading schedule with each day's lesson and I would encourage any student of prayer to read it as they work through these lessons. It will take almost 49 days to read all four gospels and I think the chronological timeline helps a reader better see how important prayer was in the life of our Lord.

-Rodney Jetton

July 29, 2015

ACKNOWLEDGMENTS

All glory and honor for putting a study like this together must first and foremost go to God alone. Without His help and guidance it would have been impossible to put something like this together. With each chapter He provided the help and direction needed to choose the right reflection questions and assemble the leaders guide. There is really no way to explain the help the Holy Spirt gave, while praying about what key points and illustrations needed to be stressed. Thankfully, the Lord sent others to help with this task as well. My parents, Bill & Judy Jetton along with Peter & Sue Westrum encouraged me when I first started thinking about organizing this study guide. Then He sent Michelle Tandy and Irene Foster to help improve the grammar and spelling. Their editing advice has been such a blessing. I also want to thank my Sunday school class at Sweet Prospect General Baptist church for agreeing to let me lead them through the study. Their answers to the questions, class discussion & comments along with their helpful suggestions were a crucial aid in refining the reflection questions for each chapter as well as the key points and illustrations for each class. Additionally, special thanks must go to Kerry Messer, Sherry Rowland and U.S. Navy Chaplin Mike Hall for taking the time to review the final draft and make suggested edits. Their careful review and prayerful examination greatly improved this final version. I also owe a special debt of gratitude to both pastor Jay Scribner and his in-home Bible study group as well as Lottie James and her Sunday school class at Harmony Congregational Methodist church. They each agreed to test the book in a small group setting and their feedback was invaluable. I know we all share the hope that this reflective study of E. M. Bounds, *The Necessity of Prayer* and Andrew Murray's, *With Christ in the School of Prayer* will encourage other Christians to pray fervently for the advancement of God's kingdom. We thank the Lord for His gracious help and pray that through this study, God would be glorified!

PRAYER WARRIOR BOOTCAMP

LEADER'S GUIDE

Top Priority - Nothing is more important than you as a leader taking time to pray. God may be pleased when we write about prayer, teach about prayer and talk about prayer, but He is moved to action only when we pray! The most important thing that will bring His presence into your class and allow you and your recruits to strengthen your prayer lives is prayer. As the leader, you will need to commit to praying for this class. Pray daily for God to help you as you lead, pray for you and your recruits to have the desire and time to pray and do the daily reading, pray that all obtain wisdom and understanding, pray that they would be kept from temptation, pray for the class requests…pray fervently, pray earnestly and pray often! This class is designed to teach Christians how to be powerful prayer warriors who move God to action. Your efforts in leading this class have the capacity to revolutionize your church and community for Christ! In 2nd Chronicles 16:9 it says, *"For the eyes of the Lord run to and fro throughout the whole earth, to shew himself strong in the behalf of them whose heart is perfect toward him."* Praying Christians have hearts that are perfect toward Him, so pray that your class will produce perfect hearts that pray! In Psalms 34:15 the psalmist writes, *"The eyes of the Lord are upon the righteous, and his ears are open unto their cry."* Then in James 5:16 it says, *"The effectual fervent prayer of a righteous man availeth much."* Praying Christians will be righteous Christians and God WILL hear their prayers. Make sure your top priority is praying for this class. Before teaching, before planning and even before studying must come prayer.

Overall responsibilities - As the leader, begin praying about who should be in this class several weeks before it starts. It will also be helpful if you can quickly read *The Necessity of Prayer* by E.M. Bounds and *With Christ in the School of Prayer* by Andrew Murray. It is also recommended that you stay a week ahead of your recruits on the daily readings. If you are a week ahead of the recruits, you should only need about 30 minutes to prepare for leading each session. You should also spend time praying for each session as you prepare for it. Keep track of any prayer requests recruits may have and continue to remember them in prayer each week in class. (Keep in mind this is just a guide, feel free to add to or skip discussion of key points and illustrations as the Spirit leads you.)

Class Activity - An optional social that we suggest is to invite all recruits and their families to your house or the church to watch the movie *War Room*. A dinner or even light refreshments and popcorn is a great way to have everyone get to know each other better. This activity can be done at the beginning before classes begin to gain interest in the study.

ORIENTATION CLASS

Focus - The focus of this first class is to get to know each of the recruits and learn more about where they are in their prayer life.

Tasks -

- Open the class in prayer.

- Stress the importance of doing one lesson each day.

- Get a commitment from each recruit that they will make doing these lessons and praying each day a priority.

- Obtain a cell phone number and email address from all recruits (This will be used to keep them updated on class meetings as well as offer them encouraging messages.)

- Have each recruit introduce themselves and answer the first four questions.

- Lead in the sharing of the answers to the last 13 questions.

- Give a quick overview of *The Necessity of Prayer* by EM Bounds and *With Christ in the School of Prayer* by Andrew Murray as well as preview class 1.

- Start a list of class prayer requests with each recruit providing one thing they need answered.

- Close with a time in prayer asking God to grant each person the desire and time to do a daily Bible reading and prayer time each day. Also pray for any other requests anyone may have.

CLASS 1

Focus - This week's focus is to show how important faith is to answered prayer.

Theme - Prayer is faith in God.

Tasks -

- Open class in prayer.
- Make sure to go over the class 1 review questions and stress the key points listed below.
- Discuss the illustrations Bounds used from the New Testament.
- Share testimonies of answered prayers.
- Memorize the week's Bible verse - Mark 11:24.
- If time permits, have the recruits share the answers from a few of the key personal response questions during week two.
- Preview next week- word, theme and key points.
- Pray for recruits and any other requests.

Key Points -

- All prayer requires faith and faith turns to trust.
- Desire for an answer improves faith and our faith can be increased. It is like a muscle that grows bigger and stronger with use.
- Fervency urges us on to pray more.
- Jesus taught us to never stop praying until we receive an answer.

Key illustrations -

- Parable of the friend seeking bread - Luke 11: 5-8.
- Parable of the unjust judge - Luke 18:1-8.
- Story of Syrophenician woman asking Jesus for healing - Mark 7:24-30.
- Story of blind men calling to Jesus for healing - Matthew 9:27-31.

Key personal reflection questions for discussion -

- Ask recruits to share their answer to questions 7 and 8 on day 5.
- Ask recruits to share their answer to questions 7 and 8 on day 6.

CLASS 2

Focus - This week's focus is to show how important obedience is to answered prayers.

Theme - God hears the prayer of an obedient child.

Tasks -

- Open class in prayer

- Make sure to go over the class 2 review questions and stress the key points listed below. <u>(This is a great week to take time as a class to confess our sins one to another and pray for forgiveness of any sin that may be hindering our prayer life.)</u> James 5:16.

- Discuss the illustrations Bounds used.

- Share testimonies of answered prayers.

- Memorize the week's Bible verse - James 5:16.

- If time permits, have the recruits share the answers from a few of the key personal response questions during week three.

- Preview next week - word, theme and key points.

- Pray for recruits and any other requests.

Key Points -

- Prayer and sinning are opposites- praying will help keep us from sinning.

- With the Holy Spirit's help, it is possible to live a sin free life.

- The foundation of faith is obedience.

- Knowing God's will is obtained by reading God's word.

- The church's top priority is to be a house of prayer.

Key illustrations -

- Paul's description of the armor of God – Prayer is the link, Ephesians 6.

- Prayers of men of faith -

    o Elijah praying for rain - promised by God, but still had to pray 7 times - 1 Kings 18:42.

    o Abraham interceding for Sodom - despite God's declaration of His wrath - Gen 18:22.

    o Moses interceding for Israelite - despite God's declaration of His wrath - Exo 32:11-14.

    o Paul asking to pray for unbelieving gentiles - promise of deliverance, but still prayed.

Key personal reflection questions for discussion -

- Ask recruits to share their answer to question 6 on day 9.

- Ask recruits to share their answer to questions 6 and 7 on day 11.

- Ask recruits to share their answer to question 4 on day 13.

CLASS 3

Focus - This week's focus is to show how God answers prayers.

Theme - Everyone who asks receives.

Tasks -

- Open class in prayer.
- Make sure to go over the class 3 review questions and stress the key points listed below.
- Discuss the key points of the Lord's Prayer.
- Share testimonies of answered prayers.
- Memorize the week's Bible verse –Matthew 7:7-8.
- If time permits, have the recruits share the answers from a few of the key personal response questions during week four.
- Preview next week - word, theme and key points.
- Pray for recruits and any other requests.

Key Points -

- Our prayers move God to action in men's lives.
- Prayer time can be anywhere and anytime, not just at church or at certain times of the day.
- We need a quiet time alone with God each day.
- God answers prayers - we ask and He gives.
- Our most important prayer request is to receive the Holy Spirit each day.
- It is easier to blame our unanswered prayers on God's unknown will than to allow the Spirit to search our lives for sin or study the Word to make sure we are praying according to God's will.

Key illustration -

- The Lord's Prayer Matthew 6:9-14 - 4 parts.
  - Part 1 - Praise - Hallowed be thy name.
  - Part 2 - God's will - Thy Kingdom, Thy will.
  - Part 3 - Our needs - our bread, our sins, our protection.
  - Part 4 - Praise - Thy kingdom, power and glory forever.

Key personal reflection questions for discussion -

- Ask participants to share their answer to question 7 on day 18.
- Ask participants to share their answer to questions 6 on day 19.
- Ask participants to share their answer to question 6 on day 21.

CLASS 4

Focus - This week's focus is to show how important believing is to answered prayers.

Theme - Have faith in the promiser.

Tasks -

- Open class in prayer.
- Make sure to go over the class 4 review questions and stress the key points listed below.
- Discuss the illustrations.
- Share testimonies of answered prayers.
- Memorize the week's Bible verse - Mark 11:22-23.
- If time permits, have the students share the answers from a few of the key personal response questions during week five.
- Preview next week - word, theme and key points.
- Pray for students and any other requests.

Key Points -

- God's chief aim or "glory of prayer" is for us to become intercessors.
- We must pray for the Lord to send laborers for the harvest.
- Our prayer requests must be specific and definite.
- Too often we blame unanswered prayers on God's unknown will instead of looking for sin in our lives or spending the time to seek God's will.
- Fasting separates us from the temporal world and strengthens our prayers.
- We must not have unforgiveness or resentment towards anyone.

Key illustrations -

- The devil uses food to tempt us - Eve in the garden - Gen 3:1-7 and Jesus in the wilderness -Matt 4:1-4.
- Jesus's story of the friend in need teaches importunity in our prayers - Luke 11: 5-8.
  - He wants to help his friend - we should pray for those around us.
  - Asks his neighbor for help.
  - His neighbor turns him down.
  - He keeps asking despite the rejection and finally receives what he needs.
- Blind Bartimaeus - Jesus asked him what he wanted Him to do - Mark 10:46-52.

Key personal reflection questions for discussion -

- Ask participants to share their answer to question 6 on day 22.
- Ask participants to share their answer to questions 4 and 23.
- Ask participants to share their answer to question 8 on day 27.
- Ask participants to share their answer to question 3 on day 28.

CLASS 5

Focus - This week's focus is to show that God's glory is the aim of all our prayers.

Theme - The chief object of prayer is God's glory.

Tasks -

- Open class in prayer.

- Make sure to go over the class 5 review questions and stress the key points listed below.

- Discuss the illustrations from the New Testament that reinforce key points.

- Share testimonies of answered prayers.

- Memorize the week's Bible verse - John 15:7.

- If time permits, have the students share the answers from a few of the key personal response questions during week six.

- Preview next week - word, theme and key points.

- Pray for students and any other requests.

Key Points -

- United prayer with other believers strengthens our requests.

- It sometimes takes time for God to bring the answer to our prayer.

- Our prayers have power because the Holy Spirit through Jesus Christ takes our requests to the Lord.

- When doing His work and praying in His name, we can be confident of our prayers being answered because we're doing His work and His power allows us to do even greater works.

- The chief aim of all our prayers should be God's glory.

- If we meet the condition and our lives abide in Christ, He will keep His promise and answer all our prayers.

Key illustrations -

- Jesus asking Peter and John to pray with Him in the garden - Mark 14:32-38.

- Paul requesting prayer for his ministry - Romans 25:30, 2 Cor 1:11, Phil 1:19.

- Unlike the Unrighteous judge, God hears and will answer speedily - Luke 18:1-8 (Day 30).

Key personal reflection questions for discussion -

- Ask participants to share their answer to question 7 on day 29.

- Ask participants to share their answer to questions 7 on day 32.

- Ask participants to share their answer to questions 5 on day 34.

- Ask participants to share their answer to question 4 on day 35.

CLASS 6

Focus - This week's focus shows how a daily life abiding with Christ and bearing fruit are important to prayer.

Theme - Faith and obedience lead to fruit bearing.

Tasks -

- Open class in prayer.

- Make sure to go over the class 6 review questions and stress the key points listed below.

- Discuss the illustrations from the New Testament that reinforce key points.

- Share testimonies of answered prayers.

- Memorize the week's Bible verse - John 15:16.

- If time permits, have the students share the answers from a few of the key personal response questions during week seven.

- Preview next week - word, theme and key points.

- Pray for students and any other requests.

Key Points -

- God's will is in His words - If they abide in us then we will be doing His will and our prayers will be answered.

- Obedience to God's will is the secret to bearing fruit.

- The power of Christ's name in our prayers is equal to the power of Christ in our daily lives.

- We must pray for the baptism of the Holy Spirit.

- Christ is depending on us to join him in interceding for sinners and to advance His kingdom.

- We must speak God's word to those in our circle that we are praying for.

Key illustrations -

- Digging up the fruit tree to help it bear - Luke 13:6-9.

- Jesus in the garden praying, gave his life - Matt 26:36-46.

- Rich young ruler giving up his riches - Luke 18:18-30.

Key personal reflection questions for discussion -

- Ask participants to share their answer to question 8 on day 37.

- Ask participants to share their answer to questions 6 on day 38.

- Ask participants to share their answer to question 4 on day 40.

- Ask participants to share their answer to question 7 on day 41.

CLASS 7

Focus - This week's focus is to show how important obedience is to answered prayers.

Theme – Believing and persistent prayer for His kingdom.

Tasks -

- Open class in prayer.

- Make sure to go over the class 7 review questions and stress the key points listed below.

- Discuss the illustrations used.

- Share testimonies of answered prayers.

- Memorize the week's Bible verse - 1 John 5:14-15.

- If time permits, have the students share the answers from a few of the key personal response questions during week one.

Preview next week - ask students to review their takeaways from all 49 days and prepare their testimony of their answered prayers and how this study helped them.

Pray for students and any other requests.

Key Points -

- It takes reading God's word slowly and prayerfully, while listening to the Holy Spirit to reveal God's will in our life.

- Christ needs us to abide in Him so He can lead our intercessions to draw down God's blessings on our fellow men.

- Faith from answered prayers creates a desire and ability to pray more.

- We should be careful not to have more confidence in other's advice than we do of God's word when seeking His direction and will.

- Our prayers must be for God's glory and not our selfish desires.

Key illustrations -

- Priest serving in the temple with God and representing his fellow man to God and blessing them for God - Deuteronomy 21:5.

- Consecrated the priest by putting blood on their right ear, right thumb, right toe, and garments, while typical Israelite just offered a burnt offering and blood was poured out on the alter -Exodus 29:20-21.

- Widow and the unjust judge an example of persevering prayer.

Key personal reflection questions for discussion-

- Ask participants to share their answer to question 7 on day 43.

- Ask participants to share their answer to questions 4 on day 45.

- Ask participants to share their answer to question 2 on day 46.

- Ask participants to share their answer to question 2 on day 47.

- Ask participants to share their answer to question 3 on day 49.

CLASS 8 TESTIMONY TIME

Focus - The focus of this last class is to allow each prayer warrior to share their testimony of how their prayer life has been strengthened by what they have learned and to share the answered prayer requests they have received over the last 9 weeks.

Tasks -
- Open class in prayer.
- Allow each student to share their personal testimony.
- Highlight key points learned from entire 9 week study.
- Review the conditional prayer promises Jesus spoke to His disciples.
- Memory verse completion - see how many recruits can say all eight weekly verses by heart.
- Go over the next steps pages and talk about what students can do to keep their prayer life strong while using their prayers to become intercessors who are advancing God's kingdom.
- Close in prayer thanking God for His grace and praising Him for answered prayers.

Key Points -
- Faith is required for answered prayer and our faith can be strengthened by prayer.
- Obedience of God's commands is required to obtain His blessings; sinning and prayer cannot survive together. Either we will stop praying and start sinning or stop sinning and start praying.
- God wants to answer our prayers. We ask and He gives. We need a daily time alone with Him to pray because our prayers move God to action on behalf of our fellow man.
- We must make specific requests to God and pray for laborers for the harvest.
- Unforgiveness in our hearts towards others will hinder any answer to our prayers.
- Joining other believers in united prayer strengthens our requests.
- Our prayers must be for God's glory and not our selfish desires.
- When we abide in Christ, are doing His work and are seeking His glory; He will answer all our prayers.
- Too often we blame unanswered prayers on God's unknown will instead of looking for sin in our lives or spending the time to seek God's will from His word.
- It takes reading God's word slowly and prayerfully while listening to the Holy Spirit to reveal God's will in our life.
- Christ is depending on us to join Him in interceding for sinners and to advance His kingdom.

Conditional Promises Jesus Gave for Answered Prayer

- We must believe or have faith -
  - *Therefore I say unto you, what things soever ye desire, when ye pray, <u>believe that ye receive</u> them, and <u>ye shall have them</u>. Mark 11:24*
  - *Jesus said unto him, <u>If thou canst believe</u>, <u>all things are possible</u> to him that believeth. Mark 9:23*
  - *Verily, verily, I say unto you, He that <u>believeth on me</u>, the works that I do shall <u>he do also</u>; and greater works than these shall he do; because I go unto my Father. John 14:12*

- We must ask -
  - *<u>Ask</u>, and it <u>shall be given you</u>; seek, and ye shall find; knock, and it shall be opened unto you: For every one that asketh receiveth; and he that seeketh findeth; and to him that knocketh it shall be opened. Matthew 7:7-8*

- Ask in His name -
  - *Verily, verily, I say unto you, Whatsoever ye shall <u>ask the Father in my name</u>, <u>he will give it you</u>. Hitherto have ye asked nothing in my name: ask, and ye shall receive, that your joy may be full. John 16:23-24*
  - *If ye shall <u>ask any thing in my name</u>, <u>I will do it</u>. John 14:14*
  - *Ye have not chosen me, but I have chosen you, and ordained you, that ye should go and bring forth fruit, and that your fruit should remain: that <u>whatsoever ye shall ask of the Father in my name</u>, he may <u>give it you</u>. John 15:17*

- Obedience to God's commands -
  - *If ye abide in me, and <u>my words abide in you</u>, ye shall ask what ye will, and <u>it shall be done unto you</u>. John 15:7*

- Must not harbor unforgiveness -
  - *And when ye stand praying, <u>forgive, if ye have ought against any</u>: that your Father also which is in heaven <u>may forgive you your trespasses</u>. Mark 11:25*
  - *For if <u>ye forgive men</u> their trespasses, your heavenly <u>Father will also forgive you</u>: But <u>if ye forgive not men</u> their trespasses, <u>neither will your Father forgive your trespasses</u>. Matthew 6:14-15*
  - *<u>Judge not, and ye shall not be judged</u>: <u>condemn not, and ye shall not be condemned</u>: <u>forgive, and ye shall be forgiven</u>: Luke 6:37*

- God must get glory -
  - *And whatsoever ye shall <u>ask in my name</u>, that will I do, that the <u>Father may be glorified</u> in the Son. John 14:13*

10 CONDITIONS OF ANSWERED PRAYER
BY ED KLEIMAN

Sometimes our prayer life actually hinders or clashes with our faith in God. When our prayers are not answered we simply believe either God doesn't hear us, God's promises concerning prayer are not true, or there is something unknowable or mystical about prayer.

It is important to be aware that God has the prerogative to answer any prayer as and when He sees fit, whether they meet any conditions mentioned in scripture or not. Yet, He has promised to always answer our prayers when the conditions He gives in the bible are met. In effect, He has bound Himself by His own Word, and we know that He cannot lie (Titus 1:2; Hebrews 6:18).

Let us now look at 10 conditions God has given in scripture, whereby He promises to answer our prayers.

We Must Ask!   The very first condition is - we must ask God and pray! James 4:2 says; *"You* do *not have, because you do not ask God"*. You say that's obvious, but is it?   Though James goes   on to deal with other matters, he begins where we need to as well. We must ask God. Asking God humbles us, and shows our dependency on and our faith in Him.

Keeping a prayer journal is a good idea. Many times our prayers are answered, but in a way and time God deems more appropriate (than immediately as we would have). Having a journal to refer to will strengthen your faith when you see the faithfulness of God, as He answers your prayers over time.

We Must Pray in Faith – Believing!   I know this is treading on dangerous ground with some. You will say that it is the object of our faith – God, and not our faith that is important and I would agree with you. Nevertheless we are told by Christ Himself in Mark 11:24; "Therefore I tell you, whatever you ask for in prayer, *believe that you have received it*, and it will be yours." In Matthew 21:22; *"If you believe*, you will receive whatever you ask for in prayer."

James tells us in 1:6-8; *"But let him ask in faith without any doubting*, for the one who doubts is like the surf of the sea driven and tossed by the wind. For let not that man expect that he will receive anything from the Lord, being a double-minded man, unstable in all his ways."

Famed nineteenth century preacher Charles Spurgeon said; "Unless I believe my prayer to be effectual, it should not be, for it will depend on a great extent to my faith. God may give me the mercy even when I have no faith. Such is His own sovereign grace. But He has not promised to do it." Even Puritan Thomas Watson said; "Prayer that is faithless is fruitless."

Friends, faith is important to God; "And *without faith it is impossible to please God*, because anyone who comes to Him must believe that He exists and that He rewards those who *earnestly* seek Him" (Hebrews 11:6). Which brings us to the next point.

We Must be Fervent or Earnest in Prayer! The above verse talks about those who earnestly seek God. James 5:16 says; "The effectual *fervent* prayer of a righteous man availeth much."

Spurgeon said; "When we ask the Lord without passion, we actually stop His hand and restrain Him from giving us the very blessing we pretend that we are seeking. We must be earnest. Otherwise, we have no right to hope that the Lord will hear our prayer." The Puritan Thomas Brooks said; "Cold prayers always freeze before they reach heaven."

We are told the early church practiced this as Acts 12:5 says; "So Peter was kept in prison, but prayer for him was being made *fervently* (*earnestly* in the NIV) by the church to God". Again to the Church at Colosse, Paul writes; "Epaphras, who is one of your number, a bondslave of Jesus Christ, sends you his greetings, always *laboring earnestly for you in his prayers…*" (Colossians 4:12).

We Must be Obedient To God's Commands (Word)! Francis Schaeffer said; "As Christians, what we are and what we do has a relationship to our power in prayer." In other words, scripture also teaches obedience is a condition of answered prayer. 1 John 3:22 says; "And whatever we ask we receive from Him, *because we keep His commandments and do the things that are pleasing in His sight.*" Jesus tells us in John 15:7; "If you abide in Me, and My words abide in you, ask whatever you wish, and it shall be done for you", and then in verse 10 adds; "*If you keep my commandments*, you will abide in my love."

Confess and Forsake Sin! The psalmist says; "*If I had cherished sin in my heart, the Lord would not have listened*" (Psalm 66:18). Isaiah tells us; "*But your iniquities have separated you from your God; your sins have hidden His face from you, so that He will not hear*" (Isaiah 59:2).

So what are we to do? First we must realize what is said in 1 John 1:8; "If we claim to be without sin, we deceive ourselves and the truth is not in us." Then we must do what is said in the very next verse; "If we confess our sins, He is faithful and just and will forgive us our sins and purify us from all unrighteousness" (1 John 1:9). We must not take the grace of confession too lightly.

Have a Forgiving Spirit! Jesus tells us in Mark 11:25; "*And when you stand praying, if you hold anything against anyone, forgive him, so that your Father in heaven may forgive your sins*". The forgiveness of our sins is critical so that as mentioned above, they don't separate us from God whereby He does not hear us.

Jesus, after teaching the disciples how to pray in the previous verses, adds in Matthew 6:14-15; "*For if you forgive men when they sin against you, your heavenly Father will also forgive you. But if you do not forgive men their sins, your Father will not forgive your sins.*"

This is also wonderful for husbands and wives to practice together. Praying together for their marriage, for their family, and for each other. But they must learn to let any bitterness go between them by taking it to the Lord, so they can first forgive each other, and then pray.

We Must Continue or Persevere (Importunity) in Prayer! Again after Jesus teaches the disciples how to pray, He immediately goes into a parable on persistent prayer in Luke 11:5 about the man who knocks on his neighbor's door at midnight asking for food to give an unexpected guest. Finally in verse 8 Jesus says; "…because of his *persistence* he will get up and give him as much as he needs". Then in verse 9 come His familiar words; "And I say to you, ask, and it shall be given to you; seek, and you shall find; knock, and it shall be opened to you."

Since it follows on the heels of Jesus telling the parable to show us to persist in prayer, we are hearing Him say in effect; Ask, and keep on asking; seek, and keep on seeking; knock, and keep on knocking. You might wonder why is this necessary. I am sure there are several reasons as we look at the scriptures, but I believe as we look to our own deceitful hearts we see an obvious one. Certainly in one way our persevering in prayer demonstrates not only to God but also to us, if what we are praying for really is something we strongly desire. Our persisting shows just how much we do desire it. Then when God does answer, it helps us appreciate the blessing all the more.

Jesus tells another parable about continuing to come and ask in the eighteenth chapter of Luke. It is the story of the pestering widow who eventually obtains help from an unrighteous judge because she refuses to stop petitioning him. At the beginning of that story is one of the clearest instructions Jesus gives on persevering in prayer; "Then Jesus told His disciples a parable to show them that *they should always pray and not give up*" (Luke 18:1).

We Must Pray in Accordance to God's Will! Jesus sets the example for us in the garden of Gethsemane, when we read in Matthew 26:39; "Going a little farther, He fell with His face to the ground and prayed, 'My Father, if it is possible, may this cup be taken from Me. Yet *not as I will, but as You will.*'"

1 John 5:14–15 drives this home to us very clearly; "This is the confidence we have in approaching God: that *if we ask anything according to His will*, He hears us. And if we know that He hears us - whatever we ask - we know that we have what we asked of Him."

Now many will say; "How do we know what God's will is, or is it even possible to know?" That is why God has given us His Word. When we approach anything in life to pray for, we should ask, what are the principles of God's Word regarding what we're praying about?

That's why it's helpful whenever reading the bible to ask ourselves, what practices in life should flow from what we're reading? What differences should it make in my life? Where does my life not conform to the Word of God? Then we will learn more of God's will and the right things to pray for ourselves and others.

That is why Jesus said in John 15:7; "If you abide in Me, and *My words abide in you*, ask whatever you wish, and it shall be done for you." Should we find ourselves praying against God's will as revealed in scripture, it is possible God would answer the prayer, but the consequences may not be worth it; "And He gave them their request; but sent leanness into their soul" (Psalm 106:15).

When scripture does not clearly speak to or address an issue, God still tells us to come to Him and pray as it states in James 1:5; "If any of you lacks wisdom, he should ask God, who gives generously to all without finding fault, and it will be given to him."

We Must Pray In Jesus Name! Believers are said to be found "in Christ" over 100 times in the epistles of Paul alone, signifying our new relationship with God through being found in Jesus Christ and all that includes. One thing it includes is the right to come boldly before the throne of God (the throne of grace) to receive mercy and find grace to help in time of need   (Hebrews 4:16).

An unbeliever has no right to expect God to hear or answer prayers, because they still do not have a right relationship with God found only in Jesus Christ. God may hear and answer, just as His common grace is shown to all men – but He has certainly not promised to.

Jesus told the world; "I am the way, the truth, and the life. No one comes to the Father except through Me" (John 14:6). So it is only through a right relationship with God, through Christ that anyone can approach God. Ephesians 3:12 tells us; "In Him (Christ Jesus our Lord) and through faith in Him we may approach God with freedom and confidence".

But for those whom Christ has redeemed and who know Him as their Lord and Savior, Jesus says; "…Whatever you ask the Father *in My name* He will give you" (John 16:23). "And I will do *whatever you ask in my name*, so that the Son may *bring glory* to the Father. You may ask me for *anything in my name*, and I will do it" (John 14:13-14).

We Must Pray with the Right Motive! Finally we hear James say; "You ask and *do not receive, because you ask with wrong motives*, so that you may spend it on your pleasures" (James 4:3).

Well if those are the wrong motives, what are the right ones? I believe scripture makes that abundantly clear. The flag that flies over every act that God has ever performed is found in Isaiah 48:11; "For My own sake, for My own sake, I will act; for how can My name be profaned? And *My glory I will not give to another.*" It is God's glory that God is most concerned with.

God created us for His glory as stated in Isaiah 43:7; "Everyone who is called by My name, and whom *I have created for My glory*, whom I formed, even whom I have made." God predestined and chose us for His glory as seen in Ephesians 1:5-6; "He *predestined us* to be adopted as His sons through Jesus Christ, in accordance with His pleasure and will - to the *praise of his glorious grace …*" He even sanctifies us for His glory shown in 2 Thessalonians 1:11-12; "To this end we always pray for you, that our God may make you worthy of His calling and may fulfill every resolve for good and every work of faith by His power, so that our *Lord Jesus may be glorified* in you, and you in Him, according to the grace of our God and the Lord Jesus Christ."

It is most appropriate to end on this point because we find here, that in all of life, including our prayer life, whatever is for God's glory is also for our good. Jonathan Edwards said in his book; *The End for Which God Created the World;* "God in seeking His glory seeks the good of His creatures, because the emanation of His glory…implies the…happiness of His creatures. And in communicating His fullness for them, He does it for Himself, because their good, which He seeks, is so much in union and communion with Himself. God is their good."

Oh friends, let us learn from and want more of such a good God. Let us draw near to Him in His Word, and through union and communion with Him in prayer. Let us rejoice in Him and that He lets us be co-laborers with Him, working together to determine the outcome of events as we pray. Let us reflect on these conditions given and practice them so we too may become - mighty in prayer!

Finally, let us remember Spurgeon's words on this God who answers prayer; "There is always an open ear if you have an open mouth. There is always a ready hand if you have a ready heart. You have but to cry and the Lord hears; nay, before you call, He will answer, and while you are speaking He will hear."

Ed Kleiman

www.praybold.org